Languaging M
and Realities

NEW PERSPECTIVES ON LANGUAGE AND EDUCATION

Founding Editor: Viv Edwards, *University of Reading, UK*

Series Editors: Phan Le Ha, *University of Hawaii at Manoa, USA* and Joel Windle, *Monash University, Australia.*

Two decades of research and development in language and literacy education have yielded a broad, multidisciplinary focus. Yet education systems face constant economic and technological change, with attendant issues of identity and power, community and culture. What are the implications for language education of new 'semiotic economies' and communications technologies? Of complex blendings of cultural and linguistic diversity in communities and institutions? Of new cultural, regional and national identities and practices? The New Perspectives on Language and Education series will feature critical and interpretive, disciplinary and multidisciplinary perspectives on teaching and learning, language and literacy in new times. New proposals, particularly for edited volumes, are expected to acknowledge and include perspectives from the Global South. Contributions from scholars from the Global South will be particularly sought out and welcomed, as well as those from marginalized communities within the Global North.

All books in this series are externally peer-reviewed.

Full details of all the books in this series and of all our other publications can be found on http://www.multilingual-matters.com, or by writing to Multilingual Matters, St Nicholas House, 31-34 High Street, Bristol BS1 2AW, UK.

NEW PERSPECTIVES ON LANGUAGE AND EDUCATION: 95

Languaging Myths and Realities

Journeys of Chinese International Students

Qianqian Zhang-Wu

MULTILINGUAL MATTERS
Bristol • Jackson

DOI https://doi.org/10.21832/ZHANG6898
Library of Congress Cataloging in Publication Data
A catalog record for this book is available from the Library of Congress.
Names: Zhang-Wu, Qianqian, author.
Title: Languaging Myths and Realities: Journeys of Chinese International Students/
   Qianqian Zhang-Wu.
Description: Bristol; Blue Ridge Summit: Multilingual Matters, [2022] | Includes
   bibliographical references and index. | Summary: "Drawing on a digital
   ethnography of Chinese international students' first semester languaging
   practices, this book examines how they use their multilingual and multimodal communicative repertoires to facilitate languaging across contexts, in
   order to suggest how universities might better serve the needs of international
   students"—Provided by publisher.
Identifiers: LCCN 2021032510 | ISBN 9781788926195 (paperback) | ISBN
   9781788926898 (hardback) | ISBN 9781788926904 (pdf) | ISBN 9781788926911
   (epub) Subjects: LCSH: Chinese students—United States. | English language—
   Study and teaching (Higher)—Chinese speakers. | Foreign study—Social
   aspects—United States. | Chinese—United States—Communication. | College
   freshmen—Services for—United States.
Classification: LCC LB2376.5.C6 Z47 2022 | DDC 428.0071/051—dc23/eng/20211006
LC record available at https://lccn.loc.gov/2021032510

British Library Cataloguing in Publication Data
A catalogue entry for this book is available from the British Library.

ISBN-13: 978-1-78892-689-8 (hbk)
ISBN-13: 978-1-78892-619-5 (pbk)

Multilingual Matters
UK: St Nicholas House, 31-34 High Street, Bristol BS1 2AW, UK.
USA: Ingram, Jackson, TN, USA.

Website: www.multilingual-matters.com
Twitter: Multi_Ling_Mat
Facebook: https://www.facebook.com/multilingualmatters
Blog: www.channelviewpublications.wordpress.com

The policy of Multilingual Matters/Channel View Publications is to use papers
that are natural, renewable and recyclable products, made from wood grown in
sustainable forests. In the manufacturing process of our books, and to further
support our policy, preference is given to printers that have FSC and PEFC Chain
of Custody certification. The FSC and/or PEFC logos will appear on those books
where full certification has been granted to the printer concerned.

Typeset by Deanta Global Publishing Services, Chennai, India

To Maria Estela Brisk, an inspiring role model
To 张一多 and 徐芳, who love and support me unconditionally
To Portia Clementine Wu, a ray of sunshine in my life
To Jason C. Wu, my cheerleader, harbor and best friend

Contents

Acknowledgements

The whole idea for this book project started on March 21, 2019, at my dissertation defense, during which Dr Zhihui Fang (one of my dissertation committee members) commented: 'I want to see your work in a book!' A few days later, I submitted my book proposal to my dream publisher, Multilingual Matters, and started this exciting journey.

I am blessed to have had so much support and encouragement along the way. Firstly, it has been my great pleasure to work with the editors and anonymous reviewers at Multilingual Matters who provided insightful suggestions and helped me improve my manuscript. I would also like to thank my graduate school mentors Drs Maria Brisk, Patrick Proctor, Zhihui Fang, Karen Arnold and Ana Martínez-Alemán who guided me throughout my dissertation. I am very proud and excited that this project was recognized by the Comparative and International Education Society as the winner of the 2021 Best Dissertation Award (Study Abroad and International Students SIG).

I am also extremely grateful to Dean Uta Poiger who made the impossible possible and my awesome colleagues at the Department of English, Northeastern University, especially my three big bosses and close mentors: Drs Ellen Cushman, Mya Poe and Neal Lerner. Ellen, Mya and Neal, thank you so much for your incredible mentorship, your faith in me, your cheering encouragement and your caring support along the way. Being able to work with you and learn from you every day has been such a blessing in my life! I am forever grateful for your trust and help in making my dream come true and am very much looking forward to our many more nerdy collaborations ahead.

Moreover, I am thankful to the companionship and empowerment from all my mentors and cohort members at the 2020–2022 CNV Fellowship, National Council of Teachers of English (NCTE) Research Foundation, USA. I am especially grateful to Dr Tonya Perry and Dr Allison Skerrett, my two role models as women of color in the academy who have inspired and empowered me professionally and individually. I also want to thank my two 'academic older sisters', Dr Yalda Kaveh and Dr Bridget Goodman for cheering me on every step of my graduate studies and helping me navigate my brand-new journey as a tenure-track assistant professor.

Last but not least, this book would not have been possible without the love and companionship of my family. I want to thank my awesome parents 张一多 and 徐芳, who love me and support me unconditionally and believe in me more than anyone else in the world. I am grateful to my daughter Portia Clementine Wu who has accompanied me throughout this research project as a fetus in my belly, a newborn in my arms and now a toddler running around me. Thank you for all your hugs, kisses and smiles that bring sunshine to my life. Finally, I want to thank my dearest husband Jason C. Wu, my forever cheerleader, harbor and best friend.

Qianqian Zhang-Wu
May 2, 2021
Boston, MA, USA

Preface

Nanjing born and Nanjing bred, I received my entire K-16 education in China. Two months after completing my undergraduate studies majoring in Japanese language and literature, I took a flight to the United States on August 27, 2012, and embarked on an exciting journey as a Chinese international student studying teaching English to speakers of other languages (TESOL) at the Graduate School of Education, University of Pennsylvania.

Growing up being the top student in my English as a foreign language classes in China and pursuing an MS Ed in TESOL with a near-perfect score on the test of English as a foreign language (TOEFL), I had been very confident in my English language proficiency. Nevertheless, on arriving at Penn, I was shocked to realize that I was wrong. Not only did my American peers talk as fast as a rocket (compared with what I had heard in the listening sections in the TOEFL), but also my professors often used discipline-specific vocabulary which was hard to digest. For example, my TESOL methodology professor kept emphasizing 'the importance of providing sufficient *scaffolding* for ESL students'. However, I had no idea about the meaning of the word 'scaffold'. After secretly looking it up in the dictionary during class, the meaning I found was 'a temporary or movable platform for workers (such as bricklayers, painters, or miners) to stand or sit on when working at a height above the floor or ground' (*Merriam-Webster Dictionary*), which did not make any sense in this context. I tried to search for images of scaffolds online, but ended up yielding tons of construction site pictures, which again had nothing to do with TESOL methodology.

I was frustrated and confused yet hesitant to ask my professor or American classmates for help. Everybody except me seemed to have understood this word and they were already at the stage of brainstorming ways to provide better scaffolding for students. For quite a few weeks, I felt like a fool. It was not until almost halfway through the semester that I finally realized that 'scaffold' was in fact a 'fancier' version of the word 'support', which people in education prefer to use. Similarly, in this process, I have also realized that instead of using everyday language such as 'education', 'speech', 'repeat' and 'slightly beyond comfort zone', people in my field are more comfortable using 'pedagogy', 'discourse', 'recast' and 'zone of proximal development'. It was the first time that I realized that language is so fluid that it only exists and makes sense in contexts; the ability to do well in standardized English language proficiency tests may not translate directly to successful languaging experiences in contextualized situations.

I encountered similar challenges beyond the academic context. For instance, ordering a cup of coffee had been a huge headache for me on arrival in the United States. One day after school, I decided to get a small iced coffee with some skimmed milk but no sugar. However, on entering the coffee shop, I was intimidated by the language on the menu – more than half of which I could not pronounce or understand. Before long, it was my turn to order. Yet, I was more terrified than excited. The customers in front of me were able to elegantly and swiftly make their order, but my brain was spinning like mad: What is and (more stressfully) how to pronounce 'macchiato'? Is 'frappuccino' a frapped cappuccino? But wait… cappuccino is a beverage not a rope, how could it be frapped? What is the difference between latte and caffe latte? Is caffe latte a latte for here instead of to-go because I am currently in a cafe?

'How may I help you?' The barista's cheerful voice made me more anxious than when I was taking the TOEFL.

'Ugh… hmm… Yes, may I have a small cup of latte with a little bit of non-fat milk but no sugar, please?' I was forced to squeeze something out of my mouth.

'Sure!' The barista smiled as she repeated my order, 'You'd like to have a *tall* skinny latte'.

I was very confused by her words, as I truly only wanted a small-sized coffee, instead of a giant, *tall* cup to carry around. Hearing my heart beating extremely fast, I nervously clarified: 'Uh… I think I meant a small skinny latte'.

'Yep, got it. A *TALL* skinny latte. Is there anything else I can help you with?'

I was extremely annoyed by the barista's insistence to have me get something bigger than what I had hoped for. Indeed, the sheer thought of carrying a giant, *tall* bucket of coffee around for the next hour or so was rather unpleasant. Nevertheless, at that moment I was more eager to escape from my nerve-wracking, soon-to-be-failed 'oral English test' than anything. So, I quickly squeezed out an awkward smile, thanked the barista and paid for my unwanted huge, *tall* bucket of coffee, while secretly hoping to flee the cafe as soon as possible.

Unexpectedly, when I finally received my coffee, I was pleasantly surprised that it was exactly what I wanted – a small-sized skinny latte. I was thrilled that after all the barista had made a mistake; instead of giving me a huge, tall cup, she ended up giving me what I wanted by accident. I felt very lucky – all the way until I looked up the meaning of *tall*, a familiar adjective that I thought I had confidently mastered as early as when I was a first grader in China. In fact, a cup of tall-sized coffee was far 'shorter' than I had thought. Being one of the smallest sizes that customers can choose from, a *tall* cup of coffee is quite the opposite to however *tall* and huge it may sound to be. This experience again made me think deeper about the mismatches between my English proficiency as measured by standardized English examinations and my actual ability to function linguistically across contexts.

When sharing my experiences with other multilingual international students, I was shocked to realize that I was by no means alone. While multilingual international students' shiny TOEFL scores could indeed demonstrate their ability to do well in standardized assessments, such successful scores may not always lead to a smooth transcultural, translingual and transnational journey at the beginning of their overseas studies. However, higher education institutions in Anglophone countries do not seem to see such a mismatch. In most cases, they tend to rely heavily on standardized English language proficiency exams such as the TOEFL and the International English Language Testing System (IELTS) as gatekeeping tools for college admission. As a result, international students with successful standardized English assessment scores are often regarded as linguistically problem-free, and then receive little if any institutional language support.

How exactly do multilingual international students function linguistically in academic and social contexts on arriving in American higher education institutions? What are their challenges, needs and successes during their initial languaging journeys in college? How do they draw on their rich multilingual and multimodal communicative repertoires to facilitate their languaging across contexts? How can university support systems better serve the needs of multilingual international students? Informed by these questions, this exploratory qualitative study explored the first-semester language and academic experiences of 12 Chinese international freshmen studying in a higher education institution in the United States. Drawing on the Bioecological Model of Human Development (Bronfenbrenner & Morris, 2006) and the concept of languaging (e.g. Canagarajah, 2011; Creese & Blackledge, 2015; García & Kleifgen, 2020; Jørgensen, 2008), I proposed an integrated theoretical framework to guide the design, analysis and discussion of the study. Adopting an insider–outsider positionality (Dwyer & Buckle, 2009), I collected multilingual and multimodal data through a combination of a four-month digital ethnography (Pink *et al.*, 2016) using a culturally relevant social media application *WeChat*, along with traditional qualitative data collection methods including semi-structured interviews, bilingual language logs, writing samples across genres, talks around texts and informal communication. Highlighting the within-group dynamics among Chinese international students and calling for a developmental perspective to understand their initial languaging journeys, the findings unpacked five commonly held myths among Chinese international students. Through in-depth investigation of a group of Chinese international students' linguistic functioning across academic and social contexts over the course of one semester, this project sheds light on ways that higher education institutions in Anglophone countries could better support their growing culturally and linguistically diverse international student population and suggests future research directions.

This book is organized in three parts. Part 1 introduces the rationale, focus, background information and study design of my project. Chapter 1 presents the overarching research problem, detailed guiding research questions, the educational significance of the study and a glimpse of the findings and implications by answering three key background questions: (1) Who are Chinese international students? (2) Why do I study newly arrived Chinese international students? (3) What do I want to explore about Chinese international students' initial college experiences? Chapter 2 reviews the relevant literature on the gap between Chinese international students' language and education experiences in China and the linguistic demands they face studying in American higher education. Based on the review and discussion, I propose an integrated theoretical framework for this project. In Chapter 3, I introduce the details of my study design and provide detailed examples to illustrate my multimodal data collection methods.

Parts 2 and 3 present the key findings of my study. In Part 2 (Chapters 4 through 7), I draw attention to within-group variabilities among Chinese international students by zooming in on five focal participants' first-semester languaging journeys in college. In Chapter 4, I propose a continuum to capture how nuances regarding participants' previous language and educational experiences could play a role in their different degrees of readiness in pursuing overseas studies in American higher education. To illustrate each of the five categories proposed in the continuum, in Chapters 5 and 6, I present the languaging journeys of five focal students through storytelling. To conclude Part 2, Chapter 7 synthesizes the findings from the five focal cases (see Chapters 5 and 6) in reference to the continuum proposed in Chapter 4 and calls for a developmental perspective in understanding multilingual international students' initial college experiences.

Part 3 of the book (Chapters 8 through 14) shifts attention from selected focal cases back to all 12 participants in the study and presents their initial college experiences in the format of debunking five commonly held myths. In Chapter 8, I present an overview of my research findings and introduce five commonly held myths/misconceptions about Chinese international students studying in American higher education. These myths, which are elaborated in detail in Chapters 9 through 13, include:

- Myth 1: TOEFL results accurately predict international students' abilities to function linguistically on college entry
- Myth 2: An English-only policy is necessary in college classrooms to help international students improve their linguistic functioning in English
- Myth 3: *First-Year Writing* guarantees international students' successful writing performances in content-area courses
- Myth 4: English is responsible for all the challenges facing Chinese international students
- Myth 5: Chinese international students are well supported in American higher education, linguistically and academically

Finally, in Chapter 14, I revisit and revise the theoretical framework based on the research findings as presented in Parts 2 and 3. Informed by the updated theoretical framework, I discuss implications for Chinese international students, for American higher education support systems as well as for research methodological innovation. In closing, I discuss the research implications and end the book with directions for future research.

This book targets a wide range of readers, including researchers, practitioners, students and a general audience who are interested in applied linguistics, multilingualism/multiliteracies, TESOL, college composition, digital ethnography as well as international higher education in Anglophone countries. While the study introduced in this book is grounded in the US higher education context with a specific focus on Chinese international students, many of its implications may facilitate deeper understanding of the languaging journeys and ways to support multilingual international students in other Anglophone contexts. There is so much more to explore and learn regarding multilingual international students' transcultural, translingual and transnational experiences in college. I cannot wait to invite you to join me and embark on this wonderful journey together!

Part 1

1 Who, Why and What about Chinese International Students

Introduction

Who are Chinese international students? Why do I study newly arrived Chinese international students? What do I want to explore about these multilingual international students' initial college experiences? In the opening chapter of my book, I present the overarching research problem, detailed guiding research questions, the educational significance of the study and a glimpse of the findings and implications.

Who are Chinese International Students? A Common Term with Messy Definitions

International students is a commonly used term in scholarly publications, the mass media, professional contexts and in the field of education at large. Despite its household name, this term has been used inconsistently across different contexts throughout the world. In other words, as simple as it may appear, there is no clear-cut answer to the seemingly easy question 'Who are international students?'.

According to the United Nations Educational, Scientific and Cultural Organization (UNESCO) Institute of Statistics (2020), international students are defined as 'students who have crossed a national or territorial border for the purpose of education and are now enrolled outside their country of origin'. This definition has been embraced by important international higher education organizations including the United Kingdom's Higher Education Statistics Agency (HESA). Based on this definition, in order to be defined as an international student, a person must (1) cross a national border for education purposes and (2) enroll in an education program outside their country of birth. Since one's country of origin has nothing to do with one's current nationality and country of residence, the UNESCO Institute of Statistic's (2020) definition implies that both temporary student visa holders and immigrants (i.e. those who hold citizenship or permanent residency in a country outside their country of origin) can be counted as international students. According to UNESCO's definition, we can infer that Chinese international students studying in

American higher education include those holding temporary student visas (e.g. F-1 visa) along with Chinese American immigrants whose country of origin is China but who later immigrated to the United States for educational purposes (e.g. a Chinese American college student who immigrated to the United States during preschool years).

Contrasting with UNESCO's definition, the New York-based Institute of International Education embraces a narrower definition of international students. According to the Institute of International Education (2020), an international student is '[a]nyone who is enrolled at an institution of higher education in the United States who is not a US citizen, an immigrant (permanent resident) or a refugee'. Based on the Institute of International Education's definition, which is another very commonly embraced school of thought around the world, Chinese international students are more narrowly defined as those non-immigrant Chinese students who hold temporary student visas (e.g. F-1 visa).

Messy definitions of the commonly used term 'international students' have led to statistical confusion. For example, Nick Clark (2009), editor of *World Education News & Review*, has pointed out that when measured by the Institute of International Education standard, the HESA data of the British Council indicated that 389,330 international students studied in Britain during the 2007–2008 academic year. Nevertheless, when calculated based on UNESCO's definition, the number immediately jumped to as high as 513,570 (an increase of 32%). These two different numbers describing international student enrollment in the same country at the same time have caused confusion across news agencies.

According to Clark (2009), 'Soon after this new data [UK's international student enrollment based on UNESCO's definition] was released, a number of media outlets suggested that Britain was now much closer to being on a par with the US in terms of international recruitment numbers'. Indeed, the figure 513,570 itself was very close to the 2007–2008 number in the United States (623,805). However, Clark (2009) wisely pointed out that while the UK number of 513,570 was generated based on the more liberal UNESCO definition of international students, the US figure was reported by the Institute of International Education which adopted a narrower definition. When put on the same scale, the UK international student enrollment (389,330) was in reality far from near the US number (623,805).

With the above-mentioned inconsistencies in mind, how exactly should we define Chinese international students? To put it another way, can we mix the two concepts of *Chinese American students* and *Chinese international students*? In an earlier critical review of the literature on Chinese international students pursuing higher education in the United States, I argued that international students are fundamentally different from immigrants due to the following reasons (Zhang-Wu, 2018).

Firstly, from the perspective of political status, international students are granted short-term student visas to stay in the host country, the length of which is determined by the duration of the academic programs in which they are enrolled. Being student visa holders, international students are not allowed to work, unlike immigrants who are citizens and permanent residents. Secondly, from the perspective of socioeconomic status (SES), international students are generally wealthier than immigrant populations who are likely to be subjected to financial burdens (Lenkeit et al., 2015). Contrasting with the case of immigrant students, only a very small proportion of international students depend on student loans to finish their college education. In the case of undergraduate international students, for instance, almost 85% have listed 'personal/family' as their major source of funding (Association of International Educators, 2018). This alone has earned American higher education a profit of $39 billion in the academic year 2017–2018 (Association of International Educators, 2018).

Thirdly, international students differ from immigrants given their different motivations for migration. The vast majority of international students are found to travel abroad mainly for educational purposes and are likely to return to their home countries shortly after completing their overseas studies. To them, pursuing overseas studies is 'a strategy for contributing to the family's cultural, economic, and social capital, which may be directly convertible into monetary gains' (Park, 2016: 238), so that they are provided with better career opportunities once they return to their own countries. Therefore, their motivation for studying overseas in order to improve their SES and social capital in their home countries is drastically different from most immigrants who have left their homeland for a better life in the host country (Ball, 1993, 2003; Brown, 1990, 1995).

Finally, international and immigrant students tend to have different language experiences and varying linguistic abilities. International students, who mostly aim to maintain their social capital back in their home countries and have relatively less desire or opportunity to socialize with local people in the neighborhood, often limit their English communication to academic contexts. In contrast, immigrant students, especially those who arrived in their destination countries during their childhood and grew up in the neighborhood, tend to have much more exposure to English through their schooling and social experiences. These students are therefore often more linguistically acculturated compared with their international counterparts.

Despite the many distinctions between international and immigrant students, the two parties have not been well distinguished in previous research. In many scholarly articles, international students have often been treated as a subgroup and lumped into the overall category of immigrants (e.g. Chang et al., 2007; Kagawa et al., 2011; Lim, 2015; Park et al., 2008). For instance, Beyond Myths: The Growth and Diversity of Asian American College Freshmen 1971–2005 (Chang et al., 2007), an award-winning project, is famous for providing 'the largest compilation and analysis of data on Asian American college students' (Wyer, 2007). While Chang and colleagues (2007) have made a remarkable contribution to enhancing knowledge in higher education research on Asian populations, immigrant and international students were poorly distinguished in the study; they were mixed together to represent the so-called *Asian American college students* (Zhang-Wu, 2018). Despite their acknowledgement in the methodology section that '[a]lthough Asian international students are included in the Asian/Asian American sample, we use the term "Asian American" in the report to describe the group' (Chang *et al.*, 2007: 5), the authors overlooked this aspect as one of their research limitations. Given the many differences between international and immigrant students, overgeneralizing the two parties as *Asian American college students* can be problematic. As I critiqued in an earlier article:

> Despite the humongous sample size of this quantitative study, blending these two drastically different populations under the same umbrella term of *Asian American college students* has certainly skewed the accuracy of its research findings, particularly concerning their reported percentages of 'low-SES Asian American freshmen' (international students tend to have much higher SES than immigrants) and 'Asian American freshmen intending to get a job to pay for college tuitions' (it is illegal for international students to work off-campus). (Zhang-Wu, 2018: 1175)

Considering the aforementioned differences between international and immigrant students, in this book, I embrace the Institute of International Education's definition, based on which *Chinese international students* refers to those who were born and raised in China but who later came to the United States on non-immigrant visas in pursuit of international studies. For the purpose of this book, *Chinese international students* is used to specifically refer to non-immigrant students from Mainland China. Students from other Chinese regions and districts such as Hong Kong and Macao are beyond the scope of the study, considering the extremely different heritage languages, educational policies and sociopolitical factors that may influence students' languaging experiences.

Why Study Newly Arrived Chinese International Students?

With globalization and the rising popularity of English as a lingua franca (Jenkins, 2006), more and more students are traveling overseas to English-speaking countries in pursuit of tertiary education. Among them, a considerable number have chosen to go to the United States, the top host country in the world for international students (Park, 2016). According to a recent report from the Institute of International Education (2018), in the academic year 2017–2018, the total number of international students enrolled in American higher education reached its peak at 1,094,792. With an increase of over 3.6% in comparison with the previous academic year, China has been the leading place of origin for international students over the past decade (33.2%), followed by India (17.9%) and South Korea (5.0%).

Chinese international students' journeys in American higher education encompass both opportunities and challenges. On the one hand, the new experiences in an English-speaking Western country could familiarize them with cutting-edge research and knowledge, endow them with a global vision and prepare them to be cultural ambassadors in the process of globalization (Li, 2020). On the other hand, the different cultural and language environments and the transition from secondary to tertiary education may pose challenges to their adaptation and acculturation. Although Chinese international students are required to pass certain thresholds in gatekeeping English proficiency standardized tests such as the test of English as a foreign language (TOEFL) prior to college entry, they are often found to be linguistically under-prepared and have difficulty functioning linguistically in English-speaking college environments (Wang, 2016; Xue, 2013). Such challenges in linguistic functioning[1] are particularly striking during the initial stage of their overseas experiences (Bayley et al., 2002).

A mismatch can be identified between Chinese international students' ability to pass gatekeeping standardized English assessment and their inability to function linguistically on arrival. This is likely because to function linguistically in American higher education, students are required not only to perform discrete academic English skills in listening, speaking, reading and writing (as emphasized in standardized tests such as the TOEFL), but also to demonstrate their ability to apply those language skills and draw on all resources in their multilingual communicative repertoires to function in authentic academic and social contexts. Nevertheless, with its main focus on reading and writing and little emphasis on spoken language (Thornbury & Slade, 2006), the kind of English that international students learned back in China has failed to prepare them for the linguistic demands of American higher education. In other words, English as a foreign language is usually taught based on the written grammar, despite the clear distinction between spoken and written English (Lippi-Green, 2012). This, together with the teacher-centered and passive-receptive education culture in China, adds to the challenges that Chinese international students face in communicating effectively in their overseas studies in Anglophone countries (Hellsten & Prescott, 2004; Sawir, 2005).

According to previous studies in educational psychology and counseling, the difficulty in linguistic functioning is not only 'the most significant prevalent problem for most international students' (Mori, 2000: 137), but also a major source of their academic and acculturation stressors (Smith & Khawaja, 2011; Yan & Berliner, 2011). Since international students' linguistic functioning is closely associated with their academic performances (Andrade, 2006; Karuppan & Barari, 2010; Rowntree *et al.*, 2016; Yeh & Inose, 2003) and social adjustments (Andrade, 2006; Robertson *et al.*, 2000; Yeh & Inose, 2003), it is crucial to understand the linguistic challenges that non-native English-speaking international students are faced with in academic and social settings (Zhang & Mi, 2010), especially during their initial overseas education experiences (Bayley *et al.*, 2002).

Despite their urgency and significance, there are no clear national, district, or regional policies regulating how higher education institutions should provide customized linguistic support in response to the increasing international student population. Furthermore, among existing studies focusing on the language and education experiences of tertiary-level Chinese international students, the vast majority have focused exclusively on graduate students (e.g. Cheng & Erben, 2011; Jiang, 2014; Lin, 2006; Xue, 2013). It remains unclear how undergraduate students, especially newly arrived Chinese international college freshmen, function linguistically during their initial transnational and transcultural languaging journeys.

What to Study about Chinese International Students' Initial College Experiences?

The guiding research questions of this study are (1) How did the 12 Chinese international students from different disciplines function linguistically in academic and social settings at the beginning of their first semester in college? (2) How did these multilingual international students meet the oral and written linguistic demands in academic and social settings throughout the semester? (3) What changed in their languaging experiences over the course of one semester?

Drawing on the Bioecological Model of Human Development (Bronfenbrenner & Morris, 2006) and the concept of *languaging* (Canagarajah, 2011; García, 2009; Jørgensen, 2008), this semester-long qualitative study explores the first-semester linguistic functioning of 12 Chinese international freshmen. This study provides a snapshot of the linguistic demands that multilingual international students are faced with in their initial journeys studying in an American higher education institution. By triangulating multimodal data from various sources, this study calls for a developmental perspective in understanding multilingual international students' initial languaging journeys in college. Following a close examination of the participants' linguistic functioning in academic and social contexts, the findings have challenged five commonly held myths/misconceptions about Chinese international students and shed light on how American higher education could better serve its growing multilingual international student population.

Examining multilingual international students' languaging arts is a transdisciplinary and interdisciplinary project. This book targets a wide range of readers, including researchers, practitioners, students and a general audience who are interested in applied linguistics, multilingualism/multiliteracies, TESOL, college composition, digital ethnography as well as international higher education in Anglophone countries. This project adopted a student-centered approach in exploring Chinese international students' first-semester languaging experiences, which contributes to the existing literature by drawing attention to the needs and challenges of multilingual international freshmen (e.g. Fraiberg *et al.*, 2017; Heng, 2018; Ma, 2020; Martin, 2009; Morton *et al.*, 2015; Sherry *et al.*, 2010). Drawing on innovative data collection methods combining digital ethnography (Pink *et al.*, 2016) with traditional qualitative methods, this study documents participants' multilingual and multimodal communication across contexts and presents commonly held languaging myths and realities about Chinese international students. Finally, focusing on the first-semester languaging journeys of Chinese international freshmen within and beyond college classrooms, this project adds to the explorations of post-secondary students' initial college experiences (e.g. Clark, 2005; Donahue & Foster-Johnson, 2018; You & You, 2013).

Concluding Remarks

In Chapter 1, I presented a brief overview of my rationale for conducting this project, its educational significance, guiding research questions and implications based on the findings. In the remainder of Part 1, I present a review of the literature on Chinese international students' language and educational experiences and their challenges in linguistic functioning during their initial college experiences in American higher education institutions. Following the review, I provide details about my theoretical framework and study design.

Note

(1) I have defined *linguistic functioning* as an individual's ability to draw on all *multilingual* and *multimodal* resources in their linguistic repertoires to navigate through and meet the linguistic demands of academic and social settings. These linguistic demands extend far beyond the four discrete areas of listening, speaking, reading and writing, and require students to be able not only to demonstrate proficiency in the four skill areas but also to use those skills properly and effectively to function in authentic academic and social contexts.

2 Languaging across Borders: Linguistic Demands, Challenges and an Integrated Framework

Introduction

To understand the linguistic challenges facing newly arrived Chinese international students, in this chapter I explore the mismatches between English as a foreign language (EFL) teaching and learning in China and the linguistic demands of American classrooms. Drawing on the mismatches identified, I discuss Chinese international students' linguistic challenges in American higher education. Echoing the call from many scholars in bi/multilingual research (e.g. Allard, 2017; Creese & Martin, 2003; Creese & Blackledge, 2010; Hornberger, 2004; Hornberger & Link, 2012) to adopt ecological approaches in examining students' multilingual journeys, I introduce the integrated theoretical framework of the study informed by the Bioecological Model of Human Development (Bronfenbrenner & Morris, 2006) and the concept of *languaging* (Canagarajah, 2011; García, 2009; Gynne & Bagga-Gupta, 2015; Jørgensen, 2008).

Policy-Driven English Education in China

Accompanied by English's rising power as a lingua franca (Jenkins, 2006), 'English fever' is a term coined to describe non-native speakers' overwhelming desire to learn English. While some researchers have cautioned against this phenomenon, unpacking the imperialist nature of English and its function as 'a segregationally class dialect' (Mignolo, 2009; Pennycook, 2019: 180; Zhang-Wu, 2021a), English is still considered in Mainland China as one of the most important skills of the 21st century. According to a recent article published by *People's Daily Online*, an official news agency of the Central Committee of the Chinese Communist Party, given its status as 'the language of international communication', English can benefit Chinese people by introducing them to 'a fresh pattern of thinking', 'a way... to discover an entirely new world' and 'a powerful tool... to connect to the outside world' (Li, 2020). With China winning bids to host international events such as the 2008 Olympic

Games in Beijing and the 2010 World Expo in Shanghai, hundreds of millions of Chinese people joined the English fever (Wu, 2006).

For decades, English education has been closely related to China's political orientation in reforming and opening up to the outside world. The necessity of teaching and learning English in China is said to be associated with the successful modernization of Chinese society (Shen & Feng, 2005; Yu, 2004), China's competitiveness in the process of globalization (Jiang, 2003) and its economic development (Feng, 2005; Song & Yan, 2004). Increasing the overall English proficiency of Chinese people has been regarded as a crucial approach to enhance China's ability to absorb advanced knowledge from the Western world (Qian, 2003; Zhang, 2003) and exert its political and economic power in the international arena (Zhu, 2004).

As the country with the largest population of EFL learners in the world (He & Li, 2009; He & Zhang, 2010), high-quality EFL education in China is considered 'a bridge to the future' (Jin & Cortazzi, 2006: 53) and a 'prerequisite' to transform leading cities such as Shanghai into 'a world-class international metropolis' (Shanghai Curriculum and Teaching Materials Reform Commission, 1999: 3). For over 1000 years, the Chinese government has been exerting tremendous influence on educational curricula, course materials, assessments and textbook selection in public schools (Feng, 2007; Neuby, 2012; Pan, 2007). In response to the increasing need to improve the overall English proficiency of Chinese people, the Ministry of Education (MOE) of China has put great emphasis on EFL education. In elementary and secondary education, EFL education has been placed as one of the central pieces in promoting quality education (Shen & Feng, 2005; Song & Yan, 2004; Yu, 2004). Over the past four decades, English has been listed as one of three compulsory subjects along with Chinese and mathematics in the National College Entrance Examination (or *Gaokao*), one of the most high-stakes standardized assessments in China. At the tertiary level, EFL education is a crucial component of Chinese students' college experience. Regardless of their various disciplinary studies and concentrations, Chinese college students are required to pass the College English Test, a standardized national EFL exam in China, in order to receive their undergraduate degree (Zhang-Wu, 2021a).

Since the start of the 21st century, the MOE has undergone multiple reforms to enhance the quality of EFL education in China. One of the most mentioned themes in those endeavors has been to advocate for communicative language teaching (CLT). According to the 2001 Chinese National English Language Curriculum for elementary and secondary education, EFL teaching and learning has shifted from being heavily grammar focused to being more student centered and task based. New textbooks and curricula have been designed and implemented in the hope of promoting CLT throughout China. EFL teachers are encouraged to resort to formative rather than summative assessment during their instructional practices to better implement CLT and support students' long-term English development.

In spite of all these efforts, CLT implementation in China is greatly challenged by various contextual factors including large EFL class sizes, low English proficiency among local EFL teachers, a shortage of instructional and human resources and the examination-oriented educational culture (e.g. Li & Baldauf, 2011; Nunan, 2003; Tran & Baldauf, 2007). For instance, after interviewing 73 elementary and secondary EFL teachers working in urban, suburban and rural public schools in China, Li and Baldauf (2011) reported that given the limited educational resources, Chinese EFL class sizes usually range from 40 to 80 students. Such overcrowded classrooms have posed practical challenges in adopting CLT on a daily basis. Beyond challenges from limited educational resources, Chinese EFL teachers are often reluctant to implement CLT due to their lack of confidence in their own oral English proficiency. As one teacher put it, 'I don't think I can teach my students using CLT if my English remains this poor...' (Li & Baldauf, 2011: 797). Consequently, CLT is something that Chinese EFL teachers use only on 'special occasion[s]' such as when being observed or doing teaching demonstrations (Li & Baldauf, 2011: 797). In most cases, EFL classes are taught mainly in Chinese.

The implementation of CLT is further challenged by China's examination-oriented educational culture. Although EFL teachers are encouraged to put more emphasis on formative assessment to facilitate CLT, there is no corresponding education policy in place to transform the overall grammar-focused testing system. Under the pressure of teaching to test, EFL teachers are discouraged from putting CLT into practice. As one local EFL teacher in Li and Baldauf's (2011: 799) study explained, '[U]nder the examination-oriented education, any educational reform will be in vain if the testing system does not change. And no matter how the curriculum reform is promoted, you are a loser if your students cannot get high marks!'.

In response to the many challenges of implementing CLT in China, some schools in metropolitan areas have started to recruit native English-speaking teachers to strengthen their teaching force. While Chinese EFL teachers are expected to teach grammar and familiarize students with test-taking skills, native English-speaking teachers are assigned EFL conversation classes in the hope of enhancing students' oral communication skills. While in theory such a method may seem an effective solution to promote CLT, in reality many challenges remain.

On the one hand, while native English-speaking teachers are desired due to their 'authentic pronunciation and intonation' and their ability to create a 'real life communicative environment' (Rao, 2010: 62), only wealthy schools in affluent cities can afford to internationalize their teaching forces given the high cost of hiring native speakers as EFL teachers. Based on the National Bureau of Statistics of China (2020), the average annual wage in China is around 90,000 CNY ($1071/month). Yet, according to the International TEFL Academy (2020), the average starting monthly salary for inexperienced, 'first-time English teachers in China from the US, Canada, the U.K. or other native English-speaking countries' is usually as high as $2600, more than 2.5 times the average monthly wage of Chinese nationals.

On the other hand, hiring native speakers does not necessarily guarantee high-quality education, since many foreign teachers have little training or teaching experience in EFL education. Research examining Chinese students' perceptions of foreign EFL teachers has found that students often cast doubt on their qualifications and their effectiveness as language teachers. Some have expressed concerns about being taught by native speakers of English who have little training in EFL teaching and who used to work in unrelated industries as 'a police officer, a shop assistant, an architect, a bus driver, and a dramatist' before coming to teach in China (Rao, 2010: 61). Others have pointed out that regardless of their native-speaking teachers' qualifications, these EFL instructors' teaching effectiveness is limited by their lack of familiarity with the local educational system and culture, Chinese students' learning styles and the unique English learning challenges for Chinese speakers (Rao, 2010).

Teaching and Learning in Chinese EFL Classrooms

As discussed earlier, despite the promotion of CLT, China's test-oriented nature in EFL education remains untouched. Under the pressure of teaching for the test, EFL education in China emphasizes rote memorization of vocabulary and grammar with very minimal focus on oral English proficiency. This is partially due to local teachers' lack of confidence in their spoken English and the large class sizes that discourage learner-centered activities. More importantly, the heavy emphasis on EFL written skills is largely determined by *Gaokao*, which assesses students' English language proficiency solely based on their written responses to listening, reading and writing problems. Since oral English communication skill is not part of the areas assessed in *Gaokao*, EFL teachers mostly use Chinese to teach students grammatical rules and vocabulary for clarification purposes. Students have little chance to engage in English conversations, and rely heavily on grammar-translation methods to facilitate their EFL learning.

With 题海战术 (preparing for tests by submerging students in oceans of practice problems) as a widely appreciated pedagogical value in Chinese society, EFL education is largely defined by test preparation. Teachers are expected to gear their pedagogical practices toward test preparation so that their students will be able to select the one and only 'correct' answer to achieve high scores in high-stakes standardized assessments. Yet, such an overemphasis on test performance and finding the black-and-white 'correct' answer have undermined the very nature of language as a tool for negotiation, communication and discussion. Using the evolvement of the word 'tweet' over the past decade on social media as an example, Zhang-Wu (2021) reminds us that English is a living language that is constantly being revised and recreated based on its users communicative needs; in the process, the definition of correctness and appropriateness is also fluid. Overlooking this important reality and grounding EFL education in test-oriented correctness limit Chinese students' capacity to function linguistically in English in the long run. For instance, Question 29 in 江苏高考英语试卷 (College Entrance Exam in Jiangsu province) in 2020 asked students to select *the* correct answer from 'absurd, abrupt, allergic, authentic' to fill in the blank: 'The outbreak of Covid-19 has meant an _____ change in our life and work'. *Abrupt*, the officially announced 'correct' answer to this question, is a key phrase (i.e. an abrupt change 突变) in China's high school curriculum which students are expected to have memorized. While this adjective certainly makes sense in this context, it is problematic to declare *abrupt* as the only answer to this question and punish those who choose otherwise by deducting their points in this high-stakes standardized assessment. Emphasizing the feelings of frustration and shock, *absurd* can be another answer to this problem. While not included as one of the key phrases in Chinese K-12 EFL textbooks, the phrase 'an absurd change' is not only used frequently in informal settings (e.g. oral communication, blogs), but has also appeared in scholarly publications such as *A Concise and Genuine Account of the Dispute Between Mr. Hume and Mr. Rousseau* written by the famous Scottish Enlightenment philosopher David Hume, and *Notes on the Text of Asklepiodotos* published in the *American Journal of Philology*.

Trained in such an examination-oriented environment, many Chinese students are demotivated to learn English and often associate EFL learning with tedious rote memorization and endless test preparation. Clearly recognizing the gap between test-oriented EFL training and their ability to function linguistically in English, these students cast doubt on the meaning of English education:

> I always ask myself the same question: what is the goal of studying English at all? To pass the exam or to gain the enough scores? I don't know. I just know that up to now, I cannot use English to communicate with foreigners…. (Cargill *et al.*, 2011: 61)

The heavy emphasis on test performance in Chinese EFL education has also demoralized teachers, who are constantly under pressure to grade students' practice tests and prepare them to achieve high scores. Describing teaching as 'a tiring job', one EFL teacher vented their frustration:

'[W]e have to mark 70 or 80 exam papers. If the students take an exam this evening, I have to finish marking all the papers before the first lesson tomorrow because I will have to give them feedback' (Gao & Xu, 2014: 158). The heavy emphasis on test preparation and rote memorization has further discouraged EFL teachers from creating a student-centered learning space to engage students in active meaning-making processes. In their ethnographic study investigating Chinese students' reticence in EFL classrooms, Sang and Hiver (2021: 10) found that the focal EFL teacher 'frequently interrupts and repairs students' languages' to make sure their grammatical errors are corrected, and their vocabulary is properly chosen. Consequently, due to 'an absence of opportunities for interaction as a result of too much teacher control', Chinese students are often stereotyped as being quiet and passive (Xie, 2010: 18).

In China, English is usually taught as a stand-alone subject in K-12 education. Beyond the EFL classrooms, students are rarely exposed to any English-speaking environment since all their content-subject courses are taught in Mandarin. In other words, regardless of their English language proficiencies, EFL learners in China are unfamiliar with authentic communication experiences in content-subjects and are unlikely to be able to function linguistically across the disciplines. At the tertiary level, in well-funded prestigious universities, occasionally a small portion of the content courses are taught in English or a mixture of both languages. However, college students have expressed concerns about content-based EFL education. In their survey study, Beckett and Li (2012) found that 99% of their participants believed that their content-subject learning was watered down due to English medium instruction, and 74% preferred the content-subject be taught in Chinese and EFL education be kept outside of the content classroom. Meanwhile, college teachers are also reluctant to integrate content and EFL education. As one instructor explained, 'Chinese universities do not focus on teaching, but use publications and grants as the main indicators for faculty promotion. So we don't have incentive to improve teaching, let alone EMI [English-medium instruction] teaching' (Macaro & Han, 2020: 228).

Linguistic Demands in American Classrooms

Academic English, or English used in academic contexts, has been referred to as the 'hidden curriculum' of schooling and is in essence 'at the heart of teaching and learning' (Christie, 1985; DiCerbo et al., 2014: 446). Although linguistic demands within and across disciplines are seldom made explicit during content-area teaching and learning, disciplinary content knowledge is expressed in language and digested by students via language. Drawing on Christie's (1985) work, DiCerbo et al. (2014: 447) have concluded that 'success in school is largely a matter of learning the patterns of discourse through which academic concepts and skills are developed, explored, and expanded'. In this process, the mastery of academic English is crucial, especially for those non-native English-speaking learners who are studying in the American educational system.

Academic English is defined as a set of linguistic resources that are necessary for teaching, learning and communication in school settings to facilitate students' knowledge acquisition (Bailey & Heritage, 2008; Schleppegrell, 2004; Snow & Uccelli, 2009). It is viewed as 'a culturally shaped resource for making meaning' in academic settings (Coffin *et al.*, 2005: 11). One of the pioneering scholars in examining academic English is Cummins (1980, 1981), who proposed the concepts of basic interpersonal communicative skills (BICS) and cognitive academic language proficiency (CALP). BICS, often referred to as social language, focuses on the conversational fluency of the target language. CALP, often referred to as academic language, relates to 'students' ability to understand and express, in both oral and written modes, concepts and ideas that are relevant to success in school' (Cummins, 2008: 71). While Cummins' (1980, 1981) classic work set a solid foundation for later research on academic language, the clear distinctions between BICS and CALP are problematized by some scholars as perpetuating dichotomous perceptions of language use (Scarcella, 2003). On the one hand, the concept of CALP has fallen short in capturing the detailed characteristics of the language of schooling (i.e. features of language across various disciplines). On the other hand, implying CALP as the language of schooling while BICS as codes outside of the school contexts may lead to deficit views on the rich cultural and linguistic resources that students bring to the classroom (MacSwan & Rolstad, 2003).

Both social and academic languages should be considered as valuable resources for students; they differ from each other in the complexity of their language features (Bailey, 2007). Based on this idea, Bailey and Heritage, 2008) have categorized academic English into school navigational language (SNL) and curriculum content language (CCL). SNL is defined as 'the language to communicate with teachers and peers in the school setting in a very broad sense' (Bailey & Heritage, 2008: 15). In contrast, CCL is defined as 'the language used in the process of teaching and learning content material' (Bailey & Heritage, 2008: 15). While complicating the concepts of CALP and BICS by pointing out the social aspects of academic language, the notion of CCL and SNL as two sets of language skills has potentially perpetuated another dichotomy which fails to account for academic practices integrating the application of both skills. For example, common tertiary education practices such as visiting professors during their office hours and collaborating with teammates in group work require a combination of CCL and SNL skills. The blurred boundary between CCL and SNL has made many scholars (e.g. Schleppegrell, 2004; Turkan *et al.*, 2014) cast doubt on the existence of so-called academic English, arguing that the language of schooling should instead be viewed as a set of registers across various disciplinary contexts.

For instance, drawing on Schleppegrell's (2007) work, Brisk and Zhang-Wu (2017: 88) summarized that the language of mathematics represents 'a multi-semiotic system that includes oral language, symbolic representations, graphs, diagrams, formulas, and written language'. The math language is particularly challenging because of its vocabulary and grammar (Dale & Cuevas, 1992). Not only does math require mastery of technical jargon (e.g. hexagon, decagon), but it also involves everyday words with discipline-specific meaning (e.g. root, face, row). Furthermore, the math language features challenging grammatical structures, featuring the frequent presence of the passive voice (e.g. X is divided by Y), logical connectors (e.g. if… then…), comparatives (e.g. greater than), prepositions (e.g. divided by, added on) and long noun groups (e.g. the surface area of a sphere with a radius of 5 inches).

Similarly, although science may be easily misunderstood as a language-free discipline with numbers and symbols, Norris and Phillips (2003: 226) suggest that language and literacy are in fact 'inextricably linked to the very nature and fabric of science'. According to Fang and colleagues (Fang, 2005, 2008; Fang *et al.*, 2010), the language of science is characterized by informational density, abstraction/nominalization, technicality and authoritativeness. Informational density is usually measured by the index of vocabulary density, or the number of lexical words in each non-embedded clause. While average lexical density in written language is between approximately four and six lexical words per clause (Halliday, 1994), the lexical density in science texts could be as high as 10 lexical words per clause (Fang, 2005). Abstraction and nominalization, the process of turning verbs and verb phrases into nouns and noun groups (e.g. construct → construction; protect rainforest → the protection of rainforest), is also common in the language of science. Technicality speaks to the frequent presence of discipline-specific jargon in the language of science (e.g. paleontologist, geosphere). Authoritativeness speaks to the fact that science texts are usually expressed in a way that distances its author (i.e. absence of first-person expressions such as 'I believe/think'). To meet the linguistic demands of science, students are expected to navigate through and become familiar with all four features.

Similar to the case with language in math and science, the language in social studies also has its unique challenges, featuring high lexical density, abstraction/normalization (e.g. colonize → colonization) and technicality (e.g. massacre, prosecution). Furthermore, in order to function linguistically in social studies, students are expected to understand logical connectors to establish cause and effect relationships (e.g. X historical event has led to Y historical event) and are required to interpret the meanings of words in contexts (Brisk & Zhang-Wu, 2017). For instance, the word 'call' has different meanings in 'The Great Depression, as it was *called*, lasted from 1929 to 1939' (history text) and 'I plan to *call* him tonight' (everyday language).

Research in K-12 education has found that academic discourses across the disciplines are difficult due to their abstract meanings, complex sentence structures, dense vocabulary and demands for precise and succinct expressions (Brisk & Zhang-Wu, 2017; Fang *et al.*, 2010; Fang & Schleppegrell, 2010; Gottlieb & Ernst-Slavit, 2014). All students, native and non-native speakers alike, are faced with more and more complicated and abstract academic language as they further their education (Christie, 2012). When it comes to their transition into tertiary education, students are challenged by even heavier linguistic demands characterized by denser vocabulary, oral discussions that require higher-level thinking, more abstract content knowledge and more academic writing in discipline-specific genres. While those who major in the humanities (e.g. English, history) are often engaged in rhetorical analysis, argumentative essays and translation projects, students in the sciences (e.g. chemistry, biology) are expected to produce lab reports, grant proposals and field-work notes (Coffin *et al.*, 2005). Thus, understanding and navigating these discipline-specific genre norms are particularly important in facilitating college students' overall academic well-being.

Despite the importance of placing academic language instruction at 'the centre of teaching and learning' in tertiary education, it remains 'an invisible dimension of the curriculum' (Coffin *et al.*, 2005: 3). There are few clear national, district or regional policies on how higher education institutions should provide linguistic support to their students, especially in addressing the needs of the increasing population of multilingual international students. The degree of institutional linguistic support varies based on the university, usually ranging from no support at all to one or two English for academic purpose (EAP) courses, the quality and disciplinary relevance of which depends on a case-by-case basis.

Chinese International Students' Linguistic Challenges in American Higher Education

English fever in China has substantially motivated Chinese students to pursue overseas studies in Anglophone countries. Over the past decade, students from China have remained the world's largest international student group. In the United States, the top international student host country, 369,548 Chinese international students were enrolled in American higher education institutions in 2019, accounting for approximately a third of the entire international student population (Institute of International Education, 2019). This number is almost twice as many as that from India ($n = 202,014$), the second largest international student exporting country in the world.

Previous studies on multilingual international students' language experiences have reported significant challenges in their linguistic functioning during overseas studies (e.g. Cheng & Erben, 2011; Wang, 2016; Xue, 2013). Terminologies such as *language barrier* (Wang, 2016), *incompetent* (Jiang, 2014), *language difficulties* (Yeh & Inose, 2003), *deficiency in English* (Xue, 2013) and *broken English* (Wang & Li, 2014: 13) are often used when describing their language experiences in Anglophone countries. Chinese international students are faced with challenges in meeting the oral and written linguistic demands across contexts. These language difficulties have exerted negative influences on them, both mentally and academically. For instance, in her qualitative case study, Wang (2016) found that Chinese international students had significant difficulties in their linguistic functioning across academic and social settings, which resulted in low self-esteem and lack of confidence. Similarly, Xue's (2013) research on 14 Chinese international students' group work experiences has shown that all participants were concerned about their lack of competence in English reading and speaking, which in turn reduced their confidence in oral participation and impeded their capability to contribute to group work in college.

The linguistic challenges that Chinese international students are faced with are, to a large extent, because when transitioning from EFL to English-speaking contexts, their previous EFL learning experiences, strategies and knowledge not only transfer, but also influence their overseas academic experiences in American universities. In this process, the different educational culture and practices between the United States and China challenge Chinese international students' linguistic functioning in American higher education institutions (Cheng & Erben, 2011; Wang, 2016; Xue, 2013).

To be specific, Chinese international students' challenges in meeting the oral linguistic demands are mainly caused by the different educational cultures between China and the United States as well as the heavily test-oriented nature of EFL education in China. On the one hand, while discussion and collaboration are emphasized in American education culture, exerting high linguistic demands on oral English, Chinese EFL educational policies and practices are more test oriented (Yu & Suen, 2005), didactic (Wong, 2004) and passive-receptive (Hellsten, 2002), emphasizing memorization of written grammatical rules and vocabulary. Since Chinese international students are used to passively listening in class without contributing to oral discussions, they are likely to find it daunting to speak up in class during their overseas studies in the United States. On the other hand, despite the MOE being a strong advocate for CLT in enhancing Chinese students' communicative competence, the implementation of new curricula and teaching practices is severely impeded due to limited resources and a lack of corresponding policy innovations to change the examination-oriented nature of Chinese education

(Li & Baldauf, 2011; Nunan, 2003; Tran & Baldauf, 2007). This has made Chinese international students linguistically underprepared for their overseas college studies. While having learned English in China for years, their EFL education features 'constantly memorizing words and doing [test preparation] exercises' (Wang & Li, 2014: 13). Although EFL education in China focuses primarily on written grammar, there are considerable distinctions between oral and written grammar (Thornbury & Slade, 2006). In other words, scoring high on grammatical tests does not guarantee high communicative competence in English. The English they learned in textbooks in China may not help them successfully navigate office hour consultations, group discussions and participation in student organizations among other activities. As a result, Chinese international students are often faced with challenges in meeting the oral linguistic demands during their overseas studies in Anglophone countries.

Chinese international students' difficulties in meeting the written linguistic demands are related to the highly abstract and contextualized nature of academic English and the gap between writing for standardized assessments and writing in contexts. As discussed earlier, academic English is difficult for all students, native and non-native speakers alike, due to its dense vocabulary, complicated grammar and abstract meaning. Furthermore, academic English is highly contextualized, with different linguistic features and demands across the disciplines. This poses substantial challenges to Chinese international students who are experienced in grammar-oriented test preparation but have limited to no exposure to authentic language in contexts. Many Chinese international students are trained to meet the written linguistic demands in standardized assessment such as the test of English as a foreign language (TOEFL), which focuses primarily on argumentative writing. Despite its importance, argumentative writing represents only one of the genres needed in college. Depending on their fields of study, students are expected to perform specific genres that meet the disciplinary requirements of college. For example, while English majors are often engaged in rhetorical analysis writing, chemistry majors frequently write research reports. Since these genres are not tested in the TOEFL and Chinese EFL education is highly test oriented, newly arrived international students are likely to be unfamiliar with the genre expectations. Yet, because the quality of academic writing is closely intertwined with students' content-subject learning and evaluation, Chinese international students' lack of familiarity with discipline-specific genre expectations may put them at a disadvantage in their overall academic well-being.

Theoretical Framework

Recently, scholars in bi/multilingual education (e.g. Allard, 2017; Creese & Blackledge, 2010; Creese & Martin, 2003; Hornberger, 2004;

Hornberger & Link, 2012) have emphasized the importance of contextualizing participants' languaging experiences through ecological approaches. Shifting away from research on decontextualized language usage, ecological approaches make it possible to unpack 'the relationships among languages, relations among social contexts of language, relationships among individual speakers and their languages, and interrelationships among these three dimensions' (Hornberger & Hult, 2008: 282).

Based on my review of the literature above, the linguistic challenges facing newly arrived Chinese international students in American higher education are closely related to their previous EFL education in China as well as their culturally informed learning styles. Echoing previous literature in favor of ecological approaches in exploring individuals' languaging experiences (e.g. Allard, 2017; Creese & Blackledge, 2010; Creese & Martin, 2003; Hornberger, 2004; Hornberger & Link, 2012), my discussion above has made it clear that it is essential to examine Chinese international students' languaging experiences across contexts and situate their languaging journeys within their cultural, educational and sociopolitical backgrounds. To fully understand Chinese international students' bilingual linguistic functioning during their initial college experiences through an ecological lens, I propose an integrated model as the theoretical framework of the study. Aimed at contextualizing Chinese international students' languaging experiences during their overseas studies, the theoretical framework integrates the Bioecological Model of Human Development (Bronfenbrenner & Morris, 2006), which examines human development in contexts, and the concept of *languaging* (Canagarajah, 2011; García, 2009; Gynne & Bagga-Gupta, 2015; Jørgensen, 2008), which explores dynamic multilingual and multimodal communication across contexts.

Bioecological Model of Human Development

Drawing on an ecological perspective to examine Chinese international students' languaging journeys in American higher education, it is important to consider both their previous language and education backgrounds in China, and their experiences navigating American higher education. The Bioecological Model of Human Development (Bronfenbrenner & Morris, 2006: 793), which addresses 'the phenomenon of continuity and change in the biopsychological characteristics of human beings, both as individuals and as groups', lends itself as a useful framework that allows a contextualized exploration of the focal participants' journey across time and space. This model suggests that human development occurs when individuals are engaged in activities with increasing complexity; such processes can only be measured when contextualized, taking into consideration individuals' interactions with time, society and life. Four layers of environments influence an individual's development, including their micro, meso, exo and macro systems. This multilayered system represents a dynamic, nested structure to analyze individuals' experiences.

The Bioecological Model (Bronfenbrenner & Morris, 2006) is an updated version of its widely cited precursor, the Ecological Model of Human Development (Bronfenbrenner, 1979, 1989, 1993). Similar to Bronfenbrenner's classic Ecological Model, the new Bioecological Model also examines human development in contexts. Yet, different from its precursor, the updated Bioecological Model puts more emphasis on the processes of individual development. It is worth clarifying that the updated model does not aim to propose a shift in paradigm but instead represents 'a marked shift in the center of gravity of the model' (Bronfenbrenner & Morris, 2006: 794). Individuals are placed at the center of the multilayered system and are perceived as both the products and the producers of their environments. Through their 'bidirectional, synergistic interrelationships' with the multilayered system (Bronfenbrenner & Morris, 2006: 799), individuals are constantly shaped by and are shaping their environments by engaging in 'the *form, power, content,* and *direction* of the proximal process' and the '*developmental outcomes*—qualities of the developing person that emerge at a later point in time' (emphasis in original, Bronfenbrenner & Morris, 2006: 798).

The Bioecological Model of Human Development (Bronfenbrenner & Morris, 2006) can be summarized as a person–process–context–time framework. The person–process model emphasizes that development happens along with close interactions between individuals and their environments. Based on this model, in order to understand the person–process model of Chinese international students, a close examination of their interactions with faculty members, classmates, peers and friends in both academic and social settings is necessary. Moreover, given the central status of the developing human in the entire model along with the bidirectional relationship between individuals and their environments, it is also important to examine the unique traits, characteristics, challenges, strategies and actions of individual Chinese international students during the developmental processes.

The context model introduces four nested systems in which human development takes place. The microsystem involves the direct, immediate environment in which developing individuals are situated. The mesosystem summarizes a second layer of environment that 'comprises linkages and processes taking place between two or more settings containing the developing person' (Bronfenbrenner, 1993: 22). The exosystem features policies and indirect environments that could also impact the growth of developing individuals. Lastly, the macrosystem entails more general and broader environments such as social norms, race and cultural expectations. In the case of Chinese international students studying in the United

States, the microsystem may include roommates, classmates, peers and friends; the mesosystem may include interactions that take place involving multiple contexts such as family and academic and social settings; the exosystem involves aspects such as immigration policies, institutional policies, faculty and curriculum; and the macrosystem situates their identities as foreign, gendered minority students in a predominantly white higher education setting in an Anglophone country.

Finally, the time model (also referred to as the chronosystem) proposes that the timing of events impacts both the outcome and the processes of human development. Such influences could take place not only at a macro-level, in which the timing of specific historical events plays a role in shaping social norms and culture, but also at a micro-level, in which the occurrence of important transitions and life events affect the processes and outcomes of human development. Based on this model, Chinese international students' high school to college transition, Eastern to Western cultural transition as well as Chinese to English linguistic transition could influence the way they function linguistically and navigate their new environment. Moreover, perceptions of immigrants and foreigners, race and diversity in current American society may also affect social norms, views and expectations toward Chinese international students, which in turn exert influences on their development.

The person–process–context–time model presented in bioecological theory is crucial in understanding the transnational languaging journeys of Chinese international students, as it simultaneously draws attention to the development, processes and outcomes of their experiences (Renn & Arnold, 2003). This multilayered system allows a close examination of Chinese international students' development from their most immediate contexts to broader sociocultural aspects. In this study, the central focus will be on Chinese international students' micro, meso and exo systems with their macrosystems serving as an important backdrop to situate and facilitate understandings of their holistic experiences. Echoing the Bioecological Model, research participants are placed at the center of their entire developmental systems and are perceived as active change agents who are both the products and the producers of their environments.

Languaging as a multilingual and multimodal social practice

Languaging, which captures multilingual communication in action, is also referred to as *ways-of-being-with-words* (Gynne & Bagga-Gupta, 2015). Because it is 'impossible to understand language as independent of human beings' (Jørgensen, 2008: 163), languaging is an interactional social practice. According to Jørgensen (2008: 169), languaging is defined as a dynamic communicative practice where 'language users employ whatever linguistic features are at their disposal with the intention of achieving their communicative aims'. From this perspective, language is fluid and constantly changing its forms based on languagers' needs and communication settings. When Chinese international students shuttle from contexts to contexts, they are constantly languaging based on the contextual situations and their interaction with their audience. For example, even when their nameable language of performance is English, Chinese international students' ways of interacting with classmates in math lectures are likely to be very different from how they communicate with peers in the cafeteria. Furthermore, even when Chinese international students are engaged 'in a "monolingual mode" and producing one namable language only for a specific stretch of speech or text', they are constantly thinking multilingually and making languaging decisions that tap into their entire multilingual linguistic repertoires (Canagarajah, 2011; García, 2009; Li, 2018: 18). This has made code-meshing a lived reality and a powerful way of identity expression among multilingual communicators' everyday languaging experiences (Canagarajah, 2011).

Drawing on Jørgensen's (2008) definition, in this book I have chosen to adopt *languaging* as an important lens to examine Chinese international students' multilingual and multimodal communication across contexts. In today's globalized world, the internationalization of higher education is rising along with increased cultural and linguistic diversity. This has made multilingualism a new norm in society. Meanwhile, in the era of Web 2.0, multimodality is a key feature of discourses (Barton & Lee, 2013). This has made it important to explore Chinese international students' languaging experiences beyond merely examining their unilingual proficiencies across academic and social settings. Because languagers constantly 'employ whatever linguistic features are at their disposal with the intention of achieving their communicative aims' (Canagarajah, 2011; García, 2009; Jørgensen, 2008: 169), I consider the term *languaging* as a broad concept that captures not only multilingual students' shuttling between their home languages and English across contexts, but also their dynamic linguistic functioning drawing on multimodal forms of communication including video, audio, image and text among others.

An integrated model

Focusing on human development in context, the Bioecological Model (Bronfenbrenner & Morris, 2006) situates the challenges of Chinese international students' linguistic, cultural and educational transitions in different layers of environments and developmental processes. Focusing on dynamic communicative practices in action, the concept of languaging (Canagarajah, 2011; García, 2009; Jørgensen, 2008) is beneficial in gauging how Chinese international students draw on all the resources in their linguistic repertoire to function linguistically in and outside of academic contexts during their cross-cultural college experiences. The two

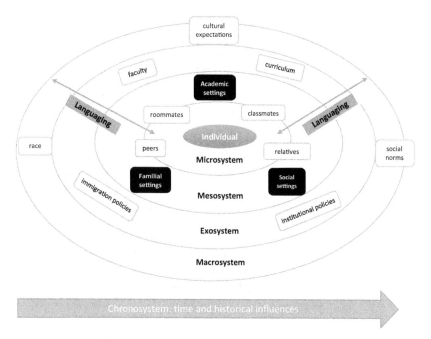

Figure 2.1   Languaging across contexts: An integrated theoretical framework

concepts are interrelated and jointly inform the theoretical framework of this book (see Figure 2.1).

The framework enables an examination of multilingual international students' dynamic multilingual and multimodal communication experiences across contexts during their translingual, transcultural and transnational overseas studies experiences. Owing to the theoretical guidance of the Bioecological Model (Bronfenbrenner & Morris, 2006), layers of external factors influencing international students have been mapped out with individuals placed at the center of the developmental processes. Moreover, influences from time and historical events at the chronosystem are also taken into consideration (e.g. previous schooling experiences in China). Throughout this multilayered system, students are constantly languaging in English, Chinese or a combination of both, or in multimodal ways based on their contextual situations. The double arrows that cut across all layers of the developmental environments show that multilingual students keep shuttling back and forth across contexts and adjusting their languaging practices based on their audience. For instance, in their microsystem, which includes factors in the direct environment with which Chinese international students are interacting, Chinese international students are likely to resort to Chinese and multimodal ways of communication to keep in touch with their parents and friends in China, mix various codes to communicate with other Chinese international students in the United States and adopt English to communicate with domestic students. Yet, when they are visiting professors during their office hours (exosystem), Chinese international students are likely to mainly adopt academic English to refer to course contents and to remain professional.

Concluding Remarks

In Chapter 2, I presented a review of the literature on EFL education in China and the academic English linguistic demands in American classrooms. Based on the review, I discussed the challenges that newly arrived Chinese international freshmen face in their initial experiences studying in American colleges. The review indicated that in order to understand Chinese international students' languaging experiences in American higher education, it is crucial to consider their previous language and education experiences in China. Echoing the call by many scholars in bi/multilingual research (e.g. Allard, 2017; Creese & Blackledge, 2010; Creese & Martin, 2003; Hornberger, 2004; Hornberger & Link, 2012) to adopt ecological approaches in examining students' multilingual journeys, I proposed the guiding theoretical framework of this book which incorporates the Bioecological Model of Human Development (Bronfenbrenner & Morris, 2006) and the concept of languaging (Jørgensen, 2008). This framework enables an examination of participants' dynamic multilingual and multimodal communication experiences across contexts. In Chapter 3, I introduce my study design informed by the theoretical framework.

3 A Four-Month In-Depth Investigation: An Overview of Study Design

Introduction

In Chapters 1 and 2, I drew readers' attention to my overarching research problem and detailed research questions (Chapter 1), presented a review of the relevant literature and proposed an integrated model of the theoretical framework (Chapter 2). In this chapter, I provide an overview of my four-month in-depth investigation. I introduce my methodological approach by presenting the study design, context, data sources, data collection methods, and analytical approaches, as well as researcher positionality. To familiarize readers with my multimodal approach to study design informed by the concept of languaging (Canagarajah, 2011; García, 2009; Jørgensen, 2008), I further provide detailed data samples to illustrate each of my data collection methods. Focusing on the languaging journeys of 12 Chinese international college freshmen studying in an American higher education institution, my study was guided by the following research questions:

(1) How did first-semester Chinese international college freshmen from different disciplines function linguistically in academic and social contexts at the beginning of the semester?
(2) How did they function linguistically in academic and social contexts for the rest of the semester?
(3) What has changed with regard to their language and academic experiences over the course of their first semester in college?

I conducted a semester-long qualitative study to closely follow the linguistic functioning of a group of Chinese international students from orientation week (Week 0) prior to school starting until the end of the semester (Week 15). This 16-week period was chosen because it is part of the major developmental phases in Chinese international students' life, transitioning simultaneously from high school to college, from Chinese- to English-speaking environments and from Eastern to Western education systems (Bronfenbrenner & Morris, 2006). While the entire processes of linguistic, cultural and educational acculturation were likely to last much longer than one academic semester, zooming in on the initial stage of the participants' linguistic functioning and academic performances could provide a snapshot of their navigating experiences during the important transition.

To explore the first-semester Chinese international college freshmen's linguistic functioning across academic and social contexts, I conducted an applied thematic analysis (Fereday & Muir-Cochrane, 2006; Guest *et al.*, 2012) on a corpus of multimodal data, including (1) semi-structured interviews ($n = 24$); (2) writing samples ($n = 29$, covering four genres); (3) talks-around-texts interviews ($n = 24$); (4) digital data from online observations informed by digital ethnography through *WeChat*[1]; (5) bilingual language logs ($n = 24$, covering a total of 576 hours); (6) informal conversations; and (7) research memos based on ongoing analysis.

Research Setting

This study took place at a private university, Hillside,[2] located in a suburb in Northeastern United States. Hillside University offers undergraduate and graduate degrees in various disciplines including but not limited to business, management, social work, arts and sciences and education. Currently, it has over 9000 undergraduates and 5000 graduate students. Among them, approximately 30% are students of color and 7% are international students, representing 41 countries around the world.

Hillside pays great attention to diversity. A Diversity and Inclusion Conference involving over 200 faculty and staff is held annually to maintain 'a diverse, welcoming, and inclusive community'.[3] In addition to having a designated webpage on the university website documenting news and events about diversity on campus, Hillside also houses multiple student organizations and cultural centers that promote cultural and ethnic diversity. From the academic years 2009–2010 to 2016–2017, the enrollment of international students doubled, with undergraduate international students increasing from 3% to 7% and graduate international students increasing from 11% to 21%. Among them, 65% are from Asia, with international students from China representing the largest ethnic group ($n = 790$), followed by Korea ($n = 160$). Based on the latest diversity news on the Hillside website, the number of Chinese international student enrollment continues to grow, with a 24% increase from 2017 to 2018.

As a prestigious university, Hillside has a very high threshold for their incoming international students' English proficiency. Regardless of their indicated majors of interest, all non-native-speaking international students are required to have a test of English as a foreign language (TOEFL) score of at least 100 out of 120 to be considered for admission. In order to achieve 100 or above in the TOEFL, students need to have an average score of 25 or above out of 30 in each of the four discrete areas of examination, including listening, speaking, reading and writing.

Based on the score interpretation guideline provided on the Educational Testing Service (ETS) official website, scoring 22 or above in reading and speaking, 24 or above in writing and 26 or above (totaling 94) in listening is considered a 'high performance level' in English proficiency (ETS, 2019a). Students at this level are expected to demonstrate 'excellent' and 'solid' skills in listening and reading (ETS, 2019b), and will be able to conduct conversations on academic and social topics and perform writing based not only on reading and listening, but also on knowledge and experience (ETS, 2019a). According to the description on the ETS website, a threshold of 100 or above as an admission requirement is rather demanding. In other words, international students admitted to Hillside have remarkably high English proficiency as measured by the TOEFL.

Pilot Study

This study's methodological approach was inspired by a pilot study that I conducted during the 2017–2018 academic year in the hope of improving the research design and testing out the appropriateness and effectiveness of the research questions (Guest et al., 2012). In the pilot study, I used convenience sampling to recruit three Chinese international students who were college freshmen at the time of the study. The three pilot participants, Yang, Xiao and Gao, were male and age 18. They had completed their high school education in China before coming to the United States as international students. Yang, Xiao and Gao took First Year Writing for Multilingual Students during their first semester in college in fall 2017.

Data collection for the pilot study occurred in spring 2018. Firstly, I conducted a one-hour in-person semi-structured interview with each student. The interview was made up of five guiding questions that tapped into (1) their previous English learning experiences in China; (2) reasons for pursuing higher education in the United States; (3) their first-semester language experiences in academic and social settings; (4) their overall experiences as an international student at Hillside; and (5) their perceptions of the linguistic support provided by the university. Based on the participants' preferences, all three interviews were conducted in Mandarin Chinese.

Secondly, I reached out to the students via email after the interview and asked them to send me all the writings they had completed for their sheltered writing course along with instructors' rubrics and the grades assigned. I yielded 11 pieces of writing from their English language learner (ELL) writing course, including students' initial outlines, multiple rounds of drafts, as well as the final versions. I selected two final pieces from each student and conducted a language analysis and text structure of student writing following Brisk's (2015) genre-based rubrics. Lastly, based on an analysis of the texts, I initiated a 15-minute talks-around-texts interview with each participant over the phone, clarifying their specific language choices and their thought processes when producing the texts.

Something worth noting was that, originally, I had also planned to conduct observations in order to obtain additional information beyond the participants' self-reported data. However, based on the pilot study, site observations turned out to be inappropriate mainly for two reasons. Firstly, none of the participants felt comfortable with this data collection method, claiming that it was 'too embarrassing' to be observed. They worried that their classmates might think them incompetent in English, attracting an outside observer to sit in on lectures to monitor their communication practices. One student further pointed out that he would feel too nervous to be observed, which would eventually lead to his reluctance to participate orally in class. Secondly, even assuming the participants agreed to be observed, given the lecture-heavy, teacher-centered nature of many freshmen courses, it was very unlikely that much information would be obtained by watching my participants sitting quietly in lecture-style classes. Therefore, I decided not to use observation as a data collection method.

The data collected were analyzed following the applied thematic analysis method proposed by Guest *et al.* (2012). Major findings from the pilot study were as follows:

(1) Despite their successful TOEFL score to meet the university threshold, the three participants reported a lack of confidence in their English at the beginning of their freshmen year, especially with regard to English speaking and writing.

(2) During their first-semester college experiences, the English linguistic demands encountered in academic settings were said to be related to both receptive and productive language skills. However, all three students reported that they were more likely to practice English reading, listening and writing than oral skills in academic settings.

(3) Participants reported that oral English was used more often in social settings than academic settings, as English served as the medium for them to perform many daily tasks in the United States, such as negotiating rents, calling customer service, ordering food and drink, and attending hospital visits. In contrast, in academic contexts, even if they did not use much oral English, they were still able to receive successful scores if the courses (e.g. mathematics) allotted less than 5% of the total grades to participation.

(4) Participants tended to draw on Mandarin to navigate in both academic and social settings. With regard to academic settings, given the large proportion of Chinese international students present, despite the 'English-only policy' in their First Year Writing class, participants reported that they sometimes communicated in Mandarin during peer or small-group work to make clarifications and exchange ideas 'in a faster and easier way'. In social settings, since none of the participants reported having native

English speakers as close friends or having stayed in any native-English-speaker-dominant student organizations for more than a few weeks, they tended to use Mandarin to socialize with peers and connect with family and friends in China.

(5)   All three participants reported daily use of *WeChat*, a popular Chinese social media software. This software was used mainly to stay connected with family and friends in China, and also to communicate with their Chinese peers in America. In addition to functioning as a culturally relevant virtual social space, the *WeChat* platform also allowed the participants to discuss course-related questions and concerns they had in academic life.

(6)   The three participants had different English learning experiences in China, depending on their parents' perceptions of overseas studies and English, the resources available and their personal preferences. However, one theme that emerged from all three participants was that the English education provided by public schools in China was described as 'unpractical', 'unhelpful' and 'boring', given its heavy focus on grammatical accuracy and the goal of learning English to pass standardized tests. The three participants claimed that both the English language used in the TOEFL and the skills required to function linguistically in an American college were drastically different from what they had been prepared for through their English education in Chinese elementary and secondary public schools. They all reported taking some TOEFL preparation courses provided by private educational companies in China. Additionally, all of them had taken the TOEFL at least three times before they eventually reached the threshold for admission.

(7)   Analysis of students' texts using a genre-based rubric informed by systemic functional linguistics (SFL) (Brisk, 2015) revealed that while the three participants had some general understanding of one of the most important academic genres, argument, they were still in need of additional academic support, especially in effectively presenting thesis statements.

(8)   In the talk-around-texts follow-up interviews, participants reported that they made many of their word choices based on direct Chinese translations, and all three participants reported that they often resorted to online Chinese-English dictionaries during writing at the beginning of the semester. Yet, by the end of the semester, they were more prone to using English-English dictionaries to avoid strange wording in writing.

The findings of the pilot study informed the design of the current study in six ways. Firstly, in the pilot study, I mainly looked at the participants' language experiences in academic settings. However, after interviewing the participants, I yielded interesting data about their language experiences beyond classroom contexts. Therefore, I found it necessary to also examine the focal students' linguistic functioning in social contexts to present a comprehensive picture of their linguistic transition. This reminded me of the importance of using ecological approaches to contextualize participants' language experiences (e.g. Allard, 2017; Creese & Martin, 2003; Creese & Blackledge, 2010; Hornberger, 2004; Hornberger & Link, 2012), which later informed my theoretical framework drawing on the Bioecological Model of Human Development (Bronfenbrenner & Morris, 2006). Secondly, while my original focus had been solely on participants' English language experiences, the findings of the pilot study indicated that it would be beneficial to examine international college freshmen's linguistic and academic transition through a multilingual lens informed by the concept of languaging (Jørgensen, 2008). Because multilingual beings never function in unilingual mode (Li, 2018), their home language, Chinese, could function as an influential factor in their English language functioning and acculturation.

Thirdly, it would be necessary to collect writing samples from within and beyond their *First Year Writing* course. On the one hand, collecting writing samples from content-subject courses could yield more diverse writing samples, which might open up the opportunity to see their performances across genres. On the other hand, because *First Year Writing* is by nature an academic English writing course aimed at enhancing the participants' English proficiency, examining writings from this course alone may fail to represent the whole picture of how participants function to meet the writing demands in content-area subjects. Given that academic writing demands of college require not only language skills, but also a mastery of content knowledge, it would be beneficial to examine students' written work from the writing course and beyond.

The findings also provided some general information indicating that Chinese and English were used differently to fulfill various social and academic purposes. However, the exact proportion of usage of the languages and how they were used throughout the day was not clear. Therefore, I found it necessary to integrate a language log (Brisk *et al.*, 2004) to document the nuances of participants' language usage during a typical weekday and weekend day (for details see data sources). Additionally, based on the pilot study, the participants were found to be frequent users of the popular Chinese social media application, *WeChat*, through which they communicated about their academic experiences and social interactions. Given its popularity and cultural relevance, it would be interesting to incorporate *WeChat* as a data collection tool to trace the focal students' social and academic language experiences throughout the semester. As discussed earlier, since the traditional shadowing and observations were not favored by the participants, online observations and interactions through *WeChat* informed by digital ethnography (Pink *et al.*, 2016) provided an alternative approach to observe the participants' experiences in a non-intrusive way. Once the participants and I were friended on *WeChat*, I would be able to observe all their public postings. This social media platform would allow the collection of multilingual and multimodal data which captured participants' languaging experiences in a non-intrusive, organic way.

Lastly, relying on convenience sampling methods, the three participants in my pilot study were of the same gender and major. This resulted in three extremely similar programs of study during their first semester, due to the limitation of which different linguistic demands across various disciplinary areas could not be identified. Therefore, I found it necessary to recruit a larger and more diverse sample of Chinese international students, which could ideally represent within-group variabilities regarding students' gender, major and background.

Design of the Current Study

I adopted inductive qualitative research methods drawing on an applied thematic analysis (Guest *et al.*, 2012) as a means to examine the focal research questions. Applied thematic analysis is an exploratory research method that searches for emerging themes in the process of describing and analyzing the phenomenon under study (Daly *et al.*, 1997). It is an inductive approach that involves various analytic techniques (Guest *et al.*, 2012). A theme is defined as 'a *phrase* or *sentence* that identifies what a unit of data is about and/or what it means' (emphasis in original, Saldana, 2009: 139), or an abstract construct that 'link[s] not only expressions found in texts but also expressions found in images, sounds, and objects' (Ryan & Bernard, 2003: 87). In the process of a thematic analysis, themes are identified through 'careful reading and re-reading of the data' (Rice & Ezzy, 1999: 258), so that fragments of ideas that may carry little meaning when examined alone can be sophisticatedly integrated (Leininger, 1985).

In this study, I integrated traditional data collection methods that included semi-structured interviews, text analysis, talks around texts, a bilingual language log (Brisk *et al.*, 2004) and informal communication, along with digital ethnography (Pink *et al.*, 2016) through the *WeChat* software to explore first-semester Chinese international college students' linguistic functioning in academic and social settings. Meanwhile, I also took research memos to document interesting findings during my encounters with the participants, preliminary thoughts and ongoing analysis based on data collected in the aforementioned approaches.

Regarding my data collection through traditional qualitative methods, I firstly conducted one round of entry interviews with each participant at the beginning of the semester to gather information on their language and education experiences prior to college entry. Around the middle of the semester, I collected at least two writing samples per student from their writing and content-subject course assignments. Informed by Brisk's (2015) genre-based text analysis, I conducted talks-around-texts follow-up interviews with each participant on their thought processes and decision-making during writing. At the end of the semester, I performed one exit interview with each participant to reflect on their first-semester languaging experiences across academic and social contexts.

Beyond these pre-planned, structured data sources, over the course of the semester, any clarification of the data collected from the afore-mentioned sources or participant-initiated contact were also included as informal communication data. This reflected my research stance as a collaborator and co-creator of knowledge, rather than the single sto-ryteller of my participants' experiences. Because knowledge production was not a one-way activity but instead a dynamic process in which ideas were generated 'through our encounters with other people and things' (Pink *et al.*, 2016: 16), I found it necessary to also document any planned or unplanned informal communication with the participants to help understand their languaging experiences during the initial stage of their translingual, transcultural and transnational journeys studying in an American higher education institution.

Along with those traditional qualitative data collection methods, throughout the semester, I also conducted online observations informed by digital ethnography in which I closely observed the participants' daily lives in a non-intrusive, digital way (Pink *et al.*, 2016) through the cul-turally relevant *WeChat* software. The data collected using this method were multimodal in nature, and included texts, videos, audios and visu-als. Finally, throughout the entire semester, I documented any thoughts, ideas and observations, as well as my preliminary analysis by keeping an ongoing research memo.

The richness of the data sources in the study required a flexible yet comprehensive study design that allowed for an analysis of data and themes 'in all shapes and sizes' (Ryan & Bernard, 2003: 87). An applied thematic analysis was particularly suitable for this project, which collected a corpus of multimodal data from multiple participants in different disciplinary areas across academic and social settings over time. The exploratory and inductive nature of the thematic analysis echoed the focus of the book, considering the sparse literature focusing exclusively on the transitional experience and linguistic functioning of undergraduate-level Chinese international students in American higher education. Moreover, because the outcome of the thematic analysis tended to be policy recommendations rather than theory building (Guest *et al.*, 2012), choosing this method addressed the ultimate goal of this book to explore how American higher education could better support the unique needs of its growing bilingual international student populations.

Sampling

In this thematic analysis study, sampling was conducted for theoretical rather than statistical reasons (Glaser & Strauss, 1967; Yin, 2003). Different from quantitative sampling, the purpose of which is to increase generalizability, theoretical sampling approaches focal participants with a set of criteria to examine them systematically and in greater detail in order to deepen the understanding of the phenomena under study (Yin, 2003).

Sampling began after all relevant procedures had been approved by the institutional review board. With support from the Office of International Students and Scholars (OISS) at Hillside, recruitment flyers were sent out to all newly arrived undergraduate Chinese students during international student orientation in late August 2018. One week after the orientation, the OISS sent out a follow-up email with the electronic version of the recruitment flyer to all Chinese international freshmen at Hillside University. Both the physical and the electronic versions of the recruitment flyer were bilingual in Mandarin Chinese and English, containing a brief description of the purpose of the study and my contact information. Interested students were encouraged to reach out to me either through email or via *WeChat*.

There were no material incentives for research participation. However, drawing on my own identity as a veteran Chinese international student in pursuit of a terminal degree at the time of the study, I incentivized participants in the following two ways. Firstly, based on participants' needs, I offered to share my own experiences and takeaways as an international student from China. Secondly, on completion of the study, I debriefed each participant on the research findings and implications and provided personalized suggestions on how he or she could better navigate linguistically and academically as an international college student in their future studies.

The recruitment criteria of the study were (1) non-immigrant undergraduate students from China; (2) those who were currently enrolled as first-semester freshmen in Hillside University; and (3) native speakers of Mandarin Chinese from Mainland China. Interested students had to meet all the aforementioned criteria to be considered as research participants.

These recruitment criteria were determined for the following reasons. Firstly, as detailed in Chapter 1, Chinese international students were fundamentally different from immigrants to the United States with Chinese descent, due to their different language, culture, education and socioeconomic backgrounds. Therefore, only F-1 visa holders (or student visa holders) were included in the study. Secondly, since the focus of this study was to explore the participants' ability to function linguistically during the initial stages of their overseas college experiences, only first-semester college freshmen were included. Finally, only native speakers of Mandarin Chinese from Mainland China were recruited because the two Special Administrative Regions of China, Hong Kong and Macau, enjoy a high degree of autonomy in their executive, legislative and educational systems. Since Chinese international students from those regions were likely to grow up in different language environments (e.g. Cantonese and English) and receive distinct educational curricula compared with their Mainland Chinese peers (e.g. Hong Kong's curricula were heavily influenced by the UK education system), I decided to exclude them from the study. After disseminating the recruitment flyers, 15 Chinese students contacted me interested in voluntary research participation. After reviewing the volunteers' candidacy based on the aforementioned inclusion criteria, 12 students were officially recruited as research participants of the study.

Participants

The participants' background information is summarized in Table 3.1, detailing the 12 participants' pseudonyms, gender information, disciplinary areas of study, disciplinary areas of courses chosen during their first semester in college and TOEFL results for college application. As shown in Table 3.1, the 12 participants, seven male and five female, majored in eight disciplinary areas, covering psychology, economics, marketing, English, computer science, biology, chemistry and mathematics. Given their various disciplinary studies, the participants were enrolled in a variety of courses during their first semester in college, such as philosophy, history, chemistry, mathematics, writing, sociology, theater arts, painting and economics. It was worth noting that the actual courses that the participants were enrolled in were far more diverse than the information presented in Table 3.1. This was because to summarize the disciplinary areas of the courses taken, I categorized all the courses based on their common content-subjects. For instance, courses such as *Asia in the World* and *Women in Modern Asian Society* offered by the history department were all noted as history in Table 3.1. By the same token, various courses offered by the mathematics department, such as *Calculus I*, *Calculus II* and *Statistics* were denoted as math. Similarly, all seminar-style courses focusing on college adjustment offered by individual departments to their first-semester students (course names varied by departments; examples include but are not limited to courses such as *Reflection and Action* and *First-Year Seminar*) were reported as seminar.

As shown in Table 3.1, among the 12 participants, 11 had taken the TOEFL prior to college entry, and their scores ranged from 103 to 117. According to my earlier discussion on the TOEFL score interpretation based on the official description of ETS, their overall successful TOEFL results (theoretically speaking) indicated their high ability to function linguistically in overseas studies. Hugo was the only student

Table 3.1 A summary of the participants' background information

Pseudonym (gender)	Disciplinary areas of studies	Disciplinary areas of first-semester course	TOEFL results for college application
Pat (male)	Psychology	Writing, psychology, math, history, seminar	110 (S 24, L 29, R 29, W 28)
Larry (male)	Psychology, Chemistry	Writing, psychology, chemistry, math, history, seminar	107 (S 20, L 30, R 30, W 27)
Bill (male)	Psychology	Writing, psychology, math, philosophy, seminar	103 (S 20, L 26, R 30, W 27)
Hugo (male)	Math	Writing, math, philosophy, history	N/A
Shawn (male)	Computer science	Writing, math, computer science, history, seminar, philosophy	107 (S 22, L 30, R 28, W 27)
William (male)	Marketing	Writing, economics, computer science, seminar, math	108 (S 26, L 29, R 30, W 23)
Matthew (male)	Economics	Writing, math, philosophy, physics, economics	103 (S 25, L 27, R 28, W 23)
Sarah (female)	Psychology	Writing, math education, seminar, psychology, computer science, philosophy	107 (S 26, L 23, R 30, W 28)
Rebecca (female)	Chemistry, Biology	Writing, chemistry, biology, math, music	117 (S 27, L 30, R 30, W 30)
Kristin (female)	Economics	Literature, math, history, economics, seminar	110 (S 23, L 29, R 29, W 29)
Lily (female)	Psychology	Writing, psychology, philosophy, math, sociology, seminar	106 (S 22, L 26, R 24, W 24)
Eva (female)	English	Writing, philosophy, painting, math, theatre arts, seminar	115 (S 27, L 30, R 30, W 28)

who did not take the TOEFL prior to college entry; due to his prolonged studies in an American high school, he was exempt from the TOEFL requirement based on Hillside's admission policy.

Data collection

Data collection occurred over a period of four months from August to December during the fall semester of the 2018–2019 academic year. I further divided the four-month investigation into 16 weeks, starting from Week 0, which referred to orientation week, to Week 15 right before the study days for the final examination. Table 3.2 summarizes the detailed timeline for the data collection of each source.

Prior to the official start of the data collection process (Weeks 0 and 1), I obtained consent from the potential participants to ensure confidentiality and protect their rights. Participants were informed that at any stage during the data collection, they had the right to skip questions or withdraw from the study. They were also notified that if they decided to drop out from the study at some point but afterwards expressed an interest in rejoining the study, they would be permitted to participate in the project again at a later stage.

Immediately after receiving consent from the potential participants, I started the first round of semi-structured student interviews (Weeks 1 and 2). Students' writing products (Weeks 5–7), talks around texts (Weeks 6–10) and bilingual language logs (Week 12) were gathered at specific time points during the semester. Toward the end of the semester, a second round of semi-structured student interviews was conducted (Week 13). Ongoing analysis, informal communication and digital ethnography were conducted throughout the four months to analyze, re-evaluate and reflect on the data collected and shed light on ways to improve future data collection. I generated research memos to record ideas, thoughts, questions and tentative interpretations (Corbin & Strauss, 2007). Throughout the data collection process, I conducted frequent member checks through informal conversations either in person or through *WeChat* with the participants in Mandarin Chinese. Member checking (also referred to as respondent validation) was beneficial in improving data quality as it helped to ensure that my observation, evaluation and tentative interpretation of participants' linguistic performances were true to their meaning (Corbin & Strauss, 2007; Creswell & Miller, 2000; Guest *et al.*, 2012; Krefting, 1991). Conducting constant member checks also echoed my stance of valuing my participants as co-constructors of knowledge.

Data sources

The exploratory and inductive nature of the thematic analysis employed in this study placed emphasis on the collection of data from a variety of sources. Multiple sources of data could enhance the construct validity and potential generalizability, although generalizability was never a goal for this exploratory qualitative study (Yin, 2003). Multimodal data were collected (texts, visuals, audios and videos) from the 12 participants majoring in eight disciplines.

To be specific, data sources included a combination of (1) two semi-structured interviews with each of the 12 participants at the beginning and end of the semester ($n = 24$); (2) writing samples from the participants' course assignments across disciplines ($n = 29$, covering four genres); (3) talks-around-texts interviews with each participant to debrief about their writings ($n = 24$); (4) digital ethnography informed observations of the participants' usage of a popular Chinese social media application *WeChat* throughout the semester; (5) two 24-hour language logs documenting each participant's bilingual usage in academic and social settings ($n = 24$, covering a total of 576 hours of self-reported language usage); (6) informal communication with the participants; and (7) research memos based on ongoing analysis.

Table 3.2 Timeline for data collection

Data collection	August W0–1	September W2–5	October W6–10	November W10–14	December W15
Participant consent	X				
Semi-structured interview (round #1)	X (W1 only)	X (W2 only)			
Semi-structured interview (round #2)				X (W13 only)	
Students' writing (texts)		X (W5 only)	X (W 6–7)		
Talks around the texts			X		
Bilingual language logs				X (W12 only)	
Informal communication	X	X	X	X	X
Online observations informed by digital ethnography	X	X	X	X	X
Ongoing data analysis	X	X	X	X	X

The rich data sources enabled a close exploration of Chinese international students' academic and linguistic experiences during their transitional period using multimodal means. The various and diverse sources of evidence not only paved the way for later triangulation of the findings, but also allowed examination of the same phenomenon from different perspectives (Miles *et al.*, 2014). To explore the participants' first-semester experiences, I simultaneously drew on self-reported data from semi-structured interviews, bilingual language logs, informal communication and talks around texts to capture the focal students' perceptions of their linguistic functioning, and I also integrated observational data from genre-based writing analysis and digital ethnography to gauge their actual linguistic performances. Table 3.3 maps out the data sources of the study and the corresponding research questions these data served to answer. In the following sections, I present details in relation to each data source.

Online observations informed by digital ethnography

Multimodal data collected through digital ethnography contributed to the three key research questions. Digital ethnography is an innovative approach that utilizes digital platforms to explore participants' daily life experiences; it allows the collection of various modes and forms of artifacts which may include but are not limited to text, voice memos, videos and pictures (Pink *et al.*, 2016). The rich sources of artifacts collected through digital ethnography could provide different angles in understanding the experiences of the focal participants, and consequently contribute to data triangulation and analysis.

According to Pink and colleagues (2016), there are five guiding principles of digital ethnography, namely multiplicity, non-digital-centric-ness, openness, reflexivity and unorthodox. By multiplicity, the authors claim that there should not be rigid rules and standards in designing and conducting digital ethnography research; each digital ethnography study is therefore 'always unique to the research question and challenges to which it is responding' (Pink *et al.*, 2016). By non-digital-centric-ness, the authors argue that the digital media adopted in digital ethnography should not be placed at the center of the research; instead, participants' feelings and experiences in using these digital tools should also be given attention (Pink *et al.*, 2016). Openness acknowledges the researchers of digital ethnography as collaborative knowledge builders rather than determiners of knowledge; by the same token, instead of being passive objects of digital observations, participants of digital ethnography research are perceived as co-producers of knowledge (Pink *et al.*, 2016). Building on the openness principle, reflexivity defines the ways in which digital ethnographers co-construct knowledge with participants as interactive and collaborative (Pink *et al.*, 2016). Finally, the unorthodox principle encourages non-traditional, multimodal ways of data collection,

Table 3.3   Research questions and data source mapping

Research questions	Data source
How did the 12 Chinese international students function linguistically in academic and social settings at the beginning of their first semester in college?	• Digital ethnography observations • Semi-structured interviews • Ongoing research memo • Informal communication
How did they meet the oral and written linguistic demands in academic and social settings throughout the semester?	• Students' writings • Talks around texts • Digital ethnography observations • Semi-structured interviews • Ongoing research memo • Informal communication
What has changed regarding their linguistic functioning over the course of one semester?	• Digital ethnography observations • Semi-structured interviews • Ongoing research memo • Informal communication • Bilingual language logs

especially through the integration of data beyond texts (e.g. visuals, audios) (Pink *et al.*, 2016).

I decided to incorporate online observations informed by digital ethnography as a supplement to traditional data collection methods because given the popularity of social media technology among young people, this data collection approach is said to be particularly appropriate for studies that involve college students (Arnold & Casellas Connors, 2017). According to recent research findings from the Pew Research Center surveying young adults between 18 and 29 years old in the United States, over 90% of the participants reported owning a smartphone (Pew Research Center, 2016). This has placed Chinese international college students in a favorable position to use social media to socialize and express feelings and experiences regarding their first-semester linguistic functioning through multimodal means such as text, videos, pictures and audios.

My intensive virtual digital ethnography observations were conducted through *WeChat*, a widely used, China-centric, multipurpose social media application. Launched in 2011, *WeChat* became the most popular social media platform for Chinese of all age groups with over 1.083 billion monthly active users (Statista, 2019). The *WeChat* software supports a variety of modes of online communication, including but not limited to instant messaging through text, one-on-one or one-to-many voice messaging, video conferencing, photo and video sharing, blog posts, video games, bill pay and location sharing. Additionally, it allows the establishment of private chat groups, meaning that any form of group postings or sharing is private and confidential.

I incorporated digital ethnography informed observations as a means to explore my participants' daily experiences throughout the fall 2018 semester. *WeChat* was reported to be culturally relevant and frequently used according to the three participants of the pilot study. Similarly, all my current research participants reported to be daily users of *WeChat*, through which they connected with families and friends both in the United States and in China. After participant recruitment, I friended each of my participants via *WeChat*, which not only allowed private correspondence through individual audio, video and text messages, but also granted permission for me to observe their public postings as well as the participants' interactions with their peers regarding the posts.

Over the course of one academic semester, I documented a total of 557 *WeChat* posts from the participants. These posts were multimodal in nature and very often simultaneously contained bilingual texts, emojis and visuals. An example of the multimodal data collected through digital ethnography is presented in Figure 3.1. In this example, the participant shared his experiences during a career fair event that he had just attended. On the one hand, he was excited that he had received many free gifts at the career fair (as shown in the picture). On the other hand, he was thrilled that although most organizations did not accept freshmen interns, one company was particularly interested in him and encouraged him to submit his resume as soon as possible. In this post, simultaneous usage of Chinese and English texts, emojis and pictures could be easily observed. Additionally, since the post was somewhat humorous, it received many likes from his Chinese peers.[4]

Semi-structured interviews

Interview data also contributed to the exploration of the three key research questions. I conducted two semi-structured interviews with each participant ($n = 24$) at the beginning and end of one academic semester about their language and academic experiences. All the interviews were conducted in private in a quiet room at Hillside University. While I had originally planned to spend approximately 60 minutes on each interview, given the open-ended nature of the semi-structured interviews, the duration of the interviews ranged between 40 and 95 minutes.

The interview protocols for the two rounds of interviews are presented in Appendix A. Questions in the anchor interview at the beginning of the semester mainly addressed the following five aspects of Chinese international students' experiences: (1) language and education experiences prior to college entry; (2) reasons for overseas studies; (3) linguistic functioning in academic and social settings after entering Hillside University; (4) experiences as non-native speakers at Hillside; and (5) perceptions of the effectiveness of support received from the university. Comparatively speaking, the end-of-semester interviews were more open-ended in nature, in which I asked participants to share their general feelings about their first semester in college, and overall academic, language and social experiences. Given the variability in each participant's experiences, I encouraged them to decide the main topics they would like to focus on and allowed them to share as much information as they

Career Fair真的是"大丰收"。这么多水杯各种小玩意。
这么多公司都不面向Freshman😓..走了狗屎运竟然有一家说可以考虑我实习。结束还发邮件说印象很深刻😄，对我很感兴趣，让我尽快发她resume。（怕是对我拿着这么多东西很深刻吧）

5 hours ago

Figure 3.1 An example of the *WeChat* posts collected

wanted to about their unique stories during this transcultural, transnational and translingual journey.

As a balanced bilingual in Mandarin and English, I made it very clear to all the participants prior to the interviews that they were free to choose whichever language they felt comfortable with during the interview, be it Mandarin Chinese, English or a mixture of both. I further assured that I would not judge their English accent or grammatical errors, as the focus of the study was to learn about their experiences. By providing my participants with the agency to determine the medium of interviews, they were more likely to be at ease when sharing their stories. All interviews were audio recorded with the participants' permission and later transcribed for further analysis.

Students' writings

To address the second research question, the students' writing samples from coursework (also referred to as texts) along with any corresponding grades and feedback from professors (if applicable) were collected around midterm (Weeks 5–7). The students were instructed to send me at least two writings, one from their writing class and the other from any content-area class (e.g. history, philosophy, psychology) to ensure that I could yield texts of various genres. For Kristin, who was not enrolled in any writing classes, I requested two essays from different content-area classes. By Week 7, I had received 29 pieces of essays, covering the following four genres: argument ($n = 12$), recount ($n = 15$), explanation ($n = 1$) and report ($n = 1$).

It is worth noting that while I had originally asked for two writing samples from each student (expected total: 24 samples), the students shared with me a total of 37 writing samples which was more than 1.5 times my original plan. Among the 37 essays, 29 fell into the predetermined data collection window (Weeks 5–7) and were eventually included in the analysis of this book.

Talks-around-texts interviews

Talks-around-texts interviews were also conducted to answer the second research question. The so-called 'talks-around-texts' interviews refer to informal conversations with student writers about their writing products (Coffin & Donohue, 2012; Lillis & Scott, 2008). Talks around texts integrated ethnographic elements into this exploratory thematic analysis study by generating conversations around and beyond texts (Lillis & Scott, 2008). It is regarded as a supplementary tool in addition to written text analysis, as it extends understandings from a 'texts in context' level to a deeper investigation of writers' perceptions of the contexts and their rationale for the texts produced (Coffin & Donohue, 2012).

I conducted two 15-minute talk-around-texts interviews with each student. The talks around texts happened after I had conducted a text analysis based on the genre-based rubrics, during which I customized questions based on the results of the text analysis. For instance, if a student received a low score in verb tense consistency, I would ask him or her to discuss the rationale behind his or her frequent shifting of tenses. Similarly, if a student did not have a thesis statement in his or her argument writing, I would try to explore whether the missing component was due to the student's intentional language choice or unclear understanding of genre-specific requirements. In all talks around texts, I also asked whether the students had received any support during their essay writing (e.g. from the Hillside Writing Center, professors or peers). If so, I encouraged the students to talk about their experiences in support-seeking as well as their perceptions of the effectiveness of the support received.

Bilingual language logs

Inspired by Brisk *et al.* (2004), I integrated bilingual language logs to document the participants' usage of English and their heritage language (Mandarin Chinese) within a 24-hour period during a typical weekday and also a typical weekend day. Data from the bilingual language logs supported the investigation of the second research question. I collected one weekday language log and one weekend day language log from each participant ($n = 24$), documenting their specific time, duration and purpose of bilingual language usage.

An example of one participant's weekday language use is included in Table 3.4. As shown in the example, the bilingual language log not only provided detailed information on when, where and for what purpose English or Chinese was used, but also documented the modes of language usage (listening, speaking, reading or writing) as well as information about interlocutors (e.g. Chinese classmates, roommate). By integrating the self-reported bilingual language logs as a source of data collection, I was able to yield detailed information about the participants' linguistic functioning. As mentioned earlier, since neither site observation nor shadowing was feasible for this study, the bilingual language logs provided valuable data on the participants' actual language usage in a non-intrusive way.

Informal communication

Data from informal communication, either through face-to-face conversations or private messaging via *WeChat*, were also included to explore the three key research questions. As mentioned earlier, the stance I took in conducting this book was as a co-constructor of knowledge; I therefore valued the agency and contributions of my participants. Informal communication data mainly consisted of (1) any form of contact initiated by me to make clarifications or get additional information from the participants (e.g. after reviewing the anchor interview data, I reached out to clarify with two participants about a few issues they mentioned during the interview); and (2) any participant-initiated communication for the purpose of sharing their experiences with me. The data collected from informal communication were usually multimodal in nature, including not only bilingual texts, but also visuals and audios.

An example of participant-initiated informal communication is presented in Figure 3.2. In this example, William initiated a conversation with me through *WeChat* personal messaging. He first sent over a picture showing a boy with an upset and tortured face to express his negative feelings. Following the visual, he continued with some bilingual texts complaining that as a student at the School of Management, he had to read the *Wall Street Journal* every week; however, since he could not understand the readings due to language barriers, William felt so frustrated that he described articles from the journal as '有毒' (poisonous).

Ongoing research memos

Throughout the data collection process, I also took notes and drafted memos to record observations, thoughts, tentative interpretations and follow-up questions (Corbin & Strauss, 2007). The research memos allowed me to pay attention to details, patterns and themes in the data collected, and facilitated later data triangulation. Information from my ongoing research memos was thus able to make contributions to my investigation of all three key research questions, especially my last question exploring any changes that occurred over time.

Table 3.4 An example of a weekday bilingual language log

Time	Activity	Place	Heritage language speaking/ listening/reading/writing	English speaking/ listening/reading/writing
7:50–8:30	Get up and shower	Dorm	n/a	n/a
8:30–9	Have breakfast with Chinese peers	Cafe	S/L	S/L/R only to order food
9–9:50	Physics	HU	n/a	L/R/W
10–10:50	Philosophy	HU	S/L with Chinese classmates	S/L/R/W
11–12	Lunch with Chinese friends	Cafe	S/L	S/L/R only to order food
12–1	Do philosophy readings assigned in class today	Dorm	S/L with roommate	R/W
1–1:50	Writing	HU	S/L with Chinese classmates	S/L/R/W
1:50–3	Do philosophy readings assigned in class today	Library	n/a	R/W
3–3:50	Mathematics	HU	n/a	L/R
4–5	Do philosophy reading assigned in class today	Library	n/a	R/W
5–6	Dinner with friends	HU	S/L	S/L/R only to order food
6–8:30	Philosophy class discussion session based on readings assigned in the morning	HU	n/a	S/L/R/W
8:30	Go back to dorm to sleep	Dorm	n/a	n/a

Figure 3.2 An example of data collected from informal communication

Data analysis

The preliminary, ongoing data analysis occurred throughout the process of data collection. I actively took analytic memos in order to (1) document tentative interpretations, questions, thoughts and ideas to inform future data collection; and (2) organize and synthesize data collected in preparation for later triangulation (Miles *et al.*, 2014).

Any audio-recorded data were transcribed for later analysis. Since data transcription is in itself an analytic process (Bird, 2005), I took notes and brainstormed ideas for later analysis while transcribing. Interviews conducted completely in Mandarin Chinese or those mainly adopting Mandarin with occasional code-switching between Chinese and English were transcribed and analyzed directly in their original language forms without translation. This decision was made considering my balanced linguistic abilities in both languages. More importantly, analyzing participants' narratives in their original forms had the advantage of 'preserv[ing] the nuance' and striving to interpret statements as true to their original meaning as possible (Blair, 2016: 112).

Constant member checks were conducted throughout data collection and analysis in the form of researcher-initiated informal communication to make sure that my transcriptions, translations and interpretations were true to participants' meaning (Creswell & Miller, 2000; Corbin & Strauss, 2007; Guest et al., 2012; Krefting, 1991). If participants pointed out any discrepancies, I would adjust my analysis accordingly to reduce researcher bias.

I adopted a combination of deductive and inductive data analyses. Utilizing a deductive approach, I conducted coding and analysis following the guidance of the theoretical framework. Conversely, in the inductive process, I explored patterns and themes that emerged from multiple sources of data and strived to come up with a new framework to understand the linguistic and academic experiences of Chinese international students. In the following sections, I present detailed information on data analytic plans by source and discuss my researcher positionality.

Analysis of all data sources except student writing

To analyze the data from semi-structured interviews, talks around texts, informal communication, digital ethnography and research memos, I conducted analysis following the procedures of applied thematic analysis (Guest et al., 2012). Thematic analysis puts emphasis on inductive analysis, in which codes and themes emerge and develop from the data collected (Guest et al., 2012).

Coding provides a 'pivotal link' between the data collected and the interpretation of the data (Charmaz, 2014: 46). Following the processes proposed by Guest et al. (2012), I performed three stages of inductive coding including segmenting text, identifying themes and content coding. Firstly, I adopted segmentation as a data reduction strategy, which allowed me to separate useful information from redundant text, thereby enhancing the overall data quality (Guest et al., 2012). The process of segmenting data, which was compared to using a compass to systematically locate the target spot (Guest et al., 2012), paved the way for my theme identification.

Immediately after segmenting the data, I started to identify major themes. As Ryan and Bernard (2003: 87) commented, 'Themes come in all shapes and sizes. Some themes are broad and sweeping constructs that link many different kinds of expressions. Other themes are more focused and link very specific kinds of expressions'. Given the flexibility of themes, I paid special attention to thematic cues including repetition, indigenous typologies (i.e. participants' unique ways of addressing constructs under examination), metaphors, transitions, comparisons, linguistic connectors and silences (i.e. participants' avoidance in addressing certain topics) (Ryan & Bernard, 2003). Moreover, since theme identification was a complex process, I constantly read and re-read the texts to extract and refine themes (Guest et al., 2012). The major themes that emerged in this book included 'linguistic functioning in academic and social settings', 'coping strategies initiated', 'perceptions of the effectiveness of support received' and 'stage of the semester'.

Once emerging themes had been identified, content coding was conducted so that the proposed themes were analyzed and assigned codes that carried well-defined meanings (Guest *et al.*, 2012). Specifically, when analyzing artifacts collected through *WeChat*, which transcended the traditional modes of data, I reflected on other sources of data including ongoing research memos, informal communication and interviews in order to interpret those artifacts in specific contexts. Additionally, to increase the reliability of the methodological approach and the data quality, I conducted double-coding and frequent rechecks (Guest *et al.*, 2012). Following Guest and colleagues' (2012) suggestion to increase coding reliability, I coded all texts twice with a two-week interval in between. Finally, the codes achieved (e.g. linguistic and cultural congruences, linguistic and cultural incongruences, using Chinese as a bridging tool, support from professors, support-seeking from Chinese peers) were reviewed and compared across participants to identify any patterns for further discussion.

Thematic analysis was performed with the assistance of the qualitative coding software *ATLAS.ti*, which allowed easy coding, a comparison of codes, assigning codes and sub-codes and generating a research report. This software was particularly helpful in comparing thematic data, as it supported the organization and summary of data from different sources.

Analysis of students' written work

I conducted text structure and language analysis of student writing informed by SFL theory. When analyzing texts, I customized my analysis to features of different genres and disciplines, since '[t]he internal organization of natural language can best be explained in the light of the social functions which language has evolved to serve' (Halliday, 1973: 34). The results from text analysis were reviewed along with the grades assigned by their professors as well as talks-around-texts interviews to see whether there were discrepancies between professors' expectations and students' interpretation.

In order to analyze students' writing samples, I adapted the genre-based writing rubrics created by Brisk (2015). The corresponding rubrics for the four genres collected in this book are presented in Appendix B. Although the rubrics were originally applied to assess the writing performances of young children from kindergarten to fifth grade, they have been found to be reliable in evaluating text produced by older writers for the following two reasons. Firstly, drawing on SFL, Brisk (2015) created rubrics based on genre rather than the complexity of texts. Thus, this genre-based approach of assessing students' writing should not be limited by the age of the writers. Secondly, this rubric has been adopted in previous research focusing on young adults and adolescents and was found to be reliable when assessing texts produced by older students. For instance, in O'Connor's (2017) dissertation, Brisk's (2015) rubric was used to analyze the writing performances of high school students, the ages of whom were extremely close to participants in the current study.

In her book *Engaging Students in Academic Literacies*, Brisk (2015) systematically introduced genre-based writing instruction and provided detailed guidance on how to analyze texts based on their genre-specific characteristics. Echoing the concept of languaging, according to which communication is a dynamic social practice (Jørgensen, 2008), Brisk's (2015) rubrics have not only examined discrete language features, but also focused on the topics of the writing (field), the relationship between the language user and audience (tenor) and the role of language during interaction (mode). Therefore, Brisk's (2015) rubrics were well-suited to evaluating the writings collected in this study, given the dual focus not only on the language aspects but also on students' ability to utilize language in contexts to meet the needs of the specific genre.

Brisk's (2015) rubrics were designed to evaluate students' performances in writing each of the common academic genres, including reports, explanations, recounts, arguments and narratives. According to the rubrics, students' writings are analyzed based on two aspects: (1) purpose and stages and (2) language. For instance, in analyzing the purpose and stages of argument writing, one of the most common genres that Chinese international students encounter, the argument rubric addresses the following areas: the purpose, verb conjugation (proper tense), title (if required), thesis statement, reasons supported by evidence, reinforcement of statement of position and cohesive text (Brisk, 2015). In analyzing the language aspects of argument writing, the rubric focuses on modality, use of person, vocabulary use, language choice and cohesion (Brisk, 2015). Similar to the rubric for argument, rubrics for other genres tap into both the purpose and language of the writing, which evaluate students' ability to function linguistically in producing written assignments to meet the course expectations.

The rubrics are customized based on common genres that students would encounter in academic settings, including (but not limited to) reports, explanations, recounts, arguments and narratives. Each rubric follows a scoring scale of 1–4 in evaluating students' performances. A rating of 1 means that the writer has minimal understanding of the genre and would need substantial guidance and support in improving his or her writing. A score of 2 means that the writer has some but still insufficient understanding of particular aspects of the genre, and thus needs a certain degree of additional instruction and practice. A rating of 3 indicates that the writer has a general understanding of the target genre and can meet the genre-specific demands except for one or two incidents for revision. Lastly, a score of 4 shows that the writer has met the expectations required by the genre.

To minimize rater bias, after completing scoring of the writing samples collected, I randomly selected four writing samples representing the four genres collected and checked inter-rater reliability with a panel of three experts, two females and one male, who had extensive knowledge of the genre-based text analysis rubric (Brisk, 2015). The three experts, self-identifying as Mandarin-English, Korean-English and Spanish-English bilinguals, respectively, all received advanced training in applied linguistics and had at least one year of experience analyzing writing samples using Brisk's (2015) genre-based rubrics. A comparison between my scoring and the panel's grading yielded an average agreement of approximately 93%. All the discrepancies lay in minor disagreements in assigning a score of 2 or 3 with regard to the different levels of support required. In other words, there was no disagreement regarding discrete aspects with severe violation (a score of 1) or successful performance (a score of 4). After open discussion about the discrete items where minor disagreement lay, the panel and I eventually reached an agreement of 100%.

Researcher Positionality

Born and raised in China, I came to study in an American higher education institution for graduate studies. The uneasy start to my language, identity and education journey as a newly arrived Chinese international student prompted me to pursue my doctoral studies with a focus on second language teaching and learning. Knowing that tens of thousands of Chinese international students travel to the United States for tertiary education each year, I felt obliged to explore their experiences during the important linguistic, academic and cultural transition in the hope of shedding light on how American higher education could better serve their unique needs and facilitate their initial college adjustment.

In conducting this study, I have taken an insider–outsider researcher positionality (Dwyer & Buckle, 2009). Being a Chinese international student, I was aware that the interviews with students might involve their personal experiences, emotions and identity struggles, all of which would be hard to share. Therefore, I decided to take an insider position to make full use of our shared Chinese culture, language, values and experiences to build common ground and establish a bond and a sense of trust to open up conversations and put participants at ease.

As a researcher, I also adopted an outsider position to try my best in 'put[ting] the objects of study *at a distance*' (Kessen, 1991: 189, emphasis added in original) throughout every stage of the study so that I could minimize the chance of inserting my own feelings and perceptions which would inhibit the participants' idea expressions and skew the data analysis. As my own identity and experiences were closely interconnected with the research questions I strived to explore, I conducted constant member checking and shared my data analysis with the participants for clarification in order to reduce any unnecessary subjectivity and increase the rigor of the study (Corbin & Strauss, 2007; Creswell & Miller, 2000; Guest *et al.*, 2012; Krefting, 1991). In the meantime, I also acknowledged that it was unavoidable to bring into the study some preconceptions, ideologies and values based on my previous experiences. Therefore, I took a reflective stance and kept memoing how the data collection and analysis might have been skewed or influenced due to my own subjectivity. This has been an ongoing process; I kept these reflective memos as part of the database and revisited them throughout every stage of the study.

Concluding Remarks

Chapter 3 presented an overview of the methodological approach of my study by introducing detailed information regarding the study design, research setting, sampling, participants, data sources, data collection and an overview of data analysis. Towards the end, a brief discussion of my insider–outsider researcher positionality was also included. In Parts 2 and 3 of the book, the findings of the study based on the multimodal data collected from various sources are presented. Part 2 zooms in on a small group of selected participants and illustrates a portrait of the first-semester journeys of five focal participants, representing students from five different high school backgrounds. The purpose of Part 2 is to (1) draw attention to the within-group variability among Chinese international students and (2) engage the audience in the vivid stories of these five Chinese international freshmen and familiarize them with some major issues that have emerged during the participants' transitional experiences. Part 3 presents patterns and themes of participants' initial college experiences in the format of revisiting five commonly held myths about Chinese international students studying in American higher education institutions. Based on the findings, I discuss research implications and end the book with directions for future research.

Notes

(1) *WeChat* is a multipurpose social media application created by Tencent, one of the leading technology companies in China. Details about this application software will be introduced in the section about digital ethnography.
(2) To protect the research participants' privacy, all names in relation to the research site and participants in this book are pseudonyms.
(3) Information extracted from the Hillside University main website.
(4) To protect participants' privacy, any identifiable information has been blurred.

Part 2

4 Chinese International Students are Not *Chinese International Students*

Introduction

'These *Chinese international students* are driving me crazy', my colleague Prof. R complained to me over coffee:

> I really have no idea how to support them in my class – they are just *so different*! Some of them remain quiet throughout my class, but others are extremely eloquent – even more so than their American peers. Among those eloquent ones, some are familiar with the basic elements and expectations of academic writing, but others simply have no idea about how to write a college essay... Didn't those Chinese students always follow a central curriculum of some sort because of *Gaokao*[1]?

My friend Prof. R is among the many instructors in American higher education institutions who are faced with an increasingly diverse student population in their classrooms, a considerable proportion of whom came from China. As a caring educator, Prof. R has always tried to tailor his instruction to provide sufficient scaffolding to students with various needs and backgrounds. However, his endeavor to support students from culturally and linguistically diverse backgrounds has been challenged by the shocking reality that there are many more variabilities than he expected. This is particularly true when it comes to Chinese international students, the largest ethnic group among international students studying in Anglophone countries (Institute of International Education, 2019).

Why are Chinese international students so different despite their common language experiences and similar educational experiences given the existence of a central national curriculum in preparing for the College Entrance Examination in China? Is there a way to capture the nuances among Chinese international students based on their previous language and educational experiences? If so, what are the specific characteristics, needs and challenges of Chinese international students from different backgrounds?

Through a close examination of my research participants' previous language and educational experiences, the main goal of Chapter 4 is to provide some explanations for the considerable within-group variabilities among Chinese international students studying in American higher education institutions. Questioning the rigid umbrella term *Chinese international students*, I propose a continuum to capture the many nuances and within-group differences regarding their previous language and education backgrounds. Further categorizing Chinese international students into five subgroups based on their varying degrees of academic, linguistic and cultural preparedness for undergraduate studies in English-speaking countries, this continuum presents a new framework in understanding the diversity, dynamics, needs and challenges of Chinese international students studying in American higher education institutions.

Beyond *Chinese International Students*: A Closer Look at My Research Participants

One common misconception about Chinese international students is the assumption that they represent a homogeneous group. In recent years, many studies have been conducted to explore the various aspects of Chinese international students' experiences studying in an English-speaking higher education environment, the focuses of which include but are not limited to their psychological distress (Wang *et al.*, 2012), acculturative adjustments (Zhang & Goodson, 2011), attitudes toward counseling (Yoon & Jepsen, 2008), social networks (Hendrickson *et al.*, 2011), satisfaction during overseas studies (Douglas *et al.*, 2006), as well as aspirations and expectations (Azmat *et al.*, 2013). In these aforementioned studies, Chinese international students are often described as a homogeneous block, the within-group variabilities of which are largely overlooked.

However, with the internationalization of higher education and global mobility, more and more scholars are calling for the need to think beyond overgeneralized terms such as international students and multilingual learners and instead pay attention to superdiversity among students (e.g. Benda *et al.*, 2018; Blommaert & Rampton, 2011; Poe & Zhang-Wu, 2020). If every individual's development is uniquely shaping and shaped by a complex multilayered bioecological system across contexts, spaces and time (Bronfenbrenner & Morris, 2006) and languaging is fundamentally a highly interactive social practice (Canagarajah, 2011; García, 2009; Jørgensen, 2008), it is problematic to see Chinese international students as a static, homogeneous group. To explore Chinese international freshmen's vivid languaging journeys, it is important to consider their previous language and educational experiences to examine the within-group differences and dynamics.

Table 4.1   A summary of the participants' background information

Pseudonym (gender)	Discipline of study	TOEFL results for college application	Length of study in the United States prior to college entry (years)
Pat (male)	Psychology	110 (S 24, L 29, R 29, W 28)	0
Larry (male)	Psychology; chemistry	107 (S 20, L 30, R 30, W 27)	0
Bill (male)	Psychology	103 (S 20, L 26, R 30, W 27)	0
Hugo (male)	Math	N/A	4
Shawn (male)	Computer science	107 (S 22, L 30, R 28, W 27)	3
William (male)	Marketing	108 (S 26, L 29, R 30, W 23)	0
Matthew (male)	Economics	103 (S 25, L 27, R 28, W 23)	0
Sarah (female)	Psychology	107 (S 26, L 23, R 30, W 28)	0
Rebecca (female)	Chemistry; biology	117 (S 27, L 30, R 30, W 30)	3
Kristin (female)	Economics	110 (S 23, L 29, R 29, W 29)	0
Lily (female)	Psychology	106 (S 22, L 26, R 24, W 24)	0
Eva (female)	English	115 (S 27, L 30, R 30, W 28)	0

Despite their common status as Chinese international students, the participants in my study demonstrated strong within-group variabilities. Consequently, this played a role in their distinct languaging journeys during their first semester at Hillside University. Based on the recruitment criteria of (1) non-immigrant undergraduate students from China; and (2) those who were currently enrolled as first-semester freshmen in Hillside University, I recruited 12 volunteers as research participants. Table 4.1 presents basic information about the participants, including their pseudonyms, self-identified gender, discipline of studies, discipline of courses chosen during their first semester in college, the test of English as a foreign language (TOEFL) results for college application and the length of educational experiences in the United States prior to their international studies at Hillside.

Regular high vs American high Chinese international students

In my study, while all the participants had been uniformly categorized as *Chinese international students* based on Hillside University's enrollment information, the students preferred to identify themselves following the dichotomy of either 普高学生 (those who attended regular high schools in China prior to college entry; also referred to as *regular high students*) or 美高学生 (those who attended US high schools prior to college entry; also referred to as *American high students*). Most of the participants received their high school education in China and thus self-identified as *regular high students* (see Table 4.1). In contrast, three students (Hugo, Rebecca and Shawn), who had at least three years' experience studying in American high schools before entering Hillside University, described themselves as *American high students*.

Regardless of their identical heritage language, ethnic background and elementary to middle school experience in China, the two groups of Chinese international students demonstrated varying abilities in linguistic functioning during their freshmen studies in an American higher education institution. Compared with their *regular high* peers, *American high* students demonstrated consistently higher capacity in English linguistic functioning across academic and social contexts throughout their first semester in college. Conversely, the *regular high* participants encountered different degrees of difficulty with regard to their English linguistic functioning across contexts and demonstrated a stronger preference for Mandarin Chinese usage, especially in social settings. Further details on the first-semester experiences of these two types of students are presented in Chapters 5–7.

Beyond the dichotomy: A continuum of readiness for international studies

The dichotomy of *regular high* and *American high* students has indeed captured some within-group variabilities among Chinese international students. However, it falls short in explaining the dynamics among members within the broad categories of *regular high* or *American high* students. How are Chinese international students who have received high school education in the same country different from each other with regard to their linguistic and academic readiness for international college studies in American higher education institutions?

Following my closer analysis of the 12 participants' previous language and educational experiences, the types of high schools that the Chinese international students attended could be further sorted into five categories, namely, (1) traditional *regular high* schools in China; (2) foreign language *regular high* schools in China; (3) international departments within traditional *regular high* schools in China; (4) one year of *regular high* in China and three years of *American high* in the United States; and (5) four years of *American high* schools (Zhang-Wu, 2019).

I identified three subgroups within *regular high* Chinese international students. The so-called traditional *regular high* refers to the most typical high school education in China, the primary purpose of which is to prepare students for *Gaokao*. Therefore, students with traditional *regular high* backgrounds generally have no experience with American high school curricula, nor do they have much exposure to native English-speaking teachers. Similar to traditional *regular high* schools, foreign language *regular high* schools also have Chinese College Entrance Examination preparation as one of their primary education goals. Yet, in addition to test preparation, foreign language *regular* high schools place great emphasis on the learning of foreign languages, English in particular. As a result, although students enrolled in foreign language *regular high* schools typically have no exposure to American high school curricula, they do have frequent encounters with native English speakers as instructors of their English as a foreign language listening and speaking courses.

International departments refers to special divisions within *regular high* schools in China where the ultimate goal of education is to prepare students for overseas studies (mostly in English-speaking countries). It is worth noting that not every *regular high* school has such a department; they are more prevalent in schools in big metropolitan cities with large populations of students from high socioeconomic backgrounds who desire overseas tertiary education. Given the overseas studies-oriented instructional goal, students enrolled in this type of high schools tend to have significantly less exposure to standard Chinese high school curricula in preparation for the College Entrance Examination. Instead, their secondary education is likely to follow the curricula of high schools in their target overseas studies countries (e.g. American or British high school curricula). Not only are students exposed to the TOEFL and the scholastic assessment test (SAT) during their high school studies, but they also have opportunities to take many advanced placement (AP) courses. Therefore, international department graduates are likely to be more prepared for overseas studies given their substantial knowledge of American high school curricula compared with their peers from the other two types of *regular high* schools in China. Depending on the school, students from international departments may or may not have experience with taking courses with native English-speaking instructors.

The *American high* Chinese international students could also be categorized into subgroups based on their previous high school educational experiences. While some students finished middle school education in China (US equivalent of ninth grade) before pursuing the last three years of education in a US high school, others completed their entire four years of high schools in America. Regardless of the different duration of their high school studies in the United States, students from both groups had substantial exposure to American high school curricula and an authentic English-speaking environment prior to college entry.

The five different sub-categories discussed above naturally fall into a continuum of academic and linguistic readiness of Chinese international students prior to their international studies in American higher education institutions (see Figure 4.1). This continuum, drawing attention to the nuances and within-group differences among Chinese international

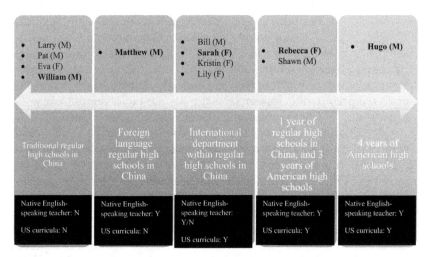

Figure 4.1   A continuum of participants' readiness for international college studies in the United States

students beyond the dichotomy of *regular high* or *American high* students, has facilitated understanding the participants' first-semester journeys at Hillside University and provided a framework to understand the dynamics and unique characteristics, needs and challenges of Chinese international students from various backgrounds.

At the very left end of the continuum were Larry and Pat from the School of Education, Eva from the School of Arts and Sciences and William from the School of Management. These students reported being from so-called traditional *regular high* schools which provided them with no previous contact with native English-speaking teachers or any American high school curriculum. These students were simultaneously faced with substantial challenges with linguistic functioning in English across academic and social settings, as well as difficulties in adjusting to and catching up with content-subject learning at Hillside University. Therefore, they were likely to be the least prepared for overseas college studies in the United States at the very beginning of the semester, not only academically and linguistically, but also culturally.

Next on the continuum was Matthew from the School of Arts and Sciences, who attended a foreign language *regular high* school in China. Compared with his traditional *regular high* peers, Matthew was in a slightly more advantageous position at the initial stage of his overseas studies; it was likely that his previous experiences taking language courses with native English-speaking teachers in high school made him more used to initiating authentic communication in English on arrival at Hillside University. Nevertheless, despite his familiarity with an authentic English-speaking environment, Matthew had no experience with US high school curricula or AP courses, putting him at a disadvantage with regard to content-subject learning in college.

In the middle of the continuum were Bill, Sarah and Lily from the School of Education, and Kristin from the School of Arts and Sciences. These students attended the so-called international departments within *regular high* schools, which potentially provided them with opportunities to experience not only native-speaking English language teachers, but also American high school curricula and AP courses. While native English-speaking teachers may or may not have been available at all international departments, these participants prolonged exposure to US high school curricula tended to put them in a more advantageous position for international college studies in the United States compared with their peers from the other two types of *regular high* schools. This was particularly because of their familiarity with the content-subjects, course expectations and the culture of the Western education system.

Finally, at the right side of the continuum were Rebecca, Shawn and Hugo from the School of Arts and Sciences, who experienced three to four years studying in authentic English-speaking environments in American high schools. They all took AP courses prior to their studies at Hillside. Compared with their *regular high* peers, these *American high* students were significantly more acculturated to the US education system linguistically, academically and culturally. This placed them in the most advantageous position during the initial stage of their international college studies at Hillside University.

Concluding Remarks

In this chapter, the main focus was to draw readers' attention to the within-group variabilities among Chinese international students studying in American higher education institutions, especially with regard to their previous language and educational experiences. Following a closer examination of my research participants, I proposed five subgroups under the broad term of *Chinese international students*. Based on my analysis of their previous language and educational experiences, I created a continuum to capture Chinese international students' varying degrees of readiness for international undergraduate studies in the United States at the beginning of their freshmen year (Zhang-Wu, 2019). Although stemming from my close examination of a small group of Chinese international students as research participants, this continuum may be applied to a much broader population. It could shed light on creating a new framework in understanding the unique needs, challenges and experiences of newly arrived international students from diverse academic, cultural and linguistic backgrounds.

In the following three chapters in Part 2, I draw on this proposed continuum as a tool to understand the distinct experiences of Chinese international students under each category. More importantly, by introducing vivid examples of the focal participants under each subgroup, I hope to familiarize readers with my proposed categorization as presented in the continuum. It is hoped that this continuum could facilitate understanding Chinese international students' first-semester bilingual linguistic functioning across academic and social contexts.

Chapter 5 focuses on the first-semester languaging journeys of three focal *regular high* students who attended traditional *regular high*, foreign language *regular high* and international departments within *regular high* schools. Chapter 6 focuses on the initial experiences of two focal *American high* students who spent three and four years, respectively, in *American high* schools prior to their college studies at Hillside University. A discussion based on the findings in Chapters 5 and 6 is presented in Chapter 7. Altogether, it is hoped that these cases pave the way for later discussions about the myths and realities regarding Chinese international students, which are introduced in Part 3 of the book.

The selected focal participants discussed in Chapters 5 and 6, William, Matthew, Sarah, Rebecca and Hugo, are emphasized in bold in the continuum (see Figure 4.1). Detailed portraits of their initial college experiences illustrate how participants with different high school education backgrounds function academically and linguistically during their first semester in an American higher education institution. My decision to focus on these five cases was made according to purposeful sampling, a widely adopted case-selecting strategy in qualitative research (Patton, 2002).

By intentionally identifying and selecting the most information-rich cases, purposeful sampling makes the most of limited resources in order to illuminate the phenomenon under study (Patton, 2002). Based on an analysis of the data collected from multiple sources, including semi-structured interviews, language logs, digital ethnography through *WeChat* observations, writing samples, talks around texts, research memos and informal communication, I identified the aforementioned students as my focal participants based on the rule of maximum variation in purposeful sampling (Patton, 2002). These students were selected due to the abundant data available for each case as well as their demonstrated varieties in gender, college major and previous language and educational experiences. It is hoped that through my detailed portraits of the journeys of these five focal students, I not only familiarize readers with the Continuum of Readiness for Overseas Studies, but I also demonstrate the heterogeneity of experiences among Chinese international students during their first semester in college.

The nature of Chapters 5 and 6 is storytelling. Echoing the storytelling nature, the following five chapters are guided by direct quotes from my focal participants throughout their first semester as headings of the portraits. These chapters aim to depict the very different transitional stories of my five focal participants in relation to their reasons for overseas studies, TOEFL histories and performances, educational experiences prior to college and major linguistic and academic experiences throughout their first semester in college. To provide readers with the best sense of the focal participants' changing experiences over time, I intentionally present their first-semester journeys in chronological order. In this process, I have drawn on a triangulation of the data collected from various sources.

While I intended to incorporate as many data sources as possible in each portrait, priority was given to data sources that best reflected each focal student's unique academic and language experiences. In other words, the data presented in each portrait are not exhaustive, but rather purposefully chosen to serve the purpose of storytelling and to highlight the different characteristics of the focal participants' distinct first-semester journeys. To be specific, in order to bring out the most interesting stories, while interview data and bilingual language logs have been included throughout all portraits, I have intentionally chosen to draw on informal communication data via *WeChat* more frequently in some cases, while putting emphasis on a text analysis of the students' writing samples in others.

Note

(1) *Gaokao* is the Pinyin version of the Chinese characters 高考, which is the National College Entrance Examination in Mainland China (see Chapter 2 on EFL education in China).

5 First Semester Languaging Journeys of Three *Regular High* Students

Introduction

This chapter focuses on the first semester languaging experiences of three *regular high* students: William, Matthew and Sarah (see Figure 5.1). William attended a traditional *regular high* school in China prior to his overseas studies in America. He was one of those traditional *regular high* students who had no previous exposure to the US high school curricula, nor did he have any experience of communicating with native English speakers before pursuing his undergraduate studies in America. Due to his language and education background, William was faced with comparatively more challenges, academically, linguistically and culturally, compared with many of his Chinese peers who attended other kinds of high school. Matthew attended a foreign language *regular high* school in China. Compared with William, Matthew was in a slightly more advantageous position on arrival at Hillside University. While also without any exposure to the US high school curricula, Matthew was more familiar with the native English-speaking environment because of his experiences taking English as a foreign language (EFL) conversation classes throughout his years at a foreign language *regular high* school. Sarah attended an international department within a *regular high* school in China prior to her overseas studies in America. Compared with William and Matthew, Sarah was relatively more academically prepared to study at Hillside University. Owing to her previous experiences studying at the international department, she was familiar with US high school curricula and had extensive opportunities in advanced placement (AP) courses as well as guided test of English as a foreign language (TOEFL) and scholarly aptitude test (SAT) preparation. Yet, having no prior experience taking classes with native-speaking EFL teachers, Sarah encountered difficulties in meeting the linguistic demands in college.

Traditional *Regular High* Student William's Languaging Journey

William's story touches on the following topics: (1) his previous language and education experiences; (2) his English language proficiency; (3) the challenges encountered; (4) his corresponding coping strategies and

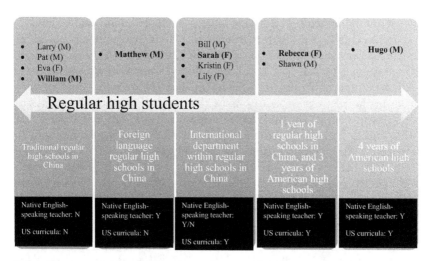

Figure 5.1 An overview of William, Matthew and Sarah on the continuum

support-seeking activities; and (5) his languaging experiences in academic and social settings. This story illustrates the initial freshman journey of a newly arrived traditional *regular high* Chinese international student, who although experiencing an extremely challenging start at the beginning of the semester, managed to function linguistically and academically toward the end of the semester.

William was an outgoing, small-figured, 18-year-old marketing major with short, curly black hair. While he performed very well on the notoriously difficult *Gaokao* in China and was admitted to a prestigious Chinese university, William's parents insisted that he pursue overseas studies in the United States to increase his competitiveness in the job market in the future. Knowing that a high TOEFL score was a prerequisite to entering an elite higher education institution in the United States, William's parents paid thousands of dollars to send him to TOEFL preparation classes provided by various private education companies. Within a year, William had taken the TOEFL five times. Through intense test preparation and repeated trials of the exam, his score almost doubled, increasing dramatically from 56 to 108.

Although receiving a 108 out of 120 on his TOEFL, William self-evaluated his English proficiency as '糟透了' (cannot be worse) during the first interview at the beginning of his college life (Interview, 8.30.18). He told me that his English proficiency was considered '最多一般般' (at most mediocre) in high school, and the TOEFL score did not reflect his real English proficiency (Interview, 8.30.18). In a private text message that he sent to me via *WeChat*, William even joked that he must have taken '假托福' (a fake TOEFL), because despite his high TOEFL score, he experienced considerable difficulty functioning linguistically in both academic and social settings on arrival (Informal Communication, 8.29.18).

William blamed his relatively humble socioeconomic background for the initial language difficulties he encountered in academic and social settings. According to William, his hometown, the City of Taiyuan in Shanxi province, was far less affluent and developed compared with major cities in China such as Beijing and Shanghai. For this reason, most students from his hometown chose to pursue their higher education in local universities in China, which made becoming an international student and studying abroad an extremely rare phenomenon in his hometown. As a result, with helping students to excel in *Gaokao* as its primary goal, William's high school put little emphasis on authentic English teaching and learning in preparation for future studies in English-speaking countries:

> 相对那些发达地区，我们不能融入英语学习。他们那些大城市的，都是真正地融入式学习，为出国而学习英语。我们这些小地方都是为了考试而考试！我们整个学校就我一个人出国，连我们整个城市都很少有人出国。谁会管你出国准备呢？

> Different from people from those more developed districts, we were not able to learn English through immersion. Those who came from big cities were really able to learn English through authentic and immersed ways. They learned English for the sake of going abroad. In contrast, people like me who were from smaller areas were purely learning English for the sake of passing exams! I was the only one who went for overseas studies in my high school; going abroad to study in a foreign college was very rare even in our city. Who would care about your overseas studies? (Interview, 8.30.18)

William further complained that 'coming from a small place' had severely limited the educational resources available to support his English language development, especially with regard to spoken English (Interview, 8.30.18). William's previous English learning experience featured large class sizes, a lack of authentic language input and an intense focus on examination-oriented education that depended heavily on rote memorization. Due to the influence of such examination-oriented education, for William and his fellow *regular high* classmates, the purpose of English learning was nothing more than to achieve high scores in examinations in the shortest time available.

> 我们学习英语是为了短时间拿个成绩而已。我们三年级才开始学英语。平时一个班都是五六十人，根本没机会练习口语。我们没外教，老师上课基本用中文，她自己口语超级差，各种美英混杂。。。每天早读课我们都是背单词，背句型，就这样中-英，中-英地死背。。。为了考托福，我就是每天狂背模板，刷题，有时候我都不知道为什么这么写这么说。反正都是背模板的，还真考了108！

All we did was nothing but to achieve high scores in exams using the shortest time possible. We did not start English learning till third grade. On average, my classes had around 50 to 60 students, leaving us absolutely no opportunity to practice English. We didn't have any [native-English-speaking] foreign teachers. Our teacher mainly used Chinese to teach English, [because] she herself spoke horrible English, with frequent mixture of British and American English... Every morning, our only task was to memorize vocabulary and sentence structures. We practiced rote memorization all the time, firstly Chinese meaning, and then the corresponding English expressions... Take my TOEFL test preparation as an example: I spent every day memorizing sentence patterns and drowned myself in doing practice problems. Sometimes I had no idea why I should write this way or speak this way. But who cares... By memorizing patterns, I did get a 108 in TOEFL! (Interview, 8.30.18)

From the beginning of the semester, William had encountered numerous challenges in meeting the oral linguistic demands across contexts. For instance, on his first day at Hillside University, William went to a nearby supermarket to buy essentials for his dormitory. However, on asking the shop assistant for help, he had trouble expressing himself in English. He described this experience as a 'total disaster' and blamed his EFL learning experiences in China on his difficulties meeting the oral linguistic demands in social contexts:

我第一天来去超市差点就委屈哭了，因为我想买床单被罩那些的，想去问营业员那些东西在哪里，却不知道怎么用英语说。在中国学了英语这么多年，也背了这多么词汇，结果发现从来都没学过怎么说这些最基本的日常生活用品。我是外向型的，但还是不敢问，找了半天都找不到，真是委屈的眼泪都要下来了。。。

I almost cried the first day I went grocery shopping. I wanted to buy things such as sheets and blankets. I decided to ask the shop assistant where they were located. However, I did not know how to say those in English. I learned English in China for so many years, and memorized so much vocabulary, but I have never learned how to express those basic daily essentials. I am an outgoing person, but I was not brave enough to ask for help. I looked for a long time and still could not find what I wanted. I felt so miserable that I was about to burst into tears... (Interview, 8.30.18)

William's challenges in his linguistic functioning in English could also be observed during our first interview at the beginning of the semester. Throughout our 90-minute conversation, William never produced one single complete sentence in English even though I had made it very clear at the beginning of the interview that he should feel free to rely on

Chinese, English or a combination of both languages (Research Memo, 8.30.18). William chose to mainly use Mandarin Chinese (around 95%) with some occasional incidences of code-meshing back and forth from Mandarin to short English phrases and a mixture of English verbs and Chinese auxiliaries (Research Memo, 8.30.18). For instance, he used 'get不到' (cannot get) five times and mentioned 'hold不住' (cannot hold) four times throughout the interview when describing the linguistic challenges he had encountered in college. During the first interview, an American classmate of William's came over to say hi. When asked how he spent last weekend, William found it challenging to engage in the conversation. He looked very nervous and started to stutter. 'I... I come to...ah how to say it... I...I go to downtown, and I... I takes the bus to the park... ah... um... I don't know how to say the park's name in English...' (Research Memo, 8.30.18). After the American student had left, William told me that he felt extremely embarrassed by the awkward conversation during which he failed to express himself. He said that he was so nervous communicating with a '外国人[1]' (foreigner) that his brain went completely blank and he had to squeeze out anything in English (Research Memo, 8.30.18).

Parallel to the many linguistic difficulties he encountered in social contexts, from the start of the semester William had faced substantial challenges functioning linguistically in academic settings. Describing himself as a 'struggler' (Informal Communication, 9.8.18), William felt 'extremely sad' when reflecting on his first week of languaging experiences at Hillside University:

> 我刚开学特别伤心，我也想像他们那样侃侃而谈，我有特别多的东西想说，但是我不知道该怎么用英语说，所以上课我不太说话.

> I was extremely sad at the beginning of the semester. I wanted to talk fast and fluently like them [his classmates]. I had so much that I would like to share, but I did not know how to express in English. Thus, I barely talked in class. (Interview, 8.30.18)

According to William, such difficulties were even more evident in classes where he was the only international student (see Figure 5.2). As shown in his *WeChat* post, even though William had hoped to seek support from his professor, he was unable to do so due to his limited oral English proficiency. To express his helplessness, William posted an image of a crying panda face to imply his Chinese identity and commented underneath in a sarcastic way: '你不用担心我 我哭一个月就会没事了' (Don't worry about me. Let me cry for a month, and I will be fine).

William reported experiencing varying degrees of language difficulties throughout his content-subject courses, especially Portico (a freshman-oriented discussion seminar course provided by the School

[Translation]
Caption under the crying panda image:
Don't worry about me. Let me cry for a month, and I will be fine.

William's post under the emoji:
Staying in a class where I am the only international student… Every day, I feel so confused and speechless… I want to ask questions, but I do not know how to pronounce… Today in class, I could not load my files, and was caught by the professor, who asked me to go to the office hour… [During office hour] she mentioned that she had been to China, and then she asked me all kinds of questions… Later, she said she could lend me a shoulder to cry on [smiling face emoji]… Finally, the professor let me out of her office…

Figure 5.2 Screenshot of public *WeChat* post by William, 9/4/2018

of Management) and business statistics (Interview, 8.30.18). In a private *WeChat* correspondence (see Figure 5.3), William described his miserable experiences in these two classes as '一个上课跟聋子一样；一个上课跟傻子一样' (in one class, I am like a deaf man; in another, I am like an idiot) (Informal Communication, 9.8.18).

On the one hand, he felt like 'a deaf man' in Portico due to his poor English listening comprehension skills and lack of familiarity with the

[Translation]
William: Yes!
William: I now realized what I was most afraid of
William: One is *Portico*
William: The other is *Business Stats*
William: These are the two courses
William: In one class, *I am like a deaf man*
William: In another, *I am like an idiot*

Figure 5.3 Screenshot of informal communication with William, 9/8/2018

course content. Because his professor and classmates often talked 'as fast as flying', it was almost impossible for William to understand the course content:

> 这个讨论课，讲述资本主义，社会主义，完全*get*不了他们的点，他们都讲的飞快，我完全听不懂.

> This discussion seminar focused a lot on Capitalism and Socialism. I really could not get what they [the professor and classmates] were saying. They all talked so fast—as fast as flying. I could not understand a thing. (Interview, 8.30.18)

On the other hand, William described himself as 'an idiot' in business statistics because he was not familiar with the technical vocabulary to express many basic programming symbols in English, such as dash, hyphen and comma. Even though William had prepared a programming symbol vocabulary list to facilitate comprehension (see Figure 5.4), he still found it extremely challenging to follow the lecture (Interview, 8.30.18). William described it as a 'mission impossible' to refer back and forth to the vocabulary list while attempting to grasp the main idea of the lecture (Interview, 8.30.18). This was because by the time he had consulted the list to figure out the technical terms that his professor was referring to, William would have already missed a considerable chunk of the instruction from the professor (Interview, 8.30.18). As a result, William's unfamiliarity with the technical words impeded his overall course comprehension, which eventually contributed to his frustration, feeling that he was not as intelligent as his American classmates.

To address the many challenges in his initial languaging journey, William developed a series of coping strategies. In particular, he depended heavily on Chinese as a bridging tool to facilitate his comprehension and

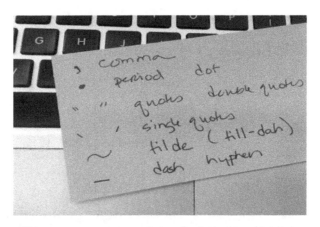

Figure 5.4 William's programming vocabulary list for *Business Statistics*

expression in English. One strategy that William adopted was to rely on an English-Chinese dictionary. Whenever he came across any unfamiliar word while reading, he would immediately look it up in his bilingual dictionary. Similarly, when hearing any vocabulary that he did not understand during conversations, William would request the interlocutor to spell the word so that he could search for the corresponding Chinese translation (Interview, 8.30.18). According to William, even though he believed it more beneficial to adopt an English-English dictionary, relying on Chinese was more efficient: '我知道用英英字典更好，但是我必须用中英字典，这样我可以在最短的时间里抓住意思' (I know it is better to use English-English dictionary. However, I have to use English-Chinese dictionary to grasp the meaning in the shortest time possible) (Interview, 8.30.18). Another coping strategy that William utilized at the beginning of the semester was to draw on Mandarin to make quick clarifications in class with his Chinese peers. In particular, William demonstrated a strong preference for seeking support from his *American high* classmates: '他们在这里呆的久，英语好，我上课有不懂的就小声用中文问他们' (They have been here [the US] for very long, and are thus good at English. If I don't understand anything in class, I will whisper to them in Chinese for help) (Interview, 8.30.18).

Resorting to the Chinese language as a bridging tool had indeed bene-fited William early in the semester, allowing him to pick up the main ideas in conversations and better follow the lectures. However, as the semester progressed, neither strategy remained effective. On the one hand, Wil-liam's strategy of relying on his bilingual dictionary became problematic because looking up every unfamiliar word was time-consuming; this habit frequently interrupted his thoughts and prevented him from grasping the main ideas in oral and written communication (Interview, 11.20.18). Fur-thermore, William's heavy dependence on bilingual translation resulted in awkward wording in his academic writing, which subsequently jeopar-dized his grades. For instance, in a paper recounting his internship experi-ences at a luxury hotel, William wrote: 'Loyally wishes you to stay at the hotel period journey to be happy, welcome your once more presence we the hotel!' (William's Recount 1, 9.17.18). This expression confused his professor who underlined this section and left a big question mark in the margin. When asked to clarify the meaning of this sentence during our follow-up talks-around-texts interview, William explained that he had intended to write '忠心祝愿您住店愉快，欢迎您再次光临' (I sincerely hope that you have had a pleasant experience staying in our hotel. Hope to see you again in the future). Yet, relying on a translation generated from his online bilingual dictionary had eventually yielded the strangely worded sentence above (Talks around Texts, 9.30.18).

On the other hand, William's strategy of using Mandarin during class to ask quick questions and seek immediate clarification from his *American high* peers also stopped working over time. As the semester progressed, William's peers started to get annoyed when interrupted during lectures and they ended up being reluctant to help him. One *American high* student confronted William directly when he tried to seek support in class, '你老问我烦不烦，别打扰我听课！' (You're being so annoying keeping on asking me questions. Don't disturb me when I'm listening to the lecture!) (Interview, 11.20.18). To make matters worse, William's frequent support seeking from his *American high* peers revealed his poor English proficiency, which subjected him to discrimination and humiliation. Around four weeks into the semester, William contacted me through *WeChat* and notified me of an incident in which he was humiliated by one of his *American high* classmates. Without his permission, that *American high* student shared one of William's course papers with a 200-person *WeChat* group and publicly shamed William for his 'Chinglish expressions' and 'poor grammar' in academic writing (Informal Conversation, 9.26.18).

After this incident, William no longer used Mandarin to seek support from *American high* students in class. Instead, he decided to record every lecture in the hope of revisiting the course content by playing back the tape at a slower speed after class (Interview, 11.20.18). Unfortunately, it was not long before William realized that this new strategy was not feasible given its time-consuming nature:

> 一个小时的课慢速回放至少要90分钟，我还得不停暂停做笔记或者重复听，这样完全是恶性循环啊，因为我没时间学其他的课，更没时间读书、做作业.

> A one-hour lecture would turn into at least 90 minutes if I played the recording at a low speed. Moreover, I had to keep on pausing to take down notes or to listen again. This was indeed a vicious circle, because I would not have enough time to prepare for other classes, not to mention finishing readings and homework. (Interview, 11.20.18)

Since neither of his original coping strategies continued to be helpful midway through the semester, William decided to seek support from his professors. Initially, he wrote an email to each of his professors, informing them of the challenges he faced during his languaging journey and expressing his determination to conquer these difficulties with hard work. Opening his email by clarifying the within-group variability among Chinese international students, William emphasized that his lack of English proficiency was largely due to his humble socioeconomic background and unfamiliarity with the authentic English-speaking environment: 'There are many students from China at [Hillside University], but we are from different cities in China, which means we have different backgrounds. As a result, our ability to understand a language is different…' (see Figure 5.5). In this way, he drew attention to the substantial

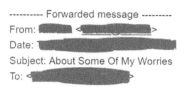

---------- Forwarded message ---------
From: ▓▓▓▓ <▓▓▓▓▓▓▓▓>
Date: ▓▓▓▓▓▓▓▓▓▓▓▓
Subject: About Some Of My Worries
To: ◄▓▓▓▓▓▓▓▓▓►

Dear ▓▓▓▓▓,

I hope this email finds you well.

I'm ▓▓▓▓▓▓, a Chinese international student, and this is my first time studying in the US.

There are many students from China at ▓▓, but we are from different cities in China, which means we have different backgrounds. As a result, our ability to understand a language is different. I was born and raised in Taiyuan, which is a less developed city in China, and I went to a traditional Chinese high school. Since I did not grow up in an environment where English is frequently used, I might need more time to get used to the new environment.

Sometimes I might have trouble understanding (Sometimes I can't follow the speed of speech. And I can't catch some of the vocabularies used.) the class and I might trouble you a lot during office hours in the future. But I will try my best to improve my English proficiency and adjust to the class as soon as possible. It's getting better every day!

Thank you. Have a good weekend!

Best wishes,
▓▓▓▓▓

Figure 5.5 William's email to his professor

challenges faced by students like him, who were from a 'less developed city' and who had attended a traditional regular high in China. William briefly shared his difficulties in meeting the linguistic demands in class and politely expressed his interest in visiting his professors during their office hours.

William's support-seeking strategy of opening himself up to his professors gained positive results. Most of his professors not only responded with empathy and understanding, but also encouraged William to come for an office hour consultation (Interview, 11.20.18). For example, one professor not only comforted him by offering to provide extensions on course projects, but also revealed the possibility to curve up his grades:

> 老师跟我说，我是中国人，英语不是母语，所以可能会写起文章慢一些，所以会给我*extension*！有的老师还会安慰－我不要担心分数，我的*lab*做的非常好，所以他会*curve up*分数的.

My professors told me that I am a Chinese, and English is not my first language. Because of this, it may take me longer to write papers. Therefore, they offered to give me extensions! One professor also comforted

You are always welcome in my office hours (or at other times by appointment); it would never be a "trouble," like you mentioned. You could come every day if you wanted! I'm here to help you however I can. Please ask questions if you have them and ask me to repeat myself or rephrase what I said if you need me to. You will never bother me.

Let me know if there's anything I can do for you.

看到professor的邮件都快流泪了。

♡ C...el ☐ Comment   ♡5 ☐

[The passage in the white area was a screenshot that William has taken from one professor's email reply]

[Translation for William's post in the black area]
When I read the email with my professor's response, I was so touched that my tears were about to come out.

Figure 5.6 Screenshot of William's *WeChat* post with professor's response, /30/2018

me that I should not worry about my grades. Since my lab work is doing very well, he will curve up my grades. (Interview, 11.20.18)

Two professors even offered to provide William with ongoing support by scheduling weekly meetings with him throughout the semester (Interview, 11.20.18). In a *WeChat* public post (see Figure 5.6), William shared a screenshot of his *First Year Writing for Multilingual Students* professor's email response. The professor assured William that she welcomed him for office hour consultations and was willing to provide as much support as she could: 'You could come [to my office hour consultations] every day if you wanted! I am here to help you however I can' (see Figure 5.6). She further emphasized that helping William to meet the linguistic demands in class would never be a 'trouble' to her (*WeChat* Observation, 9.30.18). William was so grateful for his professor's empathy, support and understanding that he felt '都快流泪了' (so touched that his tears were about to come out) upon receiving this email (*WeChat* Observation, 9.30.18).

To take the best advantage of office hour consultations, William noted all his professors' office hours in his calendar (Interview, 11.20.18). Every day, whenever he had any breaks between classes, William would visit the professors who happened to be available. For example, as shown in one of William's language logs documenting a typical weekday (Table 5.1), he utilized the three hours between classes (from 2 to 5pm) to '[v]isit all professors who have office hours during the time frame'. To

Table 5.1 William's language log: A typical weekday, Tuesday 11/13/2018

Time	Activity	Place	Heritage language speaking/listening/reading/writing	English speaking/listening/reading/writing
8–9	Get up, eat breakfast and get ready for class	Dorm	n/a	S/L
9–9:50	*Business stats*	HU	n/a	S/L/R/W
10–12	Preview readings for *Portico* class so that he can participate better	Library	n/a	R/W
12–1	Lunch	Cafe	n/a	S/L R when ordering
1–1:50	*First Year Writing for Multilingual Writers*	HU	S/L	S/L/R/W
2–5	Visit all professors who have office hours during the time frame	Prof's offices	n/a	S/L/R/W
5–6:30	*Portico*	HU	n/a	S/L/R/W
6:30–7:30	Dinner with American friends	Cafe	n/a	S/L; R when ordering
7:30–1 am	Homework	Dorm	n/a	R/W
1 am	Sleep	Dorm	n/a	n/a

him, the purpose of visiting his professors during office hours went far beyond merely asking questions. Instead, he treated communication with his professors as a valuable opportunity to practice spoken English with native speakers:

> 我所有老师的*office hour*每周都会去，而且我还把见老师当作锻炼口语的机会。我的老师都好好呀，常常告诉我这个怎么说，那个怎么说，我都学到了很多。比如我原来什么大写的*capitalize*都不会讲，但是老师教了我慢慢就知道了。

> I will always visit all professors' office hours every week. I treat visiting professors as an opportunity to practice oral English. My professors are super good. They often teach me how to say this, and how to express that. I have learned a lot from them. For example, in the past I did not know how to say 'capitalize,' but after my professor taught me [during office hours], I gradually know how to express that (Interview, 11.20.18)

During the latter half of the semester, due to his continuous support seeking from his professors, his friends nicknamed William 'the king of office hours' (Interview, 11.20.18). Enjoying his new title, William described office hour consultations as the 'most effective' coping strategy in his first-semester college linguistic adjustment (Interview, 11.20.18).

As all his professors had suggested that the best way to improve his English was through immersion, William was determined to reduce his Chinese usage and maximize the opportunity to engage in English communication throughout the rest of the semester (Interview, 11.20.18). On the one hand, William treated bilingual dictionaries as his last resort so that he could think directly in English and embrace his new identity as an English reader:

> 我现在基本上都不查中文字典了。过去我读书，都一定要把内容翻译出来，弄成中文才可以理解，现在我逼自己浸泡式读书，也不太会靠用中文才能思考了。现在有些专有名词，我都不知道对应的中文是什么，但这不理解会影响，我在英语里学了这个词，也就用英语一起思考，也能懂的文章大意。

> Now I barely use any English-Chinese bilingual dictionary. In the past, whenever I read, I had to translate all information into Chinese before I could digest the meaning. Now I have been pushing myself to get immersed in the English reading environment. Thus I no longer depend solely on Chinese translation in reading comprehension. Nowadays, even though there may be some English jargons, the Chinese meaning of which I have no idea about, it will not affect my reading comprehension. Since I learn about this particular jargon in English, I directly think in English to understand the gist of readings. (Interview, 11.20.18)

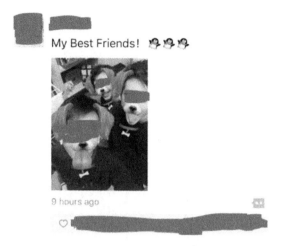

Figure 5.7 An example of William's friendship with American peers, 12/3/18

On the other hand, William intentionally maximized his opportunity to use English by establishing friendships with his American peers. Not only did he learn to use the popular social media platform *Twitter* to 'look for some common topics' to facilitate conversations with his American peers, but William also signed up for volunteering opportunities on campus in the hope of meeting more domestic students (Interview, 11.19.20). Thanks to his aggressive socialization strategy, William managed to make friends with a small group of American peers. In one of his *WeChat* public posts (see Figure 5.7), William documented a happy moment in which he was hanging out with two domestic students who he had met through volunteering. Referring to his American peers in the picture as his 'best friends' (see Figure 5.7), William adopted a puppy theme for his group selfie in honor of their friendship formed in 2018, which was the Year of the Dog (*WeChat* Observation, 12.3.18).

William considered the usage of Chinese and English an either-or choice. To maximize his chances to practice English, William became very selective in socializing with his Chinese peers, and managed to strategically hang out with only those in his immediate circle. As reflected in his language log documenting a typical weekend day (see Table 5.2), William limited his home language usage to half an hour during lunch in order to communicate with his close Chinese friends (William's Language Log, 11.17.18). Eager to enhance his ability to function linguistically in English, William even managed to improve his English by seeking support from one of his Chinese friends:

> 我觉得和中国朋友社交和提高英文必定是有影响的，所以我就没有刻意认识每一个人。我只需要认识我周边的，和他们保持关系不错就好。因为我英语还要进步，所以不能认识更多的中国人，因

Table 5.2 William's language log: A typical weekend day, Saturday 11/17/2018

Time	Activity	Place	Heritage language speaking/ listening/reading/writing	English speaking/listening/ reading/writing
Noon	Get up	Dorm	n/a	n/a
12–12:30	Get ready to go out	Dorm	S/L	S/L
12:30–1	Lunch with 'regular high' peers	Cafe	S/L	S/L only when ordering
1–6	Homework alone	Library	n/a	R/W
6–7	Dinner with Hugo (an *American high* student in this study)	Cafe	S/L (half of the conversation)	S/L (half of the conversation)
7–12	Homework	Dorm	n/a	R/W
12–12:30	Shower and sleep	Dorm	n/a	n/a

为如果就算你尽力去抵抗，最后也会一起说中文。我现在就要努力克制这方面的，虽然和我多数的普高朋友我都说中文，但是我有一个美高的朋友和我关系很好，我就会故意透露他我有哪些东西不会表达，他就会教我，我还会说哪里总是说错，如果他发现了也会纠正我。和他我也学到了很多.

I strongly believe that socializing with Chinese friends will pose threats to my improvement of English. Therefore, I did not intentionally try to know everybody [every Chinese international students]. I only need to know people close to me and keep a good relationship with them. I still need to improve my English, and because of this, I cannot know more Chinese people. Even if you try your best to resist the temptation, towards the end you will still talk in Chinese together. Currently, I am trying to work on this. Although I talk in Chinese with most of my *regular high* friends, I do have an *American high* good friend. I often intentionally tell him that I have difficulty expressing certain things, and he will teach me how to say them in English. I also let him know places where I often make mistakes, and if he catches my error in oral English, he will try to correct me. I have learned a lot from him. (Interview, 11.20.18)

William's commitment to maximizing his English usage and reducing his Chinese communication was also reflected in his bilingual language logs (Tables 5.1 and 5.2). During a typical weekday (see Table 5.1),

[Translation]
Qianqian: What did she compliment you for? [smiling face emoji]

William: I said I did not know how to pronounce something
William: She suddenly asked me where I was from
William: I said China
William: She asked don't you speak English [in China]?
William: I said no, we don't. I entered the English-speaking environment first time in my life this August.
William: She exclaimed: really!
William: [She commented] oh my god, your English is so good since you are here for only 4 months.
William: She thought I was an American-born Chinese [laughing-to-tears emoji].

Figure 5.8 Screenshot of *WeChat* text messages from William, 12/2/2018

William spent most of the day using English. The only incidence of Chinese usage occurred shortly before and after his *First Year Writing for Multilingual Writers* class (William's Language Log, 11.13.18). According to William, although an English-only policy had been mandated by his writing professor to prohibit home language usage in class, he often engaged in very brief Chinese usage especially immediately before and after class because the class was almost full of Chinese international students (Interview, 8.30.18).

Toward the end of the semester, William concluded that the biggest asset throughout this semester was to be 'the king of office hours' (Interview, 11.20.18). To William, office hour visits were especially helpful in increasing his confidence and proficiency in oral English (Interview, 11.20.18). Right before the final examinations, William messaged me via *WeChat* (see Figure 5.8) to report an incident where he was complimented on his English ability (Informal Conversation, 12.2.18). According to William, the interlocutor had mistaken him for a Chinese American, which implied that his oral English proficiency had greatly improved over the course of the semester.

Foreign Language *Regular High* Student Matthew's Languaging Journey

Matthew's story touches on the following topics including: (1) his previous language and education experience; (2) the challenges he encountered in college-level courses and the corresponding coping strategies he initiated; (3) his shifting preference in socialization; and (4) his bilingual language use in academic and social settings. This story illustrates the first-semester journey of a student, who, although had a comparatively more advantageous start compared with William at the beginning of the semester, chose to give up his efforts on linguistic and cultural acculturation toward the end of the semester.

Matthew was a tall, muscular, 18-year-old economics major at the School of Arts and Sciences. He self-evaluated as '自信' (confident) and '乐观' (pessimistic) and described himself as an 'ambitious guy with natural leadership' (Interview, 9.4.18). Matthew revealed that he chose to pursue tertiary education in the United States not only because of his parents' desire to provide him with the best educational opportunities, but also because of his own ambition to stay in the United States to further his education and become an entrepreneur with global impact in the future. '我来美国是因为我将来一定会去哈佛读MBA' (I came to the United States, because I WILL get an MBA from Harvard in the future), he told me firmly and confidently soon after the start of our first interview (Research Memo, 9.4.18).

Wearing a luxury-brand outfit from head to toe, Matthew told me that he came from a powerful, upper-class family in Shanghai, the most prosperous city in China (Research Memo, 9.4.18). According to Matthew, both his parents were highly educated and successful – his mother was a lawyer and his father was a politician in China. Matthew emphasized multiple times during the interview that he came from '不是一般的有钱' (an extraordinarily affluent family). He believed that this had provided him with the privilege to always enjoy the best educational and material resources growing up (Interview, 9.4.18).

Even though Matthew attended K-12 education in China, making him self-identify as one of the *regular high* students, his previous educational experiences were drastically different from those of William's. From elementary to secondary education, Matthew had the privilege of attending the top schools in Shanghai. He reported to have started learning EFL as early as when he was a first grader. Growing up, his English classes were taught by a combination of native-English-speaking foreign instructors and local Chinese teachers (Interview, 9.4.18).

His high school was a prestigious foreign language high school with national fame. Most of his high school peers were also from high socioeconomic backgrounds. Each year, around half of the graduates from his high school chose to pursue overseas studies in various countries such as the United States, Canada and the UK, and most of the rest would go to elite tertiary educational institutions in China. According to Matthew, this led to his high school's emphasis on the creation of an 'authentic English learning environment' (Interview, 9.4.18). To achieve this goal, all EFL classes were capped at 15 students. While most of the English classes were taught by local Chinese teachers with advanced degrees in English language education, all students enrolled at Matthew's foreign language *regular high* school had the opportunity to hone their English conversation skills by taking weekly conversation classes with native English-speaking teachers from the United States (Interview, 9.4.18).

Moreover, different from the vast majority of secondary educational institutions in China, Matthew's high school focused less on examination-oriented education in preparation for the Chinese College Entrance Exam. Instead, the school valued what was called '快乐式教育' (happiness-oriented education) which aimed to cultivate students with 'all-rounded abilities' (Interview, 9.4.18). For instance, while EFL education in most Chinese high schools is defined by a heavy homework load and a pure emphasis on written tests, Matthew's high school was among the very few in China that required an oral assessment component in English examinations. As he recalled:

我们平时英语作业其实不多，不过英语期末考试都要考口语。一般口语30%，笔试70%.

We didn't have much English homework usually. However, we had to take oral English assessment at the end of each semester. The oral part would often take up 30% of the final score, with the rest 70% being written tests. (Interview, 9.4.18)

Matthew described two main factors that contributed to his high oral English proficiency: one was his previous English learning experiences in China, especially having English conversation classes with native-speaking teachers; the other was the international community service he provided in Kenya, during which he had the opportunity to immerse himself in English conversations (Interview, 9.4.18). During his junior year in high school, Matthew heard of female genital mutilation without anesthetic, a commonly practiced ritual in Kenya. He was shocked by the cruelty of such a practice and felt obliged to help teenage girls at risk in Kenya (Interview, 9.4.18). Ambitious to make a difference, Matthew initiated fund raising in Shanghai and later flew to Kenya to collaborate with local non-profit organizations to build shelters and provide education opportunities for local teenage girls. To facilitate the sustainability of the newly established facilities, Matthew further negotiated with several Kenyan business owners who agreed to make annual donations to the project in exchange for positive social media promotion (Interview, 9.4.18). Throughout his several months in Kenya, Matthew had the opportunity to communicate, negotiate and persuade in English on a daily basis, which made him '习惯和外国人用英语交流' (become accustomed to communicating with foreigners in English) in non-academic contexts (Interview, 9.4.18).

At the beginning of the semester, Matthew regarded his linguistic functioning in social settings as 'very successful' (Interview, 9.4.18). Although his TOEFL score of 103 was just above Hillside University's baseline requirement of 100, Matthew reported that he '日常交流都没什么问题' (had no difficulties communicating in social settings) on arrival at Hillside University (Interview, 9.4.18). Confident in his linguistic functioning in social settings, Matthew further revealed his ambition of socializing with native speakers of English. In addition to his desire to make friends with American peers, he also revealed his preference to date a domestic student '我以后想要date 一个美国妹子' (I hope to date an American girl in the future) (Interview, 9.4.18).

Based on my observation during the interview (a non-academic context), Matthew indeed seemed very confident in his English, especially his spoken English. He naturally practiced code-meshing during the conversation, and frequently switched back and forth effortlessly between English and Chinese for meaning-making (Research Memo, 9.4.18). When he was describing the courses that he was taking at Hillside, he frequently adopted English (approximately 35%); however, when he talked about his overall experiences as a Chinese international student, he mainly stayed with Chinese (Research Memo, 9.4.18). Other than pronouncing the word 'FORmative' as 'forMAtive', Matthew's overall spoken English during the interview was accurate, fluent and clear (Research Memo, 9.4.18).

In contrast to his successful linguistic functioning in social settings at the beginning of the semester, Matthew reported experiencing challenges in fulfilling the linguistic demands in several college-level content-subject courses, especially philosophy and mathematics (Interview, 9.4.18).

According to Matthew, philosophy was challenging especially due to its heavy reading load and challenges in oral participation. On the one hand, he was often assigned up to 80 pages in a single day. Matthew believed that since he could not read as fast as his American classmates, he considered philosophy 'the hardest class' in his freshman year:

> 这个课真是我大一最难的课了。要读的超级多。比如昨天的课，课前要读40页，上午上完，下午有讨论课，结果讨论之前又要再读40页。。。他们美国人读的好快，我就不行，根本都不完.

> This course is indeed the hardest class in my freshman year. There are so many reading assignments. Take yesterday for example, we were required to read 40 pages before class, and then we had the *Philosophy* class in the morning. In the afternoon, we had the discussion session for *Philosophy*, and in preparation for that, we were asked to read 40 more pages... My American classmates could read so fast, but I can't. There is no way I can finish that amount. (Interview, 9.4.18)

In his public *WeChat* posts, Matthew repeatedly vented the academic stress he felt in philosophy. In the example presented in Figure 5.9, not only did Matthew compare philosophy to 'an art of dying', but he also shared a photo of his philosophy reading assignment and commented that he felt '难受' (tortured) (see Figure 5.10). He blamed his lack of exposure to authentic English language literature during secondary education in China for the difficulties he encountered in meeting the reading linguistic demands in philosophy (*WeChat* Observation, 10.4.18).

(WeChat Observation, 10.4.18).

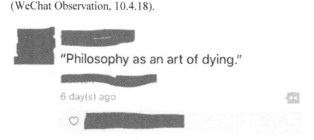

"Philosophy as an art of dying."

6 day(s) ago

Figure 5.9 Example of Matthew's *WeChat* posts complaining about philosophy, 9/10/18

[Translation]
The consequence of not reading enough books written in the English language during middle and high schools became apparent after I entered college.
Feeling tortured.
[a screenshot showing readings from the syllabus]

Figure 5.10 Example of Matthew's *WeChat* posts about philosophy, 10/5/18

On the other hand, despite his confidence in oral English communication in social settings, Mathew found it daunting to contribute to oral participation in philosophy. This, according to Matthew, was largely due to his lack of familiarity with the Western-centered course content. Despite Matthew's years of experience taking philosophy classes in China, he found it very challenging to apply his prior knowledge to facilitate class discussions in America:

> 作为一个中国人想和美国人讨论出比较有营养的点还是很难的，他们很多东西高中就学过了，而对我们中国学生来说，一切都得从头学。我们也学哲学啊，但是那都是什么马列主义毛泽东思想，他们的哲学看的都是什么亚里士多德，柏拉图，完全不一样.

> It is really hard for me, as a Chinese, to have a fruitful discussion with Americans [in *Philosophy* class]. They [American students] have learned a lot about philosophy back in high school. However, for Chinese international students, we have to learn everything from scratch. We have also learned philosophy in the past. However, the philosophy we learned focused on aspects such as Marxism, Leninism, and Mao Zedong Thought. In contrast, they [American classmates] have been exposed to the philosophy of Aristotle and Plato, which is completely different. (Interview, 9.4.18)

In fact, even when Matthew did have a clear understanding of the course content, he was still faced with additional challenges posed by the very different course expectations between Eastern and Western education system. For instance, Matthew encountered difficulties in his linguistic functioning in mathematics, a discipline area that was traditionally (and erroneously) considered language-free (Brisk & Zhang-Wu, 2017). Matthew was very confident that he could get an A in mathematics thanks to the 'super easy' course content. Nevertheless, he felt frustrated due to the oral explanation component in this class, an aspect that is absent in most Oriental mathematics education but often deemed crucial in Western contexts (Interview, 9.4.18). To be specific, mathematics education in China tends to place heavy emphasis on students' independent problem-solving skills, and getting the accurate answers to problems is regarded as the primary goal. In contrast, in addition to independent problem-solving, mathematics education in the United States also values elaboration of the thought process. Consequently, since there had been little chance for him to orally explain how to solve mathematics problems in China, he was unfamiliar with the think-aloud approach often adopted in American mathematics education.

Matthew shared with me an 'extremely embarrassing' incident that happened on the first day he attended his mathematics course in college (Interview, 9.4.18). As the only student in class who managed to solve a given problem, Matthew was called on by his professor to explain his thought processes in front of the entire class. Nevertheless, being a *regular high* school student from China who had been used to engaging in independent problem-solving with getting the correct answer as his ultimate goal, Matthew found it challenging to orally explain his thought processes in English:

有道题大家都不会，就我得出了正确答案，老师就让我上台讲讲我是怎么想的。这有什么好讲的？我们中国人都是上来就直接算，做对就行。我站在讲台上，感觉好尴尬，完全不知道怎么用英文解释。后来我只好默默转身在黑板上直接写下了做题步骤就下台了。。。

There was a question that nobody knew how to solve, except for me. I was the only one who got the answer correct. The professor asked me to go to the podium and tell everybody about my thought processes in solving this problem. What's the point of sharing the thought processes? We Chinese always just focus on doing calculation and get the answers correct. I stood in front of the whole class, feeling so embarrassed, as I had no idea how to express my math thinking in English. Finally, I had no choice but to directly go to the blackboard and write down the procedures of calculation without saying anything. Then I went back to my seat... (Interview, 9.4.18)

Matthew's lack of discipline-specific vocabulary partially contributed to his difficulties in meeting the oral linguistic demands in math. For example, Matthew's math professor once asked students to work in pairs and discuss 'in $y = kx + b$, if x increases, whether y will increase' (Interview, 9.4.18). Although Matthew was eager to persuade his partner, an American girl who insisted that the answer should be 'yes', he did not have the proper vocabulary to explain the different scenarios of this math equation. '我想说你要看k的正负决定，是正就*yes*,是负就*no*,但我不知怎么说' (I wanted to say you need to see whether k is positive: if positive, the answer should be yes; but when negative, the answer should be no. Yet, I don't know how to express myself) (Interview, 9.4.18).

Due to cultural influence and language barriers, Matthew remained quiet in almost all pair and whole-class math discussions at the beginning of the semester. This left his professor with the false impression that he could not understand the course content (Interview, 9.4.18). 'The math professor treated me like an idiot!' Matthew complained:

> 每过几秒钟他就要问我一下 'Do you understand?' 还会不停把头凑到我面前看我的笔记。搞得同学也把我当弱智，真受不了，这么简单的课程非要怀疑我的智商。不过他们把我当弱智，我也把他们当弱智。那些美国人都是自己不懂，还迷之自信，疯狂举手。。。

> Every few seconds, he [the professor] would ask me 'Do you understand?' Also, he kept on approaching me to look at my notes. Because of this, my classmates all see me as an idiot now. I can no longer tolerate this—people doubted my intelligence due to such an easy class. Although when they treated me like an idiot, I also thought of them as idiots. Those Americans were all unrealistically confident and eager to participate even though they understood nothing... (Interview, 9.4.18)

Faced with the aforementioned challenges, Matthew developed a series of coping strategies, which had undergone several different stages throughout the semester. At the beginning of the semester, Matthew mainly sought help from other Chinese international students, which included not only his freshmen peers but also some 'academic brothers and sisters' (direct translation from 学长学姐 which refers to Chinese upperclassmen at Hillside) (Interview, 9.4.18).

In order to tackle the heavy reading load in philosophy, Matthew formed a reading group with another Chinese international student from the same class. In most cases, Matthew and his peer would go through the readings independently before getting together to share their understandings in Chinese. Matthew found this method rather effective, '三个臭皮匠赛过诸葛亮。虽然我们都只理解的一小部分，合起来一聊就差不多都懂了' (Two heads are better than one. Although we both could only understand a small part of the reading, when we shared notes, we managed to get the gist of the article) (Interview, 9.4.18). Occasionally, when the reading load was overwhelmingly heavy, Matthew and his peer would share the workload by each taking responsibility for thoroughly reading half of the materials, taking down notes, summarizing the gist in Chinese, before finally explaining it to each other. According to Matthew, this approach was highly efficient and allowed them to 'go deeper' into their reading assignments (Interview, 9.4.18).

To tackle his difficulties in oral class participation in philosophy, Matthew sought support from multiple 'academic brothers and sisters' by connecting with them via *WeChat*. According to Matthew, since those students had attended the same professor's class in the past, they should be considered as 'the most knowledgeable people' to provide tips and advice to excel in the course (Interview, 9.4.18). Based on the advice from his 'academic brothers and sisters', Matthew learned to take the initiative in philosophy discussions by 'shift[ing] the context to China', a context in which he had much more background knowledge compared to his American classmates and professor (Interview, 9.4.18). For instance, when the whole class was having a heated discussion about Plato's belief that everything in the world existed in intangible ways through their imitation of forms, Matthew took advantage of this opportunity and raised his hand: 'I believe there are many similarities between the beliefs of Plato and the famous Chinese philosopher, Confucius...' (Interview, 9.4.18). According to Matthew, his American peers were faster talkers and better at cutting into ongoing conversations in class. Yet, once he connected the topic to China, nobody but the Chinese international students were able to contribute to the discussions. In this way, he managed to earn himself the floor to speak up. 'Everybody HAD to listen to me!' Matthew smiled, 'They don't know Confucius, but I do! Then I can take my time [to express my ideas]' (Interview, 9.4.18).

It is worth noting that while seeking help from other Chinese students had, to some extent, benefited Matthew's linguistic functioning in philosophy, it was not helpful in coping with his difficulties in meeting the oral linguistic demands in math. According to Matthew, his 'academic brothers and sisters' were sympathetic about his situation, since they had had similar experiences when they were taking the same class (Interview, 9.4.18). Yet, they advised Matthew to ignore the oral participation segment of the course, because his math professor would still give him an A as long as he did well in his homework and exams (Interview, 9.4.18). Matthew was not persuaded, and still tried to improve his ability to meet the oral linguistic demands in math classes. As a last resort, Matthew tried to practice oral communication using math vocabulary with two Chinese classmates. Unfortunately, his peers were uninterested in the idea and told Matthew that practicing how to participate orally in class was nothing but a waste of time (Interview, 9.4.18). Because his peers were confident that they could easily secure an A in mathematics by simply achieving full marks in the final exam, they were demotivated to contribute to oral discussions in class.

Unable to seek support from his 'academic brothers and sisters' or freshmen peers, Matthew reached the conclusion that he had to depend solely on himself to tackle the challenges in meeting the oral linguistic demands in mathematics. Yet, when asked how he planned to work toward this goal, Matthew did not have any concrete ideas:

Matthew:	这数学太弱智了，我同学上课都是在打游戏，完全不在乎参加讨论。比起来，我还是最认真的。看来，说不出说得出，只能慢慢靠自己了。
Matthew:	The math class was totally idiot-proof. My [Chinese international student] classmates always play computer games in class. They totally ignore all the discussions. Comparatively speaking, I am the most diligent one. It seems that, I can only gradually depend on myself to figure out how to orally participate.
Qianqian:	你准备怎么办？
Qianqian:	What's your plan then?
Matthew [sighed]:	我也不知道，走一步看一步吧。
Matthew [sighed]:	I have no idea. Let's wait and see. (Interview, 9.4.18)

As the semester progressed, Matthew's coping strategies along with his attitudes toward improving his linguistic functioning in academic settings had undergone some changes. Firstly, the reading partnership between Matthew and his classmate, despite its potential to reduce the reading load and facilitate comprehension, was forced to end due to the philosophy professor's interference.

Shortly after midterm, Matthew contacted me through *WeChat* and shared with me a 'super scary' incident, in which his philosophy professor accused him of cheating (Informal Communication, 11.12.18). Matthew told me that his philosophy professor requested him and his reading group partner to show up during his office hour. The professor interrogated them regarding why they had made exactly the same mistakes in the test. While the professor was concerned about their academic integrity, Matthew and his peer insisted that they had never cheated in the midterm exam. It turned out that their identical mistakes were because Matthew and his peer had been sharing all their reading notes and reflections with each other during their reading partnership. While such collaborations were beneficial in most cases, they sometimes also accidentally acquired misconceptions together. Since their understanding and misconceptions about the course content were generally the same, Matthew and his peer ended up with very similar responses in the midterm. Although the professor eventually understood the situation and decided not to report them to the university's Office of Academic Integrity, Matthew and his peer were so terrified by this experience that they decided to terminate their reading group collaboration from then on:

吓死我了，好在我们没坐在一起。要不然真是百口莫辩。听说被认为作弊就会中止 F1 遣返回国。以后再也不能什么都一起读一起复习了，一切只能靠自己。

This really scared me to death. Good thing we did not sit together [during the midterm]. Otherwise whatever we say, the professor will never believe us. I heard that if international students are reported for due to academic integrity, they are going to lose their F1 [international student visa status] and get deported. In the future, whatever the case, I will not read or review the course content together [with another student]. I have to rely all on myself. (Informal Communication, 11.12.18)

As the reading partnership was no longer an option shortly after the midterm, Matthew came up with a new coping strategy to tackle philosophy reading – to resort to technology and online resources (Interview, 11.21.18). He relied on a paid software application named *Sparknotes*, through which he was able to access summaries and critiques of countless academic literature. With regard to readings not reviewed in the software, Matthew would take advantage of online forums and book reviews, mostly in Chinese and occasionally in English, to get the gist without reading the entire articles.

Matthew was fully aware that his reliance on online resources and technology was 'sort of like cheating', since ideally, he should have read the actual philosophy readings and conduct reflections on his own (Interview, 11.21.18). Yet, Matthew argued that he had little choice but to depend on those 'shortcuts' given the unmanageable workload in philosophy:

阅读的量很多，有时候一次就要200多页，周一上完课，周三上午就要求读完。但是怎么可能读完？我还有其他课要上，还有其他作业要做，怎么可能有空读完？我只看了*Sparknotes*都抄了七八页 *summary notes*，我要是真是读的话，那我的笔记都可以写一本书了!

The reading load was indeed a lot. Sometimes, we were asked to read over 200 pages all at once. The reading was assigned after Monday's class, and we were required to finish by Wednesday morning. But how can this be possible? I had other classes to attend and had homework from other courses to do. How can I possibly finish reading that much? Even by only reading *Sparknotes*, I still took down around 7 to 8 pages of summary notes. If I were to read those readings myself, my notes would have been as thick as a book! (Interview, 11.21.18)

Matthew's stress in tackling the heavy workload in philosophy could also be observed in his language logs. According to Matthew's language log documenting a typical Wednesday (see Table 5.3), not only did he attend a philosophy lecture in the morning, but he also went to the corresponding discussion session at night. In addition, he reported spending almost every minute of his spare time in between classes reading the materials assigned in the morning class in preparation for the discussion session at night (Matthew's Language Log, 11.14.18). Based on his

Table 5.3 Matthew's language log: A typical weekday, Wednesday 11/14/2018

Time	Activity	Place	Heritage language speaking/ listening/reading/writing	English speaking/listening/ reading/writing
7:50–8:30	Get up and shower	Dorm	n/a	n/a
8:30–9	Have breakfast with Chinese peers	Cafe	S/L	S/L/R only to order food
9–9:50	*Physics*	HU	n/a	L/R/W
10–10:50	*Philosophy*	HU	S/L with Chinese classmates	S/L/R/W
11–12	Lunch with Chinese friends	Cafe	S/L	S/L/R only to order food
12–1	Do *Philosophy* readings assigned in class today	Dorm	S/L with roommate	R/W
1–1:50	*First Year Writing for Multilingual Students*	HU	S/L with Chinese classmates	S/L/R/W
1:50–3	Do *Philosophy* readings assigned in class today	Library	n/a	R/W
3–3:50	*Mathematics*	HU	n/a	L/R
4–5	Do *Philosophy* reading assigned in class today	Library	n/a	R/W
5–6	Dinner with friends	HU	S/L	S/L/R only to order food
6–8:30	*Philosophy* class discussion session based on readings assigned in the morning	HU	n/a	S/L/R/W
8:30	Go back to dorm to sleep	Dorm	n/a	n/a

language log documenting a typical weekday, Matthew reported spending a total of 6.5 hours that day on philosophy (see Table 5.3).

Toward the latter half of the semester, Matthew had gradually abandoned his strategy of entering philosophy discussions by making connections to Chinese contexts. On the one hand, Matthew explained that in order to find the link between course topics and Chinese philosophy, he needed to digest the readings and identify points of connection before class (Interview, 11.21.18). However, given the heavy reading load in philosophy and the substantial effort required by other courses, Matthew did not have enough time to do such preparation in advance (Interview, 11.21.18). On the other hand, because Matthew often relied on *Sparknotes* and Chinese online resources to get the gist of the reading assignments without reading the actual philosophy articles, he became increasingly unfamiliar with the discipline-specific vocabulary. This further prohibited him from contributing to oral discussions in class. Consequently, as the semester progressed, he talked less and less in class. Toward the end of the semester, Matthew barely took part in any oral discussions in philosophy (Interview, 11.21.18).

Shortly before the final exam weeks, Matthew seemed somewhat irritated and frustrated when debriefing with me about his experiences in philosophy (Research Memo, 11.21.18). He first sighed. After a long pause, Matthew exclaimed: '我就觉得很不公平!' (I do feel it is **very** unfair!) (Interview, 11.21.18). He complained that the philosophy professor never took the needs and background knowledge of Chinese international students into consideration, and his Eurocentric focus had put international students at a severe disadvantage:

> 这课的哲学部分还好一点，神学真的很不公平。老师让我们看*Confe ssion*，一天就是7个*book*，都不是7个*chapter*！肯定是因为老师默认为国外的人都看过了，只要复习一下就行。那我没看过呀！我也不能真的就看呀！所以我只能在网上找资料。。。老师让我们*paper*写关于圣经，但美国人都是从小读到大的，我感觉他们全都会，而且都会背了，但我们中国人都没读过，所以根本不知道该怎么写文章。完全不知道该怎么写，也不知道结构的流程怎么走，反正所有中国人都是20分只拿了13分，班上最高是18分，是个白人.

The philosophy part of this course was not too bad, but the theology section was truly very unfair. When the professor asked us to read *Confession*, he required us to read 7 books in 1 day! It was 7 books, not 7 chapters! The professor must have assumed that all foreigners [Matthew meant American students, who were foreigners to him] have already read those in the past and only needed to have a quick review. But I have never read these before! And I simply could not afford to spend that much time reading those! Thus, the only thing I could do was to search online for materials... The professor asked us to write a paper about the *Bible*. All

American students must have been reading it throughout their life, and they should have already known all the content, and even learned to memorize them. Yet we Chinese have never read the Bible before, nor did we know how to write an essay about it. I had no idea how to write it, and what the expected structure was. Anyways, all Chinese only got 13 out of 20. The highest score in class was 18, and the author was a White student. (Interview, 11.21.18)

Regarding his unsatisfactory grade, Matthew clarified that it was not because he was a bad writer; although he had no difficulty meeting the written linguistic demands in *First Year Writing for Multilingual Writers*, the type of writing he was expected to produce in his philosophy class was significantly different from what had learned in his writing class (Interview, 11.21.18). Specifically, while Matthew had learned and practiced writing narratives in his writing class, papers in his philosophy class rarely required students to draw upon their personal experiences. When asked whether he had communicated with the philosophy professor about his academic challenges and sought support accordingly, Matthew shook his head and said: 'Office hour真没必要，你除非自己听不懂，分数低，没信心才去找老师' (There is really no need to go to office hours, unless you could not understand a word, get horrible scores, and have no confidence in yourself) (Interview, 11.21.18). He added that he did not want to try out office hours because he heard from other Chinese classmates that seeking support from that professor was not helpful at all. Matthew told me:

> 我不去 office hour，不光因为和他没什么话说。因为去了也没什么用，我有个朋友去了，因为 paper 分数很低，结果去了老师帮改了改，第二次文章分数还是很低.

> I never go to office hour, not only because I have nothing to say to the professor. It is also because the office hour visit is not going to be helpful. I have a [Chinese international student] friend who went to the professor's office hours, because his paper had been given a very low grade. The professor helped him with his next paper, but it turned out that the grade was still really bad. (Interview, 11.21.18)

By the same token, as the semester progressed, Matthew gave up on his efforts to meet the oral linguistic demands in math. In contrast to his determination to work hard and practice spoken English in math, Matthew simply announced at the end of the semester that he '根本不care' (no longer cared anymore) (Interview, 11.21.18). Not only did Matthew find it too time-consuming to expand his math vocabulary to enhance his ability to speak up during discussions, but he was also extremely demotivated since the professor only assigned 3% of the final grade to class participation. He argued that regardless of his participation grade, his chance of getting an A in mathematics would not be jeopardized: '因为课堂参与比例只有3%，主要就是作业和考试，这些我都没问题，最后肯定拿A是稳的' (Class participation only takes up 3% of the grade. Determining factors of the final grades are mainly homework and quizzes, which I am good at. Therefore, I have absolutely no problem getting an A in the final.) (Interview, 11.21.18). In fact, Matthew believed that since it was so easy for him to achieve perfect scores in homework assignments and quizzes, he found it unnecessary to attend any math classes (Interview, 11.21.18). As Matthew was busy preparing for his final examinations in other courses, he barely showed up to math classes. As the class size was big, Matthew was confident that the professor would not even notice his absence (Interview, 11.21.18).

Along with Matthew's increasingly passive attitudes toward his academic work was his declining interest in socializing with domestic students. In contrast with his strong desire to make friends with Americans and date an American girl at the very beginning of the semester, Matthew announced that he was no longer interested in establishing friendships with domestic peers. Firstly, due to the growing academic stress and the substantial amount of time he devoted to his coursework, Matthew had little time to attend social events and stay connected with his American peers. Given his high academic stress, Matthew became more interested in 'surviving' than making friends with American students (Informal Communication, 11.14.18). Secondly, Matthew found it discouraging to connect with his American peers, believing that they were more interested in hearing 'new perspective[s]' than establishing friendships with Chinese international students:

> 他们可能会和你聊天，但他们从不把你当朋友，只是对你好奇，把你当成外国来的*new perspective*。比如，他会问你，你作为中国人感觉*Trump*怎样？或者中国越来越富了，你们是不是很有钱所以来这里学习？这些问题问了让我好尴尬，你说天天聊这些，我怎么和你成朋友？

> They [Americans] might want to chat with you, but they don't treat you as friends. They are merely curious about you, and regard you as a new perspective coming from a foreign country. For instance, they will ask you, 'as a Chinese, what do you think of Trump?' Or, 'China is getting richer and richer, are you guys here because you are super rich?' These questions made me very embarrassed. If you chat about these things every day, how can I become friends with you? (Interview, 11.21.18)

Finally, Matthew gave up his hope of dating an American girl because of what he described as unmanageable 'cultural differences' (Interview, 11.21.18). To illustrate his point, Matthew shared with me an incident

Table 5.4 Matthew's language log: A typical weekend day, Saturday 11/17/2018

Time	Activity	Place	Heritage language speaking/ listening/reading/writing	English speaking/listening/ reading/writing
Noon–1	Get up, shower, and get ready to go out	Dorm	n/a	n/a
1–3	Lunch with other Chinese international students	Downtown	S/L	S/L/R only to order food
3–7	Go shopping with other Chinese international students	Downtown	S/L	S/L/R only to shop
7–9	Dinner with other Chinese international students	Downtown	S/L	S/L/R only to order food
9–2	Hang out with other Chinese international students to drink, chat and play board games	Downtown	S/L	S/L/R only to order drinks
2	Go back to dorm to sleep	Dorm	n/a	n/a

of his unsuccessful experience communicating with a female American student. Because of his lack of knowledge of popular American sports, he found it challenging to engage in meaningful conversations with his domestic peers:

我们聊天不到5分钟，她就突然问我 '*Who do you think will be the winner in tonight's game*' 我当时就懵逼了。我连今晚有什么比赛都不知道，更不要说告诉她谁会赢了。太尴尬了。感觉他们美国女生都对体育特别感兴趣，什么*baseball, football*呀。我们中国人都不怎么关系这些体育项目的。文化差异太大，更不聊不到一起.

Less than 5 minutes into our conversation, she [the American girl] suddenly asked me, 'Who do you think will be the winner in tonight's game?' I was completely confused. I had no idea that there was a game that night, not to mention predicting the winner. It was too embarrassing. I feel American girls all have strong interest in sports, especially baseball and football. However, we Chinese do not care much about those kinds of sports. The cultural differences are too dramatic for us to communicate with each other (Interview, 11.21.18)

Unable to socialize with domestic students, Matthew spent his spare time exclusively with his Chinese peers, enjoying food at Asian restaurants, playing computer games, watching sports games, showing off luxury-brand clothes and occasionally studying together (*WeChat* Observation, fall 2018). Matthew clarified that when he referred to his 'Chinese friends', he actually meant *regular high* students only; he did not like those *American high* peers who tried to 'show off English' all the time that they forgot their Chinese identities (Interview, 11.21.18). His friendship preference led to Matthew's heavy usage of Chinese, a pattern that showed in his weekday and weekend language logs. As seen in Table 5.3, Matthew spent most of his typical weekday communicating with his *regular high* peers using Chinese. He preferred to resort to Chinese to connect with peers even in academic settings where a classroom-level English-only policy was mandated (e.g. in *First Year Writing for Multilingual Students*). It appeared that the only scenarios when he resorted to English were to order food from the cafeteria and to fulfill academic purposes during class and homework (Matthew's Language Log, 11.14.18). By the same token, on a typical weekend day (see Table 5.4), Matthew reported that other than when he needed to order food or go shopping, he spent almost the entire day using Chinese (Matthew's Language Log, 11.17.18).

At the end of the semester, when asked whether he felt concerned about using much more Chinese than English during his overseas studies, Matthew responded, '反正我以后也不打算留在美国，和中国人怎么开心怎么玩' (I have no plan of staying in the

United States in the future anyways, I can hang out with Chinese students as much as I want) (Interview, 11.21.18). When reminded of his earlier ambition of going to Harvard for graduate studies and working in the United States as an entrepreneur, Matthew simply answered that with all his academic stress, he had given up his hopes and dreams and could not wait to go back to China on graduating from Hillside (Interview, 11.21.18).

International Department *Regular High* Student Sarah's Languaging Journey

Sarah's story touches on the following topics: (1) her previous language and education experiences; (2) her coping strategies and support-seeking activities in response to the challenges encountered; (3) her perceptions of the effectiveness of the support received; (4) concerns about culture as an influential factor in her academic studies, especially in writing; and (5) her bilingual language use in academic and social settings. This story illustrates the first-semester journey of a student, who although had high hopes for linguistic, cultural and social acculturation, was eventually trapped in an enclaved circle toward the end of the semester.

Sarah, a psychology major at the School of Education, was a small-figured, dark-skinned girl with small eyes. She described herself as a '害羞' (shy), '安静' (quiet) and '被动' (passive) person who almost never took the initiative to start a conversation with strangers (Interview, 9.6.18). Sarah came from Nanjing, a neighboring city of Shanghai and the capital of Jiangsu province, a place known for its nationally recognized quality of education. In Jiangsu, mandatory EFL education starts from first grade in elementary school (Interview, 9.6.18). According to Sarah, growing up, she had no particular interest in the English language nor did she like Western culture. Yet, her parents insisted that she pursue higher education in the United States, arguing that an overseas college education would not only broaden her perspectives, but would also significantly increase her competitiveness on the job market in the future (Interview, 9.6.18).

Sarah pursued her high school education at the international department in one of the most prestigious high schools in Jiangsu province. Different from the rest of her high school, which focused heavily on *Gaokao* preparation, the international department was specifically established to serve students who planned to pursue college education abroad in English-speaking countries. At the international department, students were taught by local teachers following US high school curricula. While Sarah had little experience communicating with native speakers of English, owing to her high school experiences, she was familiar with US high school curricula and had opportunities to take AP courses:

我们所有的课程都是为了出国而准备的，没有任何课程是针对高考复习。班里同学都是有出国打算的，大家从高一开始就一起准备托福。我们的英语课有外教，其他课程参照美国高中课程由中国人教。我在高中已经学过*AP Psych*和*AP Calculus*.

All our curriculum was designed specifically in preparation for overseas higher education. Thus, none of the courses were designed to help us pass the College Entrance Exam. All my [previous] classmates had the plan for overseas college studies, and everybody started TOEFL preparation as early as the freshman year in high school. Our English class was taught by foreign teachers, and other courses were taught by Chinese teachers, yet designed to mirror the curriculum of American high schools. I have already passed AP in Psychology and Calculus. (Interview, 9.6.18)

Over the course of two years, Sarah took the TOEFL five times, and eventually achieved a total score of 107. Despite her satisfactory score on the TOEFL, Sarah lacked confidence in her English proficiency (Interview, 9.6.18). Firstly, Sarah was concerned about her listening comprehension since despite her high total score, she scored significantly lower in her listening subtest compared with the other three skills throughout all her attempts (Interview, 9.6.18). Secondly, although scoring high in her speaking subtest, Sarah insisted that her actual oral proficiency was much lower than the score indicated because her seemingly high performance in the speaking subtest was '完全靠背模板' (completely resulted from rote memorization of answers to the prompts) (Interview, 9.6.18). Her lack of confidence in spoken English could also be observed during the interview, in which Sarah primarily used Chinese (approximately 95%) except for occasional code-switching to English words and phrases (Research Memo, 9.6.18).

At the beginning of the semester, Sarah reported encountering difficulties in oral linguistic functioning in both social and academic settings. In social settings, the first challenge that Sarah experienced occurred during freshman orientation the second day after her arrival in the United States (Interview, 9.6.18). According to Sarah, since it was her first time communicating in an English immersion environment, she was not accustomed to how fast her American peers talked. Despite her desire to socialize with domestic students, she was embarrassed by her inability to communicate with her native-speaking peers:

我刚来这里在*orientation*见到了美国人，也很想了解对方，但是不太适应语言，也不知道有什么切入点可以和他们聊，好尴尬。感觉美国人都特别热情，都特别想和你聊，但是他们说的英语好快，都跟不上他们思路，也没法交流。虽然大家都很想聊天，但是大家说的话都听不太懂，就接不下去，只能很尴尬地看着大家。

Shortly after I arrived [in the US], I met American students at the Orientation. I was really interested in knowing more about them, but because I was not used to the English language, I did not know how to have a conversation with them. It was so embarrassing. I felt that the American students were all very welcoming and nice, and they seemed to be eager to know more about me. However, their spoken English was so fast that I could not catch up with what they wanted to express. Thus, we could not communicate. We all wanted to chat with each other, but since I could not understand what they said, I could not respond to their questions. The only thing I did was to stare at them, feeling very embarrassed. (Interview, 9.6.18)

While the university intended to support international students' cultural and linguistic adjustments by assigning international assistants (IAs) to facilitate conversations during orientation, Sarah was far from satisfied. In her opinion, Hillside University 'did a horrible job' in supporting newly arrived non-native English-speaking international students (Interview, 9.6.18). According to Sarah, the IAs contributed little except to initiate some icebreakers and push everybody to talk. Due to her culture and personality, those forced, involuntary conversations were extremely awkward (Interview, 9.6.18). Reflecting on her struggles at the orientation, Sarah shared some suggestions on how Hillside could better support international students by establishing an English-speaking environment before the beginning of the semester:

学校Orientation那里做的太不好了，太突然了， 从全中文的环境突然到全英文的环境。我刚来，就觉得：什么鬼啊？什么都讲这么快？我觉得如果有一个能在orientation之前就可以和你聊聊天的人，哪怕是在网上也好，发发邮件，语音视频，这样可以有适应过程，还可以锻炼口语，一定会好很多.

Hillside did a terrible job at the Orientation, because it happened so abrupt to us, suddenly moving from a whole-Chinese context to an immersed English environment. When I first arrived, my entire feeling was: What the hell? How come everybody talks so fast? I think it would have been better if somebody [from Hillside] could contact us prior to our arrival in America. It could have been as easy as initiating a conversation online via email correspondence, or through a voice or video chat. In this way, we surely would feel better because we could have some extra time to adjust [to the English-speaking environment], and also to practice our oral English. (Interview, 9.6.18)

To cope with her difficulty in English communication in social contexts, Sarah decided to temporarily avoid chatting with native English speakers as much as possible; instead, she preferred to socialize only with her Chinese peers, especially *regular high* students, until she felt ready to 'take that step' (Interview, 9.6.18). On the one hand, despite her strong interest in getting to know domestic students, Sarah believed this coping strategy could help her adjust to the English-speaking environment and boost her confidence in English before establishing any friendships with her American peers (Interview, 9.6.18). On the other hand, at the very beginning of the semester, Sarah found it challenging to identify common topics to enter conversations with domestic students, yet felt more comfortable communicating with other Chinese international students, especially her *regular high* peers who shared very similar language and educational backgrounds with her:'觉得自己还是和中国人在一起比较舒服，而且那些美国人和我们聊也不知道该说什么，大家都很尴尬' (I feel more relaxed chatting with Chinese. I really don't know how to communicate with Americans, and this could make all of us embarrassed) (Interview, 9.6.18).

During the first interview, Sarah told me that she was interested in volunteering to tutor children from socially, culturally and linguistically marginalized backgrounds. According to Sarah, working as a volunteer to help children from diverse backgrounds was not only meaningful to society, but also beneficial to her academic studies as a psychology major at the School of Education. Nevertheless, she was hesitant to pursue this opportunity because of the linguistic challenges she had encountered so far. Sarah told me: '真想去又不敢去' (I really want to take the opportunity but am not brave enough to go) (Interview, 9.6.18). Toward the end of the interview, Sarah announced that she did not feel linguistically ready for the tutoring opportunity and decided to reconsider it in her sophomore or junior year (Interview, 9.6.18).

Similarly, in academic settings, despite her familiarity with American high school curricula and AP courses, Sarah found it challenging to meet the oral demands in class (Interview, 9.6.18). According to Sarah, she found it difficult to understand all but one course taught by a Chinese professor who spoke English as an additional language. Sarah complained that her native-English-speaking professors talked so fast that it was almost impossible for her to keep up. To make matters worse, her American classmates tended to talk 'even faster', and because of this Sarah was intimated to participate in whole-class discussions:

老师讲的已经很快了，结果同学讲话更快，一下子就过去了。他们讨论起来都是一个接一个不停地说，我拼命想理解他们说了什么。好半天才把上一个人的观点勉强了解了，下一个人已经快说完了。我有时也有想说的，但是又不太敢举手，就是怕因为我没听清其他同学已经说过类似观点了，怕闹笑话...

The professors already talked too fast, but my [American] classmates talked even faster. They could finish expressing their opinion in seconds.

When they [American classmates] discussed, they always talked one after the other without any stop. I had to listen hard to death in order to understand what they say. Sometimes it took me so long to digest one classmate's opinion. However, by the time I have vaguely understood the first person's idea, the second person was almost done with her speech. Sometimes, I also wanted to talk. However, I was not brave enough to raise up my hand. Because of my poor English proficiency, I could not be certain whether others have already mentioned the point that I was planning to make. I was afraid to be laughed at… (Interview, 9.8.18)

To cope with this situation, Sarah had originally thought of visiting her professors during their office hours to discuss her language barrier and seek support accordingly. However, she felt very hesitant to do so, worrying that she might be the only international student who was struggling with English. '或许只有我一个人有这个问题? 我们班有其他国际生，别人好像也还好' (Maybe it's my own problem? There are other international students in class, and they seemed to be fine) (Interview, 9.6.18). For fear that sharing her linguistic challenges might leave her professors with a very bad impression, Sarah ended up asking for permission to audio record each lecture using her phone in the hope that through her hard work of repeatedly listening to the recordings after class, she would eventually catch up. Yet, due to its time-consuming nature, Sarah soon gave up recording lectures.

Around one month into the semester, I received multiple *WeChat* voice messages from Sarah, who shared her frustration and anxiety caused by her unsuccessful languaging journey. In these audio messages, Sarah's voice was a little shaky; she sounded sad, hesitant and frustrated, as she sobbed quietly, sighed from time to time, and occasionally had long pauses in between speeches (Research Memo, 9.30.18). Sarah shared her deep embarrassment and shame when failing to express herself in class:

> 有时我没法表达，课堂一片安静，教授就这样看着我，我觉得好尴尬，同学们也都看着我，我觉得真的好尴尬，很想找个地方躲起来，一头钻进地洞里，就是有种羞愧的感觉。。。

Sometimes, when I was not able to express myself in English, the whole class fell into silence. The professor did nothing but to fix his eyes on me, and this made me feel extremely embarrassed. All my classmates were also staring at me, which made me really super embarrassed. I really wanted to find a place to hide. I hoped I could just dig a hole into the floor and hide myself in it. This was how ashamed I felt… (Informal Communication, 9.30.18)

In a latter voice message, Sarah further complained about the significant peer pressure she has felt. Strongly believing all other Chinese international students must have been comfortable with linguistic functioning, Sarah perceived herself as 'the worst' among her peers (Informal Communication, 9.30.18). She was particularly intimidated by her *American high* peers, who were much better at oral English communication, owing to their years of schooling experiences in the United States. Sarah shared her anxiety in *First Year Writing for Multilingual Students* course:

> 在我写作课上，虽然大家都是中国人，我不知怎么的，就是觉得他们的口语都比我好很多。我感觉他们表达起来都比我好，有时我觉得教授问的问题只有我没法表达。。。

> My Writing class is full of Chinese international students. I don't know why, but I keep on feeling that every single one of them speak much better English than me. I feel they are all able to express themselves better than me. Sometimes I feel I was the only one who could not express my idea [in English] to answer the professor's questions... (Informal Communication, 9.30.18).

Owing to substantial peer pressure and her constant negative self-perceptions, Sarah was reluctant to seek support from her professors and she did not feel comfortable sharing her anxieties with peers. Feeling helpless, Sarah ended up calling her family in China to seek emotional support. With comfort from her mother, Sarah gradually realized that it was completely normal to encounter challenges in oral communication on arrival in an Anglophone country. All she needed to do was to stay patient and allow time for her to adjust to the English-speaking environment:

> 我不会太纠结这些，就慢慢让它过去，我告诉自己毕竟口语提高是一个过程，我需要慢慢来，不能期待一下子口-语就像母语一样和别人没有交流障碍，我就准备一点点适应，提高。

> I won't be too worried about these [feelings and experiences] anymore. I plan to let them go with the passage of the time. I comfort myself that since improving oral English is going to be a long process, I need to take it slow. It is not realistic to hope that I will not encounter any communication breakdown and my oral English can immediately become as good as my mother tongue. I plan to take it slow to make adaptations in order to improve [my English proficiency]. (Informal Communication, 9.30.18).

With the emotional support of her family, Sarah recognized the prolonged nature of language development and became less stressed about her situation. In academic contexts, she tried to push herself to speak up at least once in each class, which gradually helped to conquer her anxiety in oral participation. In social settings, Sarah decided to continue avoiding contact with domestic students until she felt linguistically ready. Meanwhile, she kept socializing exclusively with her *regular high* peers so that they could communicate in Chinese, which according to Sarah reduced her languaging anxiety. Sarah's best friend was her roommate, a *regular high* student who happened to be another psychological major and was enrolled in the same classes with her. Sarah was grateful to have her company, as they were able to go to classes, do homework, have meals and explore the city together.

Around midterm, with the increasing written linguistic demands across all subjects, Sarah started to encounter new challenges in academic writing (Interview, 11.20.18). According to Sarah, because professors in different disciplines often had very different expectations of academic writing, she ended up receiving inconsistent grades on similar articles: '差不多的文章，有的老师给分高，有的老师给分低' (for articles written in similar ways, some professors gave me high scores, but others graded me down) (Interview, 11.20.18). Sarah believed this was largely due to her professors' different perceptions on international students' grammatical mistakes in writing: while to some, grammar in writing was not as important as the content, others treated grammar equally, if not more, important compared with content (Interview, 11.20.18). In support of her point, Sarah drew on her different experiences with her philosophy and education professors:

> 我很喜欢哲学老师，因为他不会对语言点扣分，主要看内容。有时候他会给我留个言，说我的内容很好，但是有语法错，建议可以去找*tutor*，不过这不影响我拿高分。*Education*那个课就不一样了，我第一篇文章只拿了*90*，老师评语说我的内容写的非常好，但是就是语法错了太多，于是老师就扣了分。

> I really like my *Philosophy* professor, because he never deducted any point due to my language problems. He mainly focused on content. Occasionally, he mentioned in his comments that the content of my writing was good, but I had some grammatical errors. He also provided me the suggestion to find a [writing] tutor. However, this did not jeopardize my chance of receiving high scores in his class. In contrast, it's a different story in my Education class [a freshman discussion seminar required by the School of Education]. I only received 90 [out of 100] in my first essay. The professor commented that my content was really good, but I made too many grammatical mistakes, because of which he had to deduct some points. (Interview, 11.20.18)

Sarah clarified that it would be 'totally reasonable' for her *First Year Writing for Multilingual Students* professor to deduct points for grammatical errors, as she considered the course to be 'a language class' (Interview, 11.20.18). Yet, according to Sarah, all content-subject professors should evaluate international students' writing solely based on content, unless the language issues were so severe that they hindered reading comprehension. This was clearly not the case with Sarah. Based on a text analysis of the writing samples collected from Sarah's course writings using the genre-based rubric adapted from Brisk (2015), there were indeed some imperfections with her language expressions. Nevertheless, those language issues did not appear to compromise her content-meaning expression. For instance, in her writing samples including two arguments and one recount, Sarah clearly expressed her main ideas despite some occasional incidences of redundant article use (e.g. 'academic performance in **the** college'), inappropriate modality (e.g. overuse of low modality expressions such as 'might', 'could' and 'be likely to' in persuasive argument) and errors in third-person singular (e.g. 'he **like** to teach me') among other minor language problems. Reflecting on her experiences in academic writing, Sarah pointed out that compared with domestic students, non-native-English-speaking international students were naturally prone to imperfections in their language expressions. Under such circumstances, deducting points on grammar was 'super unfair' and it put multilingual writers at a severe disadvantage:

> 我就觉得不太公平，老师明明知道我是国际生了！不能明白为什么我内容写的好，因为语法问题还要扣分。美国人他们就只看内容给分，而国际生他们同时还会在语言上扣分，这意味着我们国际生比他们有更多的地方可以被扣分！哎，超级*unfair*...

> I feel this was unfair. Those professors have already known that I am an international student! I cannot understand why they had to deduct points on my grammar even though I did well in terms of the content of writing. They always evaluate American students only based on their content. However, when it comes to international students, they look at both language and content. That means we, as international students, have more potential areas to have our points deducted! Ah, this is super unfair... (Interview, 11.20.18)

Beyond her concerns with inconsistent grammar evaluation in academic writing across disciplines, another challenge that Sarah encountered during the latter half of the semester was the remarkably different genre expectations in Chinese and American argumentative writing (Interview, 11.20.18). Sarah explained that in contrast to the common Western-style five-paragraph argumentative writing featuring a clear presentation of the thesis statement in the opening, in Chinese argumentative writing, writers are expected to provide abundant evidence and background information to guide readers to discover the theme at the very end.

While fully aware of the preferred way of argument writing based on Western culture, Sarah was resistant to presenting her argument in such a straightforward way. She regarded following the Western way of argumentative writing a betrayal of her Chinese identity, insisting that '我们中国人不这么写' (We Chinese do not write this way) (Talks around Texts, 11.2.18). Sarah further pointed out that, based on the genre norms in Chinese argumentative writing, presenting a thesis statement right at the beginning to express the main ideas of the article was considered highly undesirable and even shallow, as it could not '发人深思' (generate deep reflections among readers) (Talks around Texts, 11.2.18). According to Sarah, Chinese argument writing values the generation of readers' depth of thinking. To support her view, Sarah introduced the concept of '铺垫' (to lay a foundation), a commonly adopted strategy in Chinese argument writing that aims to present adequate background information and evidence without directly presenting the thesis. In order to understand the writer's argument, Chinese readers are expected to 'do some detective work' by putting together the bits and pieces of evidence in order to understand the main argument (Talks around Texts, 11.2.18).

Sarah's intentional, culturally informed decision not to present a clear thesis statement was confirmed based on results from text analysis using Brisk's (2015) genre-based rubric. Her two argument writing samples earned scores of 1 and 2, respectively, in the section evaluating thesis statement, indicating that she either failed to present any thesis statement or provided a very vague one that did not clearly demonstrate her points. For instance, in her argument paper in fulfillment of her psychology professor's requirement to 'create a persuasive argument about the importance of a topic', Sarah chose to open her essay with some background information about child maltreatment without presenting a clear thesis statement demonstrating her perceived urgency to address child maltreatment. In her opening paragraph, she wrote:

> With the rapid development of economics and society, more people promoted child welfare system which played an important role to ensure children grow up in a good environment. However, Child Maltreatment report by the Administration on Children, Youth and Families (Collins, L.M., 2017) noted 683,000 victims of child maltreatment or 9.2 victims per 1,000 children... (Sarah's Writing Sample, 10.24.18)

While not demonstrating her stance right from the beginning, Sarah succeeded in indirectly expressing her stance by synthesizing research findings from previous studies. In other words, although without directly putting her thesis upfront, Sarah did present abundant supporting evidence along the way to scaffold readers to understand her main argument toward the end. Such a collective reasoning strategy reflected the Eastern tradition of building argument on consensual agreement, in that Sarah succeeded in leading the readers to arrive at the same conclusion that child maltreatment was an important topic that deserved research

Table 5.5 Sarah's language log: Example of a typical weekday, Monday 11/12/2018

Time	Activity	Place	Heritage language speaking/ listening/reading/writing	English speaking/listening/reading/ writing
8–8:20	Get up, and get ready for school	dorm	L/S	n/a
8:20–9	Breakfast with roommate	Cafe	L/S	L/S/R only when ordering food
9–9:50	*Philosophy* with roommate	HU	L/S	L/S/R/W
10–12	Homework with roommate	Library	L/S	R/W
12–12:50	*Mathematics Education* with roommate	HU	L/S	L/S/R/W
1–1:30	Lunch with roommate	Cafe	L/S	L/S/R only when ordering food
1:30–4:30	Homework with roommate	HU	L/S	R/W
4:30–5:45	*Computer Science* with roommate	HU	L/S	L/S/R/W
5:45–6:30	Dinner with roommate	Cafe	L/S	L/S/R only when ordering food
5:45–11	Homework with roommate	Dorm	R/W with *WeChat* L/S with roommate	R/W
11–11:30	Shower and sleep	Dorm	L/S	n/a

Table 5.6 Sarah's language log: Example of a typical weekend, Saturday 11/17/2018

Time	Activity	Place	Heritage language speaking/ listening/reading/writing	English speaking/listening/reading/ writing
9–11:30	Get up and watch TV with roommate	Dorm	S/L	n/a
11:30–12:30	Lunch with roommate	Cafe	S/L	S/L/R only when ordering food
1–9	Shopping and dinner with roommate	Downtown	S/L	S/L/R only when shopping/ordering food
9:30–11	Return to dorm, shower and sleep	Dorm	S/L	n/a

and practical attention. Unfortunately, Sarah's culturally informed decision of painting a big picture first before clarifying her thesis confused her professor, who prompted her to '[b]e clearer' about her thesis statement in opening instead of presenting her thesis at the very end. Consequently, Sarah received an unsatisfactory grade for her psychology essay.

Shortly before the end of the semester, to cope with her challenges in academic writing, Sarah decided to seek support from her professors and tutors from the Hillside Writing Center (Interview, 11.20.18). Her rationale for resorting to both professors and tutors was that they could help her writing in different ways: '老师可以帮我的文章搭框架, *tutor*可以帮我改语法' (professors are helpful in building the structure of my papers, and tutors can edit my papers for grammatical errors) (Interview, 11.20.18). Sarah's support-seeking strategy earned positive results. By visiting office hours before the writing assignment due date, Sarah was able to gain a better understanding of the expectations of her professors, which were sometimes 'beyond the rubric' (Interview, 11.20.18). For example, in her *First Year Writing for Multilingual Students* class, even though the assignment rubric of the fictional narrative project did not specify whether the authors were required to put emphasis on the main character's thoughts and emotions, the professor told Sarah during her office hour consultation that she 'personally like[d] those fictional narratives with heavy emphasis on thoughts and emotions' (Interview, 11.20.18). Based on this hint, Sarah revised her paper and added many vivid descriptions of how the main character felt. Shortly before the due date, she sent the paper to a tutor who helped to proofread and check for grammatical errors. Consequently, she received an A on this paper (Interview, 11.20.18).

At the end of the semester, reflecting on her languaging journey throughout the semester, Sarah celebrated her progress in meeting the linguistic demands in academic contexts and proudly announced that she finally felt psychologically and linguistically ready to socialize with American classmates (Interview, 11.20.18). Despite her desire to establish friendships with domestic students, Sarah believed that her earlier decision to avoid native speakers of English and socialize exclusively with *regular high* peers prevented her from valuable opportunities to improve her English communication skills and experience local culture. Sarah pointed that that she was 'only one step away' from realizing her dream of making friends with Americans, yet 'it was too late' (Interview, 11.20.18). According to Sarah, the most critical period for establishing a friendship is at the very beginning of the semester, when people are only starting to bond with each other. At the end of the semester, when such bonding was already established, it became extremely challenging to make meaningful connections with her American peers beyond the classroom settings:

感觉美国人都自己有自己的圈子，他们上课也都坐在一起。美国同学，都是课上说说，下了课就各走各了，没有办法有更多联系.

I feel American students have already had their own friend circles. They always sit together in class. My relationship with American peers is limited to our communication during class time. Once class is over, we will walk to different directions, and have no additional contacts with each other. (Interview, 11.20.18)

Sarah regretted her earlier decision to socialize almost exclusively with her *regular high* roommate, which resulted in her enclaved and monotonous social experiences. As shown in Tables 5.5 and 5.6, Sarah spent almost every minute of the day with her roommate. Sarah told me that, originally, she had intentionally chosen to live with a Chinese roommate from the same program in the hope of reducing loneliness. Yet, after spending an entire semester '和室友捆绑在一起' (sticking together with her roommate), Sarah started to feel that she spent so much time chatting in Chinese and doing everything with her roommate that it defeated the purpose of her overseas studies:

我觉得现在过的还是高中的生活，过的太单调了，每天就游离于宿舍，图书馆，食堂。一天24小时，可能有18小时我都和我的室友在一起，其他的那几个小时睡觉，虽然是在同一个屋里，呼吸同一个空气，但好歹眼睛是闭上的。有时，真希望我室友是美国人.

I feel there is no difference between my current and high school life. It was too boring and simple. I spend every day moving between the dormitory, library, and cafeteria. Within the 24 hours of a day, I spent approximately 18 hours with my roommate [who is another Chinese international student]. For the rest hours [when we are sleeping], even though we are still in the same room, and breathe the same air, at least our eyes are closed [and won't see each other]. Sometimes I really hope that roommate were an American. (Interview, 11.20.18)

When I comforted her by suggesting that she could still apply through the residential service to change her roommate to an American student next year, Sarah simply shook her head and insisted 'that's not an option anymore' (Interview, 11.20.18). Although she longed for an American roommate to experience 'authentic college life' in the United States, Sarah was worried that doing so would anger her current roommate and other *regular high* friends. Because her close peers were satisfied with socializing exclusively within the Chinese international student community, Sarah was concerned that switching to an American roommate would make her 'a betrayer' of the group (Interview, 11.20.18). At the end of the interview, Sarah concluded that she was desperate to make a change to facilitate her acculturation, yet she was 'stuck firm' due to her lack of courage to leave her current friendship behind. As she remarked, 'I am really just one step away, yet stuck firm...' (Interview, 11.20.18).

Concluding Remarks

This chapter presented the languaging journeys of three *regular high* students, William, Matthew and Sarah. The three students' varying language, education and socioeconomic backgrounds positioned them at distinct starting points and brought them unique languaging challenges at the beginning of the semester. Holding various perceptions about their multilingual identities, relationships with peers and the ability to function linguistically across academic and social contexts, the three students initiated different coping strategies to address the challenges they encountered. Consequently, this contributed to their different languaging journeys throughout the semester. In Chapter 6, I provide a semester-long linguistic portrait of two *American high* students, Rebecca and Hugo.

Note

(1) Chinese international students tend to refer to any non-Chinese as 'foreigners'. Here, William's usage of 'foreigners' specifically meant Americans.

6 First-Semester Languaging Journeys of Two *American High* Students

Introduction

This chapter focuses on the first-semester languaging experiences of two *American high* students: Rebecca and Hugo (see Figure 6.1). Before coming to Hillside University, Rebecca and Hugo had spent three and four years, respectively, studying in American high schools. Owing to their familiarity with English-medium instruction and American high school curricula, both students were able to meet the linguistic demands of college. Despite their similarly high English proficiency, however, the two students held different perceptions of their multilingual identities, which contributed to their different languaging journeys throughout the semester.

Three-Year *American High* Student Rebecca's Languaging Journey

Rebecca's story will mainly touch on the following topics: (1) her previous language and education experiences; (2) her English language proficiency; (3) perceptions of her *regular high* peers; and (4) her bilingual language use in academic and social settings. This story illustrates the first-semester journey of a culturally, linguistically and academically acculturated student who had no difficulty functioning in American higher education given her previous language and educational experiences.

Rebecca was a biology and chemistry combined major. She wore a pair of thick-framed glasses and had long, straight hair. Before coming to Hillside University, Rebecca completed her K-9 education[1] in Beijing, China, and later spent from tenth to twelfth grade in an elite, private high school in Pennsylvania. Rebecca told me that since elementary school, she had been 'determined to study in an American high school' (Interview, 9.6.18). She chose to pursue her education far from home because of her poor relationship with her parents. According to Rebecca, although born into an upper-class family with highly educated parents, she was seldom happy growing up. Since both her parents were workaholics, Rebecca had spent most of her childhood with her grandparents (Interview, 9.6.18). Reflecting on her childhood experiences, Rebecca firmly stated: '我父母每天都是工作，几乎很少管我，那我就想与其不开心，不如

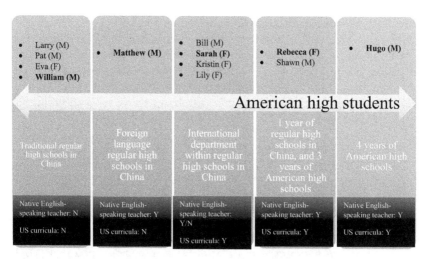

Figure 6.1   An overview of Rebecca and Hugo on the continuum

出国，离开他们!' (My parents were busy working every day, and barely had time to attend to me. Thus, I came up with the idea of going abroad. I would rather stay away from them than be unhappy!) (Interview, 9.6.18). In her ninth grade, Rebecca decided to pursue high school education in the United States, despite her parents' strong disagreement, arguing that she was too young to study thousands of miles away from home.

Rebecca started her English as a foreign language (EFL) learning as early as in first grade. Growing up, she had always been one of the top students in class (Interview, 9.6.18). Yet, according to Rebecca, EFL education in China, despite its claimed focus on communicative language teaching, was 'nothing like actual English, not even close' (Interview, 9.6.18). She described EFL education in Chinese public schools as 'super teacher-centered' and students were given little chance to practice their spoken English (Interview, 9.6.18). Therefore, Rebecca firmly believed that the EFL education received at school was far from adequate to help her excel in standardized English language assessment such as the test of English as a foreign language (TOEFL). She commented, '你要想出国读高中，就一定要在外面学托福' (If you want to pursue high school studies abroad, you must learn TOEFL outside) (Interview, 9.6.18). By 'outside', Rebecca meant taking classes from private tutors and educational companies. In preparation for her American high school application, Rebecca had spent months taking intensive one-on-one TOEFL classes with a private tutor. At the age of 14, she took TOEFL three times, and her score skyrocketed from 60 to 96, and finally to 103. Rebecca's successful TOEFL performance later earned her the opportunity to study in a prestigious high school in the United States.

Rebecca recalled that she had witnessed the greatest progress in her English proficiency during high school. On arriving in the United States, despite her successful TOEFL score, she was overwhelmed by the 'fast-paced conversations', 'crazily hard readings' and 'mission-impossible writings' (Interview, 9.6.18). Yet, since her high school was predominantly White with very few international students or students of color, her teachers were severely underprepared to support multilingual students. Through her high school experiences in the United States, Rebecca understood the importance of relying on herself and taking the initiative to seek support:

> 我的美高老师对我毫无怜悯心，我在美高充分认识到了作为一个国际生，你在用第二语言写作，人家对你毫无怜悯心。*You don't know how to write in English? Then we don't care!* 人家打分都是对着一个*rubric*，你有达不到要求的，那天经地义，没有办法。你要想分数高，就要自己寻求帮助！

> My American high school teachers were not sympathetic to me at all. As an *American high* international student, I fully understood that people would not feel sorry to you when you had to write in your second language. You don't know how to write in English? Then we don't care! They always referred to the rubrics to grade your paper. If you did not meet the requirements, then there was no other option except to have your points deducted. If you want a high grade, then you must seek help on your own! (Interview, 11.20.18)

During her three years in an American high school, Rebecca constantly pushed herself out of her comfort zone to seek language support from her American peers (Interview, 9.6.18). This not only facilitated her English development, but also helped Rebecca establish friendships with her American peers:

> When I first arrived in high school, my English sucked. So I just asked questions about everything and anything, and people would explain to you, and then you would get used to it. If you don't understand a joke, then ask your friend. That's how you get a friend! If you don't know the meaning of a question, then ask your friends to explain to you! I have many American friends who know that I am not good enough. I have many good friends who I am still in touch with. They explained so much stuff to me... That's how you live. That's how it works out. (Interview, 9.6.18)

By the time of college application, Rebecca had been studying in the United States for around three years. Based on the admissions policy at Hillside, the TOEFL requirement could be waived due to her prolonged educational experiences in an English-speaking country. Nevertheless, Rebecca decided to take the TOEFL test again right before college application 'simply to impress the universities' with her high English proficiency (Interview, 9.6.18). Without much test preparation, Rebecca yielded a near-perfect score of 117 out of 120. However, Rebecca was not satisfied, believing that her 'real English [proficiency] is way better than this [what the TOEFL indicated]' (Interview, 9.6.18). Rebecca claimed that if it were not for her severe cold on the day of the exam, she ought to have received a perfect score on the TOEFL (Interview, 9.6.18).

Throughout her first semester of college life, Rebecca experienced no difficulties languaging across academic and social settings. According to Rebecca, this was because she had already 'accomplished all those [linguistic] transitions and adaptions back in high school' (Interview, 11.20.18). In social settings, owing to her near-native English pronunciation, Rebecca had no difficulty communicating with native speakers, and was able to make friends with her American peers right from the very beginning of the semester. To demonstrate her strong ability to function linguistically in social contexts, Rebecca shared with me an incident when she was mistaken for Chinese American due to her superior oral English proficiency:

> After I talked, people were like, instead of saying 'How come your English is so good,' they said 'How come your Chinese is so good?' I said 'dude, I've learned to talk in Chinese for 14 years!' So, they were like 'so you are an international student?' I said 'yeah...' 所以我在这里已经语言没问题了 (Therefore, I have no language problems anymore here in the US). I don't need more transition... (Interview, 11.20.18)

Based on my *WeChat* observation throughout the semester, Rebecca indeed demonstrated no signs of struggle in terms of her English performance in college. In fact, she often used English skillfully as a medium to convey humor in relation to her experiences in content-subject learning, especially in chemistry and biology, her two majors (Research Memo, 12.9.18). For instance, as shown in Figure 6.2, through her demonstration of a humorous conversation between a student and her chemistry instructor (*WeChat* Observation, 10.13.18), Rebecca expressed her confusion and struggle during her 'overwhelmingly difficult Chemistry course' (Interview, 11.20.18). In this conversation, she drew on the different meanings for the word 'mass' in chemistry and theology to show that she, as a student, was completely lost in her chemistry professor's explanation of certain concepts (Interview, 11.20.18). In another example, in order to describe the intense peer pressure she experienced in her biology class (Interview, 11.20.18), Rebecca posted a joke on *WeChat*: 'Sometimes I think we are about the same, cuz I weigh 8oz and they weigh half a pound. But as I look closer, wait... I am 8oz of TRASH, and they are half a pound of GOLD...' (*WeChat* Observation, 10.7.18).

Echoing her successful linguistic functioning in social contexts, Rebecca compared her overall academic English performance in college to '如鱼得水' (like putting fish into the water; metaphorical meaning:

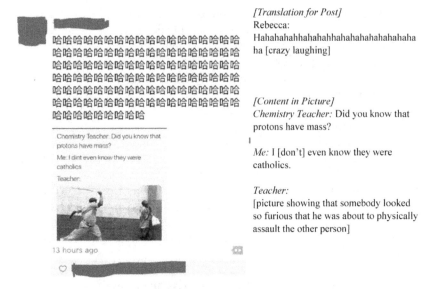

[Translation for Post]
Rebecca:
Hahahahahhahahahhahahahahahahahahaha
ha [crazy laughing]

[Content in Picture]
Chemistry Teacher: Did you know that
protons have mass?

Me: I [don't] even know they were
catholics.

Teacher:
[picture showing that somebody looked
so furious that he was about to physically
assault the other person]

Figure 6.2 Example of Rebecca's *WeChat* posts about *Chemistry,* 10/13/18

easy and successful) (Interview, 9.6.18). With regard to meeting the oral linguistic demands in academic contexts, Rebecca was able to fully engage in academic conversations, be it in class or in office hour visits (Interview, 9.6.18). As for meeting the written linguistic demands in academic contexts, Rebecca stated that since she was a science major, the only reading and writing intensive course was *First Year Writing for Multilingual Writers*, which she considered 'extremely easy' (Interview, 9.6.18).

Due to her high performance on Hillside's writing placement test prior to the beginning of the semester, Rebecca had originally been assigned to the regular *First Year Writing* class in which the majority of the students were native English speakers. Nevertheless, Rebecca requested to be placed into one of the *First Year Writing for Multilingual Writers* sections instead (Interview, 9.6.18). Clarifying that this decision was not made due to her lack of confidence in academic writing, Rebecca explained that she chose to join the multilingual section as she strongly believed that this course would be more beneficial in 'getting rid of the accent in writing' by paying attention to detailed language aspects:

我觉得听说读写里最难的就是写，特别是第二语言。你如果不写出来，你是不会意识到*there are so many mistakes.* 你如果不写出来，你是不会知道这么多*mistake*你都在一直在不停地不停地犯，所以我觉得写作还是非常有必要加强的，因为你只有常写才能发现你的不足，和你容易犯的错误。*Multilingual*班里肯定会更注意语法语言细节什么的，更有利让我发现自己的潜在不足。

I feel the hardest aspect among listening, speaking, reading and writing should be writing, especially writing in a second language. Without writing, you won't realize there are so many mistakes [in your language expression]. Without writing, you won't realize you are constantly making those mistakes. Thus, I believe it is very necessary to strengthen my writing skills. Only by writing more often can you discover your weakness and frequent errors. The *First Year Writing for Multilingual Writers* will certainly put more emphasis on grammar and other details of the language, which is more beneficial for me to realize my hidden weaknesses. (Interview, 11.20.18)

Rebecca told me that she always '严格按照一个美高学生来要求自己' (strictly followed the standards as an 'American high' student) and had 'zero tolerance for grammar mistakes and Chinglish expressions' (Interview, 9.6.18). By analyzing Rebecca's writings in partial fulfillment of her coursework in music and writing courses, I found that her texts consistently yielded the highest scores possible for all detailed aspects under the categories of both 'purpose and stages' and 'language' according to the genre-based rubric (Brisk, 2015). This, based on the rubric, indicated that Rebecca did not need any additional language or instructional support in accomplishing her academic writing assignments from the perspective of both structure and language.

While there were few observable changes in her academic and social linguistic functioning over the course of one semester due to Rebecca's already high English proficiency since high school, I did notice some gradual shifts in her attitudes toward *regular high* Chinese international students.

At the beginning of the semester, Rebecca revealed a rather unfavorable attitude toward *regular high* students, describing them as 'lazy', 'childish' and 'impolite' (Interview, 9.6.18). Firstly, Rebecca felt sorry for those *regular high* students who were reluctant to push themselves out of their comfort zone and take advantage of the resources available (Interview, 9.6.18). According to Rebecca, most *regular high* students had a tendency to rely solely on their enclosed support system, which could have negative effects on their long-term academic well-being. To illustrate her point, Rebecca shared an incident that happened in her math class. One of her *regular high* classmates had great difficulty solving a homework problem. Yet, instead of seeking support from the math professor or the teaching assistant, that student reached out to Rebecca and suggested because they were both Chinese, they needed to 'help each other' (Interview, 9.6.18). By 'helping', the student meant that Rebecca should share her homework so that he could copy her answer. Rebecca immediately rejected the student's request and suggested that he make an appointment with their math professor so that he would not only get the correct answer but also understand how to solve related problems in the future. Nevertheless, she soon found out that instead of visiting the office hours, the student approached another *regular high* student and managed to copy the answer to the question (Interview, 9.6.18). 'I really don't understand why he was so lazy and childish!' Rebecca sighed (Research Memo, 9.6.18).

Secondly, Rebecca thought negatively of her *regular high* peers due to their overall lack of motivation to participate in student organizations. According to Rebecca, Hillside had various student organizations, some social and others academic, which she believed were very valuable channels to meet American friends, practice English, know more about Western culture and learn new skills (Interview, 9.6.18). Rebecca reported that she was part of multiple student organizations, thanks to which she enjoyed socializing with American peers. In contrast, based on her observation, *regular high* Chinese international students hardly participated in any student organizations. For instance, one of the organizations that Rebecca took part in was a freshmen leadership program, in which a small group of first-year students at Hillside with ambition, leadership and academic excellence got together to socialize, participate in group discussions and hone their public-speaking skills. Yet, in spite of the fact that the Chinese international students represented the largest international student group on campus, very few demonstrated interest in the leadership program (Interview, 9.6.18). Realizing that she was the only Chinese face during the first leadership group meeting, Rebecca felt 'ashamed' of her Chinese peers: 'Come on... There are so many of them [*regular high* students], but nobody came! This is such a wonderful opportunity to boost up your resume, why not give it a try?' (Interview, 9.6.18).

Rebecca observed that even in rare cases when *regular high* students did participate in student organization events, their involvement was usually confined to the Chinese circle. She speculated, 'The most they do is probably the Chinese Student Association' (Interview, 9.6.18). Yet, Rebecca pointed out that since a particular student organization was primarily made up of *regular high* Chinese international students, joining it defeated the purpose of expanding their friend circle to get to know peers from diverse cultural and linguistic backgrounds and enhance their English proficiency (Interview, 9.6.18).

In response to Rebecca's negative attitudes toward *regular high* students, I suggested an alternative explanation that perhaps the *regular high* Chinese international students' unwillingness to approach professors and their reluctance to participate in student organizations might be due to concerns about their lack of English proficiency (Interview, 9.6.18). Nevertheless, Rebecca immediately objected to my assumption. Re-emphasizing her own experiences seeking support in adjusting to the English-speaking environment in high school, Rebecca argued that her *regular high* peers 'simply didn't try hard enough' to push themselves out of the comfort zone (Interview, 9.6.18). She explained,

When you're studying abroad, nobody is going to come and babysit you. If you're not sure, just ASK! You don't cheat or avoid. Ask your professor for help, ask your classmates for help, ask the tutoring center for help! You should take advantage of resources and give everything a try. What do you have to lose? Again, if you're not sure, just ASK! (Interview, 9.6.18)

Last but not least, Rebecca viewed *regular high* students very negatively because they were 'very, very, very impolite' (Interview, 9.6.18). Rebecca recalled her experiences in her *First Year Writing for Multilingual Students* class, in which all but three students were *regular high* Chinese students, including Rebecca and two other international students from Korea and Nepal, respectively. According to Rebecca, although the writing professor had made it clear that only English was allowed in class, the *regular high* students always '抱团' (stuck together like a rice ball) and chatted exclusively in Chinese before, during and after class (Interview, 9.6.18). On the one hand, Rebecca was disappointed by her regular high peers' reluctance to participate orally in class: 'They definitely knew the answer, cuz I heard them whisper in Chinese. But they were just too lazy to say anything to the class in English…' (Interview, 9.6.18). On the other hand, Rebecca found their Chinese usage rude and inappropriate because they not only failed to show respect to the writing professor, but also marginalized the two international students who could not understand a word of Chinese:

> I think that's very, very, very impolite. Situation really varies, if you are having a personal conversation [with another Chinese], then using Chinese is fine. If you are with other people [who are non-Chinese speakers], then ANYTIME you should use English, because otherwise you will exclude other people… Before class everyone is chatting in Chinese and I am the only one chatting in English, because they [the two non-Chinese speakers] might want to chat too! I don't know… They [the two non-Chinese speakers] must feel so bad…We are all talking in Chinese, and they are SO alone. We are all Chinese; this is just SO unfair… (Interview, 9.6.18)

Rebecca was fully aware that her resistance to using Chinese before, during and after the *First Year Writing* class had led to her *regular high* classmates' dissatisfaction. She sensed that she was resented by her *regular high* peers due to her exclusive English usage: 'They all hate me because they think I am purposefully showing off my English' (Interview, 9.6.18). Nevertheless, Rebecca was not bothered. As far as she was concerned, since all international students at Hillside had passed the TOEFL exam, English should be seen as the default language in college communication:

Other students think I am weird. I know! But I am ok with that, because I think you [*regular high* students] are weird too. Different perspectives, I guess… In the US, I assume English should be the most comfortable language for everyone, because you passed TOEFL! So, I use English as a language to approach people, while you [*regular high* students] use Chinese to exclude people… (Interview, 9.6.18)

Rebecca's tensions with *regular high* Chinese international students led to her decision to socialize exclusively with American students right from the beginning of the semester. She claimed that she never followed other Chinese international students on social media to '抱团' (stick together like a rice ball), nor did she intentionally participate in any group activities hosted especially for Chinese international students. Although Rebecca was included in the Hillside Chinese international freshman *WeChat* group, she muted all chat notifications because she was not interested in establishing any friendships with her *regular high* peers (Interview, 9.6.18). Toward the end of our first interview, Rebecca mentioned that so far, she had fewer than five *regular high* acquaintances, among whom none she considered a friend. When asked whether she would like to know more Chinese peers in the future, Rebecca answered without hesitation: 'Nope! I need what I need, and I don't need to know who they are!' (Interview, 9.6.18).

Rebecca's bilingual language logs also echoed her lack of interest in socializing with other Chinese international students. As shown in Tables 6.1 and 6.2, Rebecca hardly used any Chinese during a typical day in her first semester in college. English was her preferred language when socializing with her American peers and languaging across academic and social contexts. It appeared that the only incidence when she practiced Chinese listening was when she took the *First Year Writing for Multilingual Students* class. Yet, Rebecca made it clear that her reported Chinese usage was solely passive and even against her will because her writing class was dominated by *regular high* students: 'I listened [to Chinese] cuz I could not change my environment; but the fact that I listened does not mean that I said a thing in Chinese' (Interview, 11.20.18).

Slightly in contrast with her self-reported bilingual usage documented in the language logs, however, my observation of Rebecca's *WeChat* usage indicated that she had been involved in increasing interactions with other Chinese students, especially her *regular high* peers, over the course of the first semester (Research Memo, 12.10.18). At the beginning of the semester, Rebecca did not update her *WeChat* posts very often, and her posts during that period were largely about non-academic topics such as computer games and manga, which mostly generated conversations between her and her middle school friends in China. Yet, as the semester progressed, her *WeChat* posts touched more and more on academic-related topics in relation to her college experiences at Hillside

Table 6.1 Rebecca's language log: A typical weekday, Tuesday 11/13/2018

Time	Activity	Place	Heritage language speaking/listening/reading/writing	English speaking/listening/reading/writing
7–8	Get up and have breakfast	Dorm	n/a	n/a
8–9	Calculus discussion group	HU	n/a	S/L/R/W
9–10:15	Chemistry	HU	n/a	S/L/R/W
10:30–11:45	Biology	HU	n/a	S/L/R/W
11:45–12:45	Lunch with American friends	Cafe	n/a	S/L/R
12:45–1:30	Homework	Library	n/a	R/W
1:30–2:45	First Year Writing	HU	L	S/L/R/W
3–4:15	Music	HU	n/a	S/L/R/W
4:30–5:30	Student organization meeting	HU	n/a	S/L/R/W
5:30–6:00	Dinner with American friends	Cafe	n/a	S/L/R
6–8	Student organization meeting	HU	n/a	S/L/R/W
8–9	Shower and sleep	Dorm	n/a	n/a

Table 6.2 Rebecca's language log: A typical weekend day, Sunday 11/18/2018

Time	Activity	Place	Heritage language speaking/ listening/reading/writing	English speaking/listening/ reading/writing
9:30–10	Get up and have breakfast	Dorm	n/a	L/S/R
10–12:30	Homework	Dorm	n/a	R/W
12:30–1:30	Lunch with American friends	Cafe	n/a	S/L
1:30–4:30	Hang out with friends	Downtown	n/a	S/L
4:30–6:30	Student organization meeting	HU	n/a	L/S/R/W
6:30–7:30	Dinner with American friends	Cafe	n/a	L/S/R
7:30–11	Homework	Dorm	n/a	R/W

University, which generated closer interactions between Rebecca and her *regular high* peers mainly for the purposes of seeking emotional support. Figures 6.3 and 6.4 illustrate two examples of Rebecca's interactions with other Chinese international students which happened around the midterm examinations. In Figure 6.3, Rebecca revealed her stress about the upcoming chemistry midterm exam. Her post was liked by a few *regular high* students, and some left comments comforting her and wishing her the best of luck in the exam (*WeChat* Observation, 10.22.18). In another post illustrated in Figure 6.4, Rebecca expressed anxiety about her upcoming midterm exams. In order to stay motivated during test preparation, she requested her Chinese peers to stop her from procrastinating. Determined to devote herself to studying, Rebecca publicly invited her *WeChat* friends to 'slap her face' if she was caught not concentrating on midterm preparation. This post was again liked by a group of her Chinese peers (*WeChat* Observation, 10.24.18).

With her increased interactions over *WeChat*, by the end of the semester, Rebecca's attitudes toward her *regular high* peers also became more positive. Firstly, instead of blaming her *regular high* peers for their impoliteness of '抱团' (sticking together like a rice ball) and exclusive usage of Chinese (Interview, 9.6.18), Rebecca started to show understanding of the rationale behind this behavior (Interview, 11.20.18). She pointed out that their 'sticky rice' behavior was '可以被理解的' (something understandable) because it is human nature to socialize with people who are more similar:

> 如果我和你的相似度比我跟其他人的相似度更多，那我就更喜欢和你做朋友。所以你把我放到一群陌生人里，我会去找你.

> If you and I have more similarities compared with those between me and other people, then I will be more inclined to make friends with you. Therefore, if you throw me into a group of strangers, my first instinct is to find you. (Interview, 11.20.18)

[Translation]
Post content: Tomorrow, please do not give me the midterm exam. Please, give me one more day to do my practice problems.

[Picture: depressed panda; caption: I'm fine, followed by curses in Chinese showing that in reality I am not fine at all]

[Post liked by a group of Chinese international students]
Rebecca: Who can rescue my Chemistry? Who can rescue my biology? Where are my lifesavers? Please raise up your hands, and I will find you now
Another Chinese student: Good luck!!! [lucky leaf emoji]

Figure 6.3 Example of Rebecca's *WeChat* posts: Chemistry midterm, 10/22/18

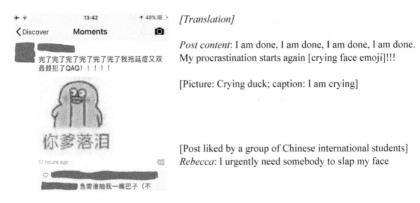

Figure 6.4 Example of Rebecca's *WeChat* posts: Anxiety due to upcoming midterms, 10/25/18

It is worth noting that although Rebecca demonstrated understanding of her *regular high* peers' inclination to socialize with people who share the same language, she insisted that the 'sticky rice behavior' was harmful, as it limited Chinese international students' opportunities to establish friendships with domestic students. She argued, '你既然就愿意交高昂学费来美国了，那你和其他人做朋友也未尝不可' (Now that you are willing to pay so much money to come for overseas studies in the US, it is not a bad idea to make friends with other [non-Chinese] people) (Interview, 11.20.18). Rebecca also added that while it was natural for people to establish friendships with others who were similar to themselves, the perceived 'similarities' should be extended beyond merely the color of the skin or the country of origin. Reflecting on her own experiences, despite the differences in their physical appearance and culture, Rebecca was able to make friends with many domestic students because of their similar interests and personalities (Interview, 11.20.18).

Beyond becoming more understanding of *regular high* students' tendency to socialize within an enclosed friend circle, Rebecca also changed her perception of many *regular high* students' passiveness in academic settings. Instead of referring to *regular high* Chinese international students' lack of oral participation and office hour visits as 'lazy' and 'childish' as she did early in the semester (Interview, 9.6.18), Rebecca told me that with the passage of time she started to realize that those behaviors may have been influenced by their previous educational experiences in China:

我知道他们并不是不会，而是不想说。。。我觉得这可能是中国教育体系里培养出的习惯，因为我在中国也不说话呀，你想象谁没事在高中的课堂说话？我觉得，他们，他们就是看惯了老师自*high*了。而且也没有*office hour*这种概念。这个其实我很理解的.

I know they ['regular high' students] barely speak up in class, not because they do not understand the content, but rather because they have chosen to stay silent... I feel this is probably a habit cultivated in the Chinese education system, because I myself never spoke up in class back in China. Can you imagine any student speaking up in a [Chinese] high school classroom? I feel, they, they must have been so used to watching their teachers' passionate solos. Also, there is no such thing as 'office hours' in China. I can fully understand this [their lack of oral participation and reluctance of approaching teachers for help]. (Interview, 11.20.18)

Reflecting on her initial experiences trying to simultaneously adapt to an authentic English-speaking environment as well as a new educational system during her three years studying in an American high school, Rebecca claimed that she no longer wanted to blame her *regular high* peers (Interview, 11.20.18). She came to the realization that at the initial stage of non-native English-speaking international students' overseas experiences, such passiveness in oral participation and support seeking that she had observed in her regular high peers was nothing unusual. Although it might be a long process, she hoped that the *regular high* students could eventually understand the expectations of their American professors and function better in academic contexts (Interview, 11.20.18). In a later private *WeChat* text message correspondence at the very end of the semester (see Figure 6.5), Rebecca revealed her empathy toward 'regular high' Chinese international students. She confessed that being an international student in an American university was indeed challenging for everybody, herself included (Personal Communication, 12.10.18). Quoting *Lu Xun*, one of the most famous writers in Chinese history, Rebecca pointed out that it was their different language and educational

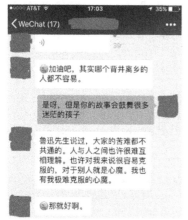

[Translation]
Rebecca: [face-palm emoji] We should fight on. Honestly speaking, it is difficult [to pursue higher education in a different country] for everybody who is so far away from home.
Qianqian: I agree. Your story will inspire many students who are currently confused [about how to take the initiative in support-seeking and make the best use of school resources].
Rebecca: Lu Xun once said: "Because people have different pains, it is very hard to fully understand each other's difficult situations. Something that seems to be easy to handle to me, could be impossible to cope with for others. I, too, have my own trouble that I could hardly concur."
Rebecca: [face-palm emoji] I hope so.

Figure 6.5 Screenshot of private conversation with Rebecca, 12.10.18

experiences in the past that had contributed to her sometimes biased assumptions and failure to fully understand the challenges facing her *regular high* peers (Personal Communication, 12.10.18).

Four-Year *American High* Student Hugo's Languaging Journey

Hugo's story touches on the following topics: (1) his language and education experiences; (2) his English language proficiency; (3) his concerns about losing his heritage language; (4) his preference for socialization; and (5) his bilingual language use in academic and social settings. This story illustrates the journey of a culturally, linguistically and academically acculturated student who started to have concerns about losing his cultural and language roots and therefore preferred to socialize mainly with his Chinese peers.

Hugo was a mathematics major at the School of Arts and Sciences. Wearing thick glasses and interested in solving math problems, Hugo joked that he was a 'typical, nerdy math guy' (Research Memo, 8.27.18). Hugo told me that he came from Zhengzhou, Henan province, in Central China. He spent his elementary to middle school education in his hometown before coming to the United States for his high school education (Interview, 8.27.18). According to Hugo, growing up, he had never had the idea of studying abroad as an international student, nor was he good at English in China. Although he started learning English as early as when he was a first grader, he barely passed any English exams up to graduating from elementary school (Interview, 8.27.18). When he was an eighth grader, Hugo accidentally sat in on a lecture about pursuing high school education in the United States and became interested in overseas studies. With the support of his parents, Hugo went to a Catholic high school in the United States and started his journey as a Chinese international student (Interview, 8.27.18). It is worth noting that Hugo's decision to attend that particular high school in the United States was not made for religious reasons; instead, he applied for a Catholic high school because he found out that many religious high schools did not require the TOEFL for admission (Interview, 8.27.18). Since Hugo was poor at English, applying to a religious high school would increase his chances of admission.

When Hugo first started his journey as an international student four years previously, he faced substantial challenges in functioning linguistically in high school. On arrival in the United States, Hugo had difficulty understanding all his high school lessons, especially the English language arts and theology classes, in which he '完全听不懂' (was not able to understand even a single word) (Interview, 8.27.18). Hugo recognized three major factors contributing to his linguistic challenges. Firstly, he pointed out the gap between EFL education in China and English communication in Anglophone countries. According to Hugo, his elementary and middle school English education had been heavily teacher centered, grammar focused and examination oriented, with oral participation never considered as part of the requirements. Furthermore, growing up, he had never experienced any English classes taught by a native English speaker; all his lessons had been taught by local Chinese teachers who spoke English with heavy accents (Interview, 8.27.18). Altogether, this made it extremely challenging for him to adjust to English-medium instruction on arriving in an American high school. Secondly, because Hugo self-considered as 'a nerdy introvert', he often felt too shy to reach out to teachers and classmates to seek support in facilitating his linguistic transition and adaptation to an English-speaking environment (Interview, 8.27.18). Finally, as his high school was 'white dominant' with very few multilingual international students, Hugo did not receive sufficient instructional support from his teachers (Interview, 8.27.18). He specifically pointed out that his high school English curriculum, especially writing instruction, was designed to meet the needs of domestic students, which was unhelpful to his initial linguistic adaptation:

> 在美高的时候，写作都教的比较马虎，也不知道到底应该怎么写。说到底，那些什么ELA之类的课，都是针对美国人设计的.

> When I was in high school in the US, I did not receive high-quality writing instruction, and was often confused about how to write. Toward the end, those [high school] courses such as the *English Language Arts* were all designed solely for Americans. (Interview, 11.19.18)

It took Hugo around seven months to be able to understand his high school teachers' lectures, and an additional year to finally adapt fully to American high school teaching and learning (Interview, 8.27.18). In order to cope with the challenges posed by his lack of English proficiency on arriving in an American high school, Hugo came up with two strategies. The first was to use Chinese as a bridging tool (Interview, 8.27.18). According to Hugo, he mainly relied on two Chinese resources. To understand the course instruction, he frequently resorted to an English-Chinese dictionary in class. In order to comprehend the readings, he often utilized online search engines to find corresponding Chinese versions of the same reading material to help him get the gist. The second coping strategy that Hugo adopted was to predict his teachers' '套路' (patterns and styles) (Interview, 8.27.18). For instance, Hugo found out that some of his high school teachers had the tendency to draw on certain reference books and websites in preparing their course design, instructions, assignments and quizzes. By identifying and previewing those reference materials prior to class, Hugo gained early access to course contents, activities and even homework, which allowed him extra time to digest the knowledge points and look up any unfamiliar vocabulary in advance (Interview, 8.27.18).

Because of these two coping strategies, Hugo gradually caught up with content learning in high school and also made significant progress in his adaptation to studying and living in an English-speaking environment (Interview, 8.27.18).

Hugo referred to himself as a 'lucky guy' who, although an international student, had never attended any TOEFL preparation course or the actual exam (Interview, 8.27.18). This was because by the time he had applied for Hillside, he had already been studying in the United States for four years, under which circumstances the TOEFL requirement could be waived based on the admissions policy.

At the beginning of his freshman year in college, Hugo self-evaluated his English proficiency as '除了听和读外，问题不小' (having obvious problems in all aspects except listening and reading) (Interview, 8.27.18). Nevertheless, when asked to explain in detail the problems in speaking and writing that he perceived to have experienced, Hugo changed his mind and claimed that he had no real language difficulties, be it functioning in academic or social contexts. He clarified that by saying 'apparent problems in speaking and writing', he had originally meant that he was not able to speak or write as well as his domestic peers (Interview, 8.27.18). Although Hugo was aware that his spoken and written English had some 'accent' compared with native English speakers, he was very confident that his English proficiency was much higher than his *regular high* peers:

> 我的英语其实在社交，在课堂听说读写都能应付。可是我是理科生，众所周知理科生英语都不太好。当然，但是要和普高的人比起来，那我的英语肯定好很多。但是你要和人家美国当地人比，肯定还是有很大差距的，不光说话有*accent,* 写起来也没人家自然.

> In reality, my English is good enough to function with no difficulty in social or academic settings, be it in listening, speaking, reading or writing. However, I am a science major, and as known to all, science majors [from China] are stereotyped to be weak in English. Of course, if you compare me with those *regular high* peers, my English proficiency is surely far better. Yet, if you compare me with those American students, then the gap in our English proficiency remains very large. Not only do I have an accent while speaking, but also I cannot write as well as them. (Interview, 8.30.18)

To get rid of his 'accent in [English] writing', Hugo insisted that since English education in his high school had never catered to multilingual students' needs, he would benefit from systematic instruction designed specifically for non-native English speakers in college: '我觉得自己虽然能完成写作要求，　但是肯定需要一些系统训练才能提高一些细节问题' (I knew that I could fulfill the writing requirements of the courses, but it was certain that I needed some systematic training [specifically for nonnative speakers] to improve some detailed problems in my writing) (Interview, 11.19.18). Hugo decided to take *First Year Writing for Multilingual Writers* to further improve his academic writing. For fear that his high English proficiency would prevent him from being placed on the course, Hugo refused to take the first-year writing placement test and explicitly requested to join one of the multilingual sections: '我直接和英语系说，我不要参加考试，就把我分到班上' (I directly contacted the English Department, and told them there was no need for me to participate in the assessment; please assign me to the multilingual writing section) (Interview, 8.30.18). Owing to his strong agency, Hugo ended up gaining a place in the *First Year Writing for Multilingual Writers.*

Throughout his first semester in college, Hugo reported that he had not encountered any challenge in functioning linguistically in English. Regarding his oral communication, my observation, interviews and informal communication also indicated no sign of language barriers. For instance, during the initial interview, Hugo translanguaged effortlessly between English (approximately 50%) and Chinese (Research Memo, 8.30.18). Even with a slight accent, Hugo's oral English appeared to be clear, fluent and easy to understand (Research Memo, 8.30.18). Echoing my observation, Hugo self-evaluated that he encountered little difficulty functioning linguistically across academic and social settings. At Hillside, Hugo was able to 'understand all the lectures' and 'speak up when necessary', despite his slight Chinese accent in English which prevented him from 'talk[ing] just like an American' (Interview, 8.30.18). In his social life, Hugo not only remained connected with several of his native English-speaking friends from high school, but he also got into the habit of chatting with his American roommate every night (Interview, 8.30.18). For example, as shown in the screenshot of one of Hugo's public *WeChat* posts (see Figure 6.6), Hugo had a great time teaching his American roommate how to sing a famous Chinese song. In the video, Hugo was able to communicate freely with his native-speaking roommate in English and was capable of providing clear instructions and explanations to facilitate his peer's music learning (*WeChat* Observation, 8.27.18).

Similarly, Hugo reported no difficulties in meeting written linguistic demands throughout his first-semester languaging journey. In social settings, his confidence in written communication could be observed in his *WeChat* posts (Research Memo, 12.11.18). For instance, as shown in Figure 6.7, Hugo observed a small detail on Hillside's career service website in which the content of 'STEM' was described as 'Science, Technology, *Environment*, Math' rather than the traditionally recognized composition of STEM as Science, Technology, *Engineering*, Math (*WeChat* Observation, 9.14.18). Hugo highlighted the word 'environment' in pink and commented humorously that Hillside managed to play a language

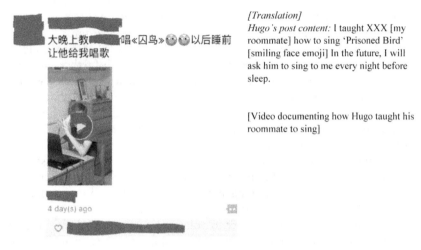

[Translation]
Hugo's post content: I taught XXX [my roommate] how to sing 'Prisoned Bird' [smiling face emoji] In the future, I will ask him to sing to me every night before sleep.

[Video documenting how Hugo taught his roommate to sing]

Figure 6.6 Screenshot of Hugo's public posting: Socializing with roommate, 8.27.18

game in order to hide its weakness of not having a College of Engineering (*WeChat* Observation, 9.14.18).

In academic contexts, as he was a math major, Hugo did not face heavy written linguistic demands during his first semester. Most of the reading assignments came from his philosophy class, which Hugo considered 'a piece of cake', since he had already learned similar content in high school and was familiar with discipline-specific vocabulary (Interview, 8.30.18). Hugo's *WeChat* posts confirmed his reported struggle-free experiences reading in academic settings, in which he demonstrated the ability to comprehend the course readings by both commenting on them

[Translation]
Hugo's post content: Hmmm... *Hillside* did a very good job hiding the fact that it does not have an Engineering School [thinking emoji] [wicked smile emoji]

[screenshot of an email notice about the career fair at Hillside, which says 'Employers want to meet you! The STEM (Science, Technology, Environment, Math) Career & Internship Fair is a customized event featuring organizations with full-time and internship opportunities in diverse STEM...'] Hugo used pink to highlight the word "Environment" in The STEM (Science, Technology, Environment, Math)

Figure 6.7 Screenshot of Hugo's public posting: Reading in social contexts, 9.14.18

[*Translation*]
Hugo's post content: Love is like wind, which will disappear right after it blows [wind-blowing emoji]
The content in Aristotle's book is much too realistic

[Picture of one page from the Philosophy reading] Hugo annotated only the following content: "Young people are amorous too; for the greater part of the friendship of love depends on emotion and pleasure; this is why they fall in love and quickly fall out of love, changing often within a single day. But these people do with to spend their days and lives together; for it is thus that they attain the purpose of friendship."

Figure 6.8 Screenshot of Hugo's public posting: Reading in academic contexts, 9.28.18

and establishing connections between the readings and his own life. For instance, as shown in Figure 6.8, Hugo was able to make an explicit association between his philosophy reading assignment and his recently ended relationship with his girlfriend. In his photo showing a few paragraphs of the course reading, Hugo annotated a quote from Aristotle, suggesting that young people had the tendency of 'fall[ing] in love and quickly fall out of love, changing often within a single day'. In his *WeChat* post (Figure 6.8), Hugo commented that Aristotle's point was 'much too realistic'. Reflecting on his own recent break up, Hugo echoed Aristotle's wisdom by comparing love to a gasp of wind, always coming and leaving swiftly and quietly (*WeChat* Observation, 9.28.18).

Throughout the semester, Hugo reported extremely positive experiences in his academic writing (Interview, 11.19.18). Describing *First Year Writing for Multilingual Writers* as 'the best course' in his freshman year, Hugo told me that through this course, he was able to learn how to effectively structure his writings in response to the genre-specific requirements, something he had never learned in high school. More importantly, on account of this writing course, Hugo was able to identify his 'accent in writing' (which he defined as 'some systematic grammatical mistakes') that he had never noticed in his writings before (Interview, 11.19.18). To take full advantage of this course, Hugo frequently visited his professor's office hours to enhance his ability to structure his writings in response to the genre requirements. Additionally, he also requested his professor to arrange a graduate student from the English department to be his writing tutor, who proofread his articles and provided him with feedback on how to eliminate certain grammatical mistakes (Interview, 11.19.18).

Hugo told me that he found the support from his professors and tutors extremely helpful, enabling him to become more confident in academic writing (Interview, 11.19.18).

Something particularly worth noting toward the end of the semester was that Hugo's high proficiency and confidence in English led to his deep concerns about losing his Chinese (Interview, 11.19.20). In order to maintain his Mandarin, Hugo attempted to maximize his opportunities to use his mother tongue. Based on information from his language logs, Hugo spent a good portion of his day communicating with peers in Chinese, be it a typical weekday or at the weekend. During a typical weekday in the latter half of the semester (see Table 6.3), Hugo reported practicing Chinese listening and speaking almost throughout the day, except for when he was in his dorm chatting with his American roommate. This, according to Hugo, was because he usually went to class, had meals and participated in student organization activities with other Chinese international students (Interview, 11.19.18). Similarly, his description of a typical weekend (Table 6.4) revealed that Hugo spent the majority of his day socializing with Chinese peers using Chinese. Despite his frequent usage of Chinese every day, however, Hugo was still concerned about losing his mother tongue, as it had become increasingly difficult to express himself in Mandarin:

> 感觉自己的中文在不断退步，自己虽然每天都在用中文，不知为什么中文就不断退步。我本来觉得中文说了十几年，怎么也不会退步，但是没想到才来美国四五年，就感觉中文已经说不好了，特别是课堂里面学到的很多新的概念，都是在美国高中和大学学到的，我都没法用中文表达。比如什么*cultural identity*之类的，都不知道该怎么翻译。这些在国内都没听过，我感觉会现在中文表达起来会有很多障碍.

> I feel my Chinese is constantly getting weaker and weaker. Although I use Chinese every day, I don't know why my Chinese keeps on becoming worse. I originally thought that since I have talked in Chinese for over a decade, there would be no way that I lose my Chinese. However, to my great surprise, I have only been in the US for around 4 to 5 years and have already felt difficulty using Chinese. This is particularly true when it comes to explaining in Chinese about the many new concepts that I have learned from my American high school and college. I cannot express those ideas in Chinese. I have no idea how to translate things like 'cultural identity.' These are concepts that I have never heard before back in China, and I feel lots of trouble trying to express them in Chinese (Interview, 11.19.18)

I comforted Hugo, telling him that what he was experiencing was not unusual given the fact that language existed in contexts; some

Table 6.3 Hugo's language log: A typical weekday, Thursday 11/15/2018

Time	Activity	Place	Heritage language speaking/ listening/reading/writing	English speaking/listening/ reading/writing
8–9	Get up and get ready for class	Dorm	n/a	S/L
9–12	Mathematics	HU	S/L	L/R/W
12–12:50	Lunch with friends	HU cafe	S/L	S/L/R only when ordering
1–1:50	*First Year Writing for Multilingual Students*	HU	S/L	S/L/R/W
2–5	Student organization: volunteer middle school math tutor	A local neighborhood	S/L	S/L/R/W
5–7	Go back to school and have dinner	Train/cafe	S/L	S/L/R only when ordering
7–11	Homework	Library	S/L	R/W
11–11:30	Go back to dorm and get ready to sleep	Dorm	n/a	S/L

Table 6.4 Hugo's language log: Example of a typical weekend, Saturday 11/17/2018

Time	Activity	Place	Heritage language speaking/ listening/reading/writing	English speaking/listening/reading/ writing
Last night till 3am	Go drinking with peers	Downtown	S/L	S/L only when ordering
3–10	Sleep	Dorm	n/a	n/a
10–11	Get up, shower and eat breakfast	Dorm	n/a	n/a
11–12	Inquire about insurance at HU health center	HU health center	n/a	S/L/R/W
12–7	Hang out with old friends	Downtown	S/L	S/L/R only when shopping/ordering
7–9:30	Watch a movie with friends	Downtown	S/L	L
9:30–10	Take the train home with friends	Train	S/L	L/R
10–midnight	Chat with roommate till asleep	Dorm	n/a	S/L

context-specific concepts in English, including his example of 'cultural identity', were simply not present in Chinese (Interview, 11.19.18). Furthermore, I shared my own experiences as a then doctoral student, who was about to receive a terminal degree with expertise in bilingualism and teacher education, yet still could not clearly explain what my research focuses were in Chinese to my family and friends in China (Interview, 11.19.18).

Hugo was grateful for my efforts in trying to comfort him. Yet, he went on expressing his concerns about losing his mother tongue. According to Hugo, in comparison with his *regular high* peers, his Chinese was way worse. In support of his self-evaluation, Hugo shared with me an example. When seeing their first snow at Hillside, one of his *regular high* peers was immediately able to improvise a short Chinese poem describing the beautiful snow scene. Nevertheless, despite Hugo's effort, the most he could produce was nothing more than some very basic descriptions such as '今天下雪了, 雪很漂亮' (Today it's snowy, and the snow looks very pretty) (Interview, 11.19.18).

Reflecting on his declining Chinese language proficiency, Hugo commented that sacrificing his roots and mother tongue for education in the United States was too much for him. This made Hugo feel somewhat regretful about studying overseas as early as high school (Interview, 11.19.18). He added that if he had been given a second chance, he would have chosen to complete his high school education in China before coming to the United States for college education, as his *regular high* peers had done (Interview, 11.19.18).

According to Hugo, there were two types of *American high* Chinese international students. The first type represented those who became fully acculturated, had strong preferences to socialize primarily with American peers, self-perceived as 'half an ABC' (half an American-born Chinese) and were likely to look down on newly arrived *regular high* students. In contrast, the second type were those who had lost interest in learning about American culture and making friends with American people, and only wanted to stay with other Chinese international students, especially those who attended high school in China. While acknowledging that the majority of the *American high* students studying at Hillside may belong to the first type, Hugo announced proudly: 'I am a Type II "American high" student!' (Interview, 11.19.18). He described his lack of interest in getting to know American culture and its people in college:

我对美国完全丧失了新鲜感，完全没有了解美国人的欲望。除了我的室友，大学里遇到的其他美国人对我来说都是路人.

I have completely lost interest in the US as well as its people. Except for my roommate, I regard all other Americans that I met in college merely as random passersby in life. (Interview, 11.19.18)

[Translation]
Hugo's post content: Happy Mid-Autumn Festival, my hometown family and friends [moon-face emoji] [cat emoji]

[Video posted: A Chinese music video named 'when love is approaching' by artist Ruoying Liu]
Hugo commented: It's my happiest day in September [laughing emoji]

Figure 6.9 Screenshot of Hugo's public posting: Mid-autumn festival, 9.24.18

More interested in maintaining his language and cultural roots, Hugo's *WeChat* posts revealed his homesickness and deep connection with China (Research Memo, 12.11.18). For instance, during the Mid-Autumn Festival, a traditional Chinese holiday that was not widely known or celebrated in the United States, Hugo extended his best wishes to his family and friends in China through a *WeChat* post; he further described that day as his 'happiest day of the month' (see Figure 6.9). In another example (see Figure 6.10), Hugo explicitly expressed his deep love for China and missing his family and friends. On October 1, the National Day in China, Hugo posted an image symbolizing Beijing, the capital of China, and wrote '无需想起，因为从未忘记' (there is no need to remember [China], because I have never forgotten) (*WeChat* Observation, 10.1.18).

Hugo explained that his strong preference for hanging out with other Chinese international students, especially those *regular high* ones, was because '新鲜感退去，留下的就只剩孤独和 *homesickness*' (when his feeling of curiosity [in Americans and American culture] faded away, what was left was only loneliness and homesickness) (Interview, 11.19.18). According to Hugo, he felt '心里很温暖' (warmth from his heart) when spending time with newly arrived Chinese peers who not only shared the same culture, but also communicated with him in his

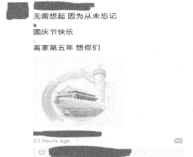

[Translation]
Hugo's post content: There is no need to remember, because I have never forgotten.
Happy National Day.
It's my 5th year away from home, miss you all

[picture posted: image of the signature building in Tian'an Men Square, Beijing, China]

Figure 6.10 Screenshot of Hugo's public posting: National Day in China, 10.1.18

mother tongue (Interview, 11.19.18). Furthermore, Hugo pointed out that the many linguistic challenges his regular *high peers* were going through during their first semester in college reminded him of his own journey adapting to an English-speaking environment four years previously on entering an American high school. This made Hugo feel obliged to connect with his *regular high* peers and support them in any way.

At the very end of the semester, Hugo told me that overall he was happy with his first semester in college, especially because of the friendships he had established with other Chinese international students, the *regular high* ones in particular. Echoing what he had documented in his bilingual language logs (see Tables 6.3 and 6.4), Hugo reported that his close friendships and frequent contact with his *regular high* peers, be it going to classes, having meals, doing homework, discussing math problems via *WeChat* together or participating in the same student organizations, allowed him to immerse himself in a Chinese-speaking environment and enjoy the companionship of his friends. Toward the end of our second interview, Hugo mentioned that his future goal was to pursue graduate education in the United States before returning to China. He told me, 'In this process, however long it is, I hope to continue our friendship [with *regular high* students], and help them with their [language and culture] adjustment, as much as I can... Because they always reminded me of myself in high school...' (Interview, 11.19.18).

Concluding Remarks

Chapter 6 focused on the first-semester languaging journeys of two *American high* students, Rebecca and Hugo. While neither student encountered any difficulties functioning linguistically in college because of their previous high school education in the United States, Rebecca and Hugo experienced their initial college adjustment differently. Rebecca's high English proficiency led to her negative attitudes toward *regular high* students. Although she grew increasingly empathetic toward her *regular high* peers as the semester progressed, Rebecca still preferred to socialize almost exclusively with domestic students. In contrast, Hugo's high English proficiency triggered his concern about losing Chinese. To maintain his language and cultural roots, Hugo decided to socialize primarily with his *regular high* peers. In this process, Hugo felt more connected to his Chinese identity and felt obliged to support his *regular high* peers. In Chapter 7, I synthesize the findings from Chapters 5 and 6 to explore how participants' previous language and education experiences played a role in their first-semester languaging journey in college.

Note

(1) In Chinese public schools, there are six years of elementary school, three years of middle school and three years of high school. Therefore, K-9 education indicates from kindergarten to middle school education.

7 Revisiting Within-Group Variabilities among Chinese International Students

Introduction

To draw attention to the within-group variability among Chinese international students, in Chapters 5 and 6, I introduced the first-semester languaging journeys of five focal students, William, Matthew, Sarah, Rebecca and Hugo, who came from different high school backgrounds. The three *regular high* students graduated from different types of high schools in China, including the so-called traditional *regular high* (William), foreign language *regular high* (Matthew) and international department within a regular high school (Sarah). The two *American high* students, Rebecca and Hugo, spent three and four years, respectively, in American high schools prior to their college studies at Hillside. In this chapter, I synthesize the five focal students' first-semester languaging experiences to discuss how participants' previous language and education backgrounds could play a role in their first-semester languaging journeys in college. This chapter aims to draw readers' attention to the within-group variability among Chinese international students and calls for a developmental perspective to understand their initial college experiences.

Challenging the Homogeneity of Chinese International Students

Chapters 5 and 6 presented a portrait of the very different journeys of five focal students during their first semester in college. William successfully coped with the challenges through his active support-seeking behavior; Matthew gave up completely; and Sarah was trapped in a dilemma. In contrast, the two *American high* students did not report any challenges in meeting the linguistic demands in English across academic and social contexts. Rebecca and Hugo, while not facing challenges posed by the English language, went down completely different paths in their first-semester college experiences, especially in their languaging preferences and attitudes towards their *regular high* peers. The distinct languaging journeys of these five students demonstrated that international students' cultural, linguistic and academic acculturation started long before their college entry, positioning them at different starting points for their overseas studies at Hillside University. This has challenged the homogeneity of Chinese international students, drawing attention to their within-group variability.

At the very beginning of the semester, the three *regular high* students, William, Matthew and Sarah, experienced varying degrees of difficulty with regard to their linguistic functioning in academic and social settings. Faced with the challenges, the three students came up with corresponding coping strategies which led to their distinct outcomes at the end of the semester. Traditional *regular high* graduate William (see Figure 4.1 at the left most end of the continuum) was the least culturally, linguistically and academically acculturated for overseas studies at the beginning of the semester. Having had no experience with English-medium instruction or US high school curricula, William faced the most challenges in his initial languaging journey. On arriving at Hillside, William was unable to meet the oral and written linguistic demands across academic and social contexts. Not only was he unable to follow the lectures, but he was also unable to express himself in oral and written communication in English. To overcome the challenges, William devised a series of coping strategies including relying on Chinese as a bridging tool and seeking support from his *American high* peers. However, as neither strategy remained effective as the semester progressed, William decided to seek support from his professors. Following advice from his professors, William intentionally maximized his opportunity to practice English while minimizing his reliance on Chinese. By the end of the semester, despite his rough start, William had made substantial progress in his ability to function linguistically across contexts.

Compared with William, foreign language *regular high* graduate Matthew (see Figure 4.1 second from the left on the continuum) was in a slightly more advantageous position at the start of the semester. Because of his educational experiences at a foreign language high school in China, Matthew had had native English speakers as his English as a foreign language (EFL) conversation class teachers. Yet, similar to William, Matthew had no exposure to US high school curricula prior to college. On arriving at Hillside, Matthew found that despite his previous experiences communicating with his native-speaking EFL conversation teachers, he encountered substantial challenges in meeting the oral and written linguistic demands across contexts due to perceived cultural incongruences. For instance, although he was able to solve math problems, Matthew could not orally explain his thought processes and engage in math discussions, a practice that was seldom emphasized in Chinese education, but highly valued in Western education. Similarly, while Matthew had had experiences learning philosophy in China, the philosophy he had learned focused on Eastern wisdom, which put him at a severe disadvantage when studying Western-centered philosophy in college. To address these challenges, Matthew devised the coping strategies of drawing on his home language as a scaffold and relying on within-group support systems to seek help from other regular high students. While these strategies worked for a short time, they became less effective with his increasing academic stress as the semester progressed. Reluctant to seek support from his professors, Matthew gave up his initial ambition to excel in his overseas studies and explore American culture, and ended up skipping classes and socializing exclusively with his *regular high* peers.

Sarah received her high school education from an international department within a regular high school in China, through which she had experienced learning US high school curricula and AP courses taught by local Chinese teachers (see Figure 4.1 in the middle of the continuum). This positioned Sarah in a slightly more advantageous position compared with her traditional and foreign language *regular high* peers in preparation for her college studies at Hillside. While Sarah was able to catch up with content-subject learning throughout the semester due to her familiarity with US high school curricula, she faced significant challenges in meeting the linguistic demands of college due to her lack of experience with English-medium instruction and communication with native speakers of English. From the very start of the semester, she had encountered considerable difficulties languaging across academic and social contexts. Not only was Sarah constantly under peer pressure from her *American high* classmates, but she was also unable to engage in meaningful conversations with domestic students. To cope with her challenges in English communication, Sarah made the decision to socialize exclusively with her *regular high* peers and temporarily avoid English usage as much as possible so that she could gradually adapt to an English-speaking environment. This strategy helped reduce Sarah's psychological stress in the short term. With the increasing written linguistic demands across the disciplines as the semester progressed, Sarah faced new challenges in negotiating her multilingual writer identity in academic writing. To address her difficulties in writing, Sarah sought support from her professors and writing tutors, enabling her to eventually meet the written linguistic demands of college. Toward the end of the semester, Sarah became much more linguistically adjusted compared with earlier in the semester and was hoping to socialize with domestic students and learn more about American culture. Nevertheless, due to her earlier decision to avoid contact with her domestic peers, Sarah found herself trapped in her small Chinese social circle unable to make a change.

Contrasting with the three *regular high* students' many difficulties meeting the English demands across academic and social contexts in college, the two American high students Rebecca and Hugo (see Figure 4.1 toward the right end of the continuum) did not report such challenges. Owing to their previous high school experiences in the United States, both students had already undergone their initial linguistic adjustment years previously and were familiar with American high school curricula and English-medium instruction. Despite their high ability to function linguistically in English, however, Rebecca and Hugo had very different languaging journeys during their first semester in college. Using English throughout the day, Rebecca's high English performance led to her decision to socialize almost exclusively with her American peers. She developed negative perceptions of her *regular high* peers because of their heavy reliance on Chinese. On the contrary, Hugo's high proficiencies in English made him concerned about losing his heritage language and culture. Despite his ability to communicate with domestic students, Hugo chose to primarily hang out with his *regular high* peers to preserve his home language and culture.

Looking across the five focal cases, *regular high* students were more likely to experience varying degrees of difficulty meeting the linguistic demands across contexts since the start of their first semester in college. Such challenges, while possible to be tackled with appropriate coping strategies, often remained throughout the rest of the semester. In contrast, American high students were much more linguistically prepared for college studies from the beginning of the semester, and were able to meet the English language demands across academic and social contexts. Yet, beyond the overgeneralized dichotomy between *regular high* and *American high* students, the five distinct languaging journeys above demonstrated that participants' linguistic, cultural and academic acculturation began long before the start of their college studies. Their previous language and educational experiences, specifically their familiarity with US high school curricula and English-medium instruction, played an important role in positioning them at different starting points during their initial undergraduate experiences (see Figure 4.1). This finding draws attention to the within-group variability among Chinese international students and sheds light on future research endeavors to see them as a dynamic group instead of a homogeneous block as implied in many previous studies (e.g. Ma, 2020; Zhang & Goodson, 2011).

It is worth noting, however, that while the five focal students' high school language and educational experiences positioned them at different starting points of their initial college experiences, their familiarity with US high school curricula and English-medium instruction was by no means linearly predicted by their previous language and educational experiences. Individual students' agency and support-seeking activities played an important role in mediating the results of their language proficiency and usage by the end of the semester. For instance, while William started college as the least prepared for US education and language, he made substantial progress and was able to function successfully in both academic and social settings by the end of the semester, owing to his determination to improve his English proficiency through his support-seeking from his professors. In contrast, although Sarah started college in a more advantageous position, her decision to avoid contact with domestic students resulted in her enclaved social experiences. By the same token, despite their similarly high English proficiency and familiarity with US education, Rebecca and Hugo held contrasting perceptions of their *regular high* peers and adopted distinct socialization strategies. The non-linear relationship between the focal participants' initial degree of academic and linguistic acculturation and their end-of-semester outcomes reflected the importance of individuals' agency as a strong force to change their developmental outcomes. This echoes the bidirectional nature of human development, in which students take the role of active change agents who are constantly shaping and are shaped by their layers of developmental environments (Bronfenbrenner & Morris, 2006).

Linguistic (In)Ability or Different Developmental Stages?

One important theme that persisted throughout the semester was the divide between *American high* and *regular high* Chinese international students. Whether it was the participants' linguistic functioning in academic and social settings or the coping strategies they utilized, there were substantial differences between the two groups. The participants were clearly aware of such distinctions, which to some extent influenced their decisions around socialization and support-seeking. Such an obvious divide led to persistent tensions between the two groups. While *regular high* students were often intimidated by their *American high* peers who liked to 'show off' their high English proficiency, some *American high* students compared their *regular high* counterparts to 'sticky rice' who stuck together talking in Chinese (see Rebecca's case) and openly discriminated against them due to their lack of English proficiency (see William's case).

Interestingly, although the participants demonstrated varying degrees of linguistic and academic acculturation prior to college entry (see Table 4.1), the Chinese international students themselves did not seem to notice the existence of such a continuum. Instead, they continued to categorize themselves based on the dichotomy of *American high* and *regular high* students. The constant divide between the two groups of Chinese international students, however, did not infer that the seemingly linguistically struggle-free *American high* students were superior or more intelligent compared with their *regular high* counterparts. Instead, it illustrated the unique stages the participants were at in terms of their linguistic acculturation into higher education in an Anglophone country. In other words, the participants' distinct languaging experiences could be better understood from a developmental perspective.

Compared with their *regular high* peers, *American high* students had been immersed in the American education system for at least three years before the start of their college studies. This placed them at a more advanced stage in their linguistic transition. In other words, rather than being superior or completely problem-free linguistically, *American high* students might be better referred to as 'ex-strugglers' who had already undergone the many challenges and difficulties of linguistic accultura-tion during their high school education in America. Contrasting with *American high* students' advanced stages in their acculturation, *regular high* international freshmen were at the beginning stage of their linguistic transition. Therefore, they were more prone to various linguistic, aca-demic and cultural challenges.

From a developmental perspective, it seems that the tensions between the two groups of students were largely due to their lack of awareness of the different acculturation stages they were in. Instead of interpret-ing *American high* students' frequent English usage and close socializa-tion with American peers as them trying to show off their high English proficiency, it was more likely that such behaviors simply naturally reflected the characteristics of those multilingual international students at advanced stages during their linguistic acculturation. It is possible that when *regular high* students reach similar stages later in their overseas studies, they might also demonstrate such a tendency of preferring Eng-lish and socializing with domestic students. By the same token, *regular high* students were likely to socialize with their own kind and frequently resorted to their heritage language because they were at earlier phases during their linguistic transition. They needed the additional linguistic, emotional and academic support from peers with similar language and education backgrounds to facilitate their transition into the English-speaking academic and social contexts. It is again highly possible that the so-called 'sticky rice' behavior that some *American high* students criticized their *regular high* peers for might have been something they themselves had already gone through years previously in high school.

Understanding their initial college experiences from a developmental perspective could benefit *American high* and *regular high* students alike. To be specific, not only would it reduce their biases and hostility toward each other, but it could also encourage these developing individuals to actively seek support to cope with the challenges from their layers of surrounding external systems. On the one hand, it may be true that *American high* Chinese international students are already at relatively advanced stages of their academic and linguistic acculturation. Yet, by helping and witnessing their *regular high* peers to 'relive' their initial transcultural, translingual and transnational transitions in American high schools years ago, *American high* students are offered the oppor-tunity to reflect on their own experiences and strengthen their cultural roots (see Hugo's case). On the other hand, *regular high* students are still at the early stages in their academic and linguistic acculturation and thus they are often faced with various challenges studying in an unfamiliar cultural, academic and linguistic environment. If they were able to view the two groups' differences in linguistic functioning from a developmental perspective, *regular high* students would be more willing to seek support from their *American high* peers. Given their shared heritage language, cultural background and experiences with Chinese elementary and middle school education, *American high* students are wonderful candidates to function as peer mentors to support *regular high* students. Such peer mentorship could be extremely important when the university support system has failed to provide culturally and linguistically responsive assistance to multilingual international students as needed (e.g. see Matthew's case).

Concluding Remarks

Part 2 of the book drew on five focal students' first-semester languaging journeys to illustrate the within-group variabilities among Chinese international students and the need to adopt a developmental perspective to understand multilingual international students' experiences. As the concluding chapter of Part 2, this chapter synthesized the findings from the five focal cases (see Chapters 5 and 6) in reference to the continuum proposed in Chapter 4 and challenged the commonly held misconception that perceives Chinese international students as a homogeneous block. In Part 3, I shift readers' attention from these five focal cases back to all the participants in the study to explore five languaging myths and realities among Chinese international students studying in American higher education.

Part 3

8 An Overview of Myths and Realities

Anchor Remarks

In Part 2 of the book, I drew attention to the dynamics and within-group variabilities among Chinese international students and proposed a continuum to capture the nuances of their academic and language experiences prior to college. To familiarize readers with each of the categories proposed on the continuum, I presented in-depth case studies of five focal participants' first-semester journeys. Through these cases, readers' attention was drawn to the various needs, challenges and experiences of participants from different language and educational backgrounds, who have been traditionally stereotyped as a homogeneous group – Chinese international students. The findings of the five focal cases allowed readers to challenge commonly held misconceptions about the homogeneity of Chinese international students and understand their experiences from a developmental perspective. Shifting the focus back to all 12 participants in the study, Part 3 provides an overview of the answers to the research questions and reports on the detailed findings of the study in the form of questioning five commonly held myths about Chinese international students.

An Overview of the Answers to the Research Questions

This study was guided by three research questions: (1) How did the 12 Chinese international students function linguistically in academic and social settings at the beginning of their first semester in college? (2) How did they meet the oral and written linguistic demands in academic and social settings throughout the semester? (3) What changed regarding their linguistic functioning over the course of one semester? In this section, I provide an overview of the participants' first-semester languaging experiences following three time points, namely the beginning of the semester (Weeks 0–4), around midterm (Weeks 5–9) and toward the end of the semester (Weeks 10–15).

Languaging experience at the beginning of the semester

At the beginning of the semester (Weeks 0–4), *American high* students reported no difficulty in their linguistic functioning in college. In addition to being able to function linguistically in classroom settings, they also demonstrated frequent contact with native speakers of English in beyond-classroom contexts. To be specific, the three *American high* participants were able to initiate office hour consultations with their professors and establish friendships with their domestic peers. Additionally, none of the *American high* students used Chinese to facilitate their linguistic functioning in academic and social settings at the initial stage of their overseas studies in college; however, they all reported relying on Chinese as a bridging tool when they first started high school in the US, a coping strategy that they later abandoned due to its ineffectiveness.

In contrast, the nine *regular high* students reported varying degrees of difficulty in linguistic functioning in academic and social contexts at the beginning of the semester. Four patterns could be observed based on their experiences. Firstly, due to the mismatch between their successful test of English as a foreign language (TOEFL) performance and various linguistic barriers on college entry, the *regular high* students reported having some shocking experiences at the initial stage of their overseas studies. Secondly, compared with their *American high* peers, the *regular high* students had significantly less contact with native English speakers. On the one hand, they rarely took advantage of office hour consultations. On the other hand, the *regular high* students' contact with American peers was very context based, and hardly extended beyond the classroom setting (i.e. required in-class discussions). Their friend circle was rather limited, as *regular high* students almost exclusively socialized with and sought support from their Chinese peers during this period. Thirdly, cultural and linguistic congruences were found to be related to Chinese international students' academic experiences. When courses were found to be culturally and linguistically congruent (e.g. *First Year Writing for Multilingual Writers, Asian History*), they were likely to have positive academic experiences. On the contrary, when the courses were perceived as lacking in cultural and linguistic congruences (e.g. philosophy, mathematics, music), the students were more prone to negative academic experiences. Last but not least, all *regular high* participants showed favorable attitudes toward the coping strategy of using Chinese as a bridging tool to facilitate their linguistic functioning in academic and social contexts, and reported frequently relying on Chinese at the initial stage of their overseas studies.

The 12 participants generally perceived the support they received from their professors and Chinese peers as effective and exerted positive influences on their initial linguistic functioning and college adjustment.

However, multiple participants showed dissatisfaction toward the support from the Office of International Students and Scholars (OISS), especially regarding international student orientation and the international assistants (IAs) assigned. They described the support as non-tangible and argued that the services provided by the OISS were 'nothing but a format' (Interviews, 8.30.18, 9.4.18, 9.6.18). Lily was the only student who thought highly of the support from the OISS. Yet, she was also the only participant with a Chinese IA from the same major.

Languaging experience around the middle of the semester (Weeks 5–9)

As the semester progressed, the gap between the *regular high* and *American high* students' ability to function linguistically in academic and social contexts continued. The *American high* participants continued to demonstrate significantly higher abilities in their linguistic functioning across contexts. Not only were they able to meet the linguistic demands in classroom settings, but they also initiated frequent contact with native English speakers in social contexts. With regard to the *regular high* students' language and academic experiences, many aspects remained unchanged compared with the beginning of the semester. The *regular high* participants continued to encounter varying degrees of linguistic challenges across academic and social contexts. Socializing exclusively with and seeking support from their close circle, cultural and linguistic congruences remained and were reported to be an important factor affecting their course experiences.

However, some progress could be identified regarding their linguistic functioning and college adjustment. Firstly, more and more *regular high* students started to seek support from their professors and tutors. In fact, by the end of Week 9, all but one student reported having initiated meetings with their instructors during their office hours. Secondly, while the majority of the *regular high* students primarily socialized with other Chinese international students, their overall contact with native English-speaking peers increased. Half of them expressed interest in communicating with their American peers, and three took concrete action to approach domestic students. In the most extreme case, Eva decided to socialize almost exclusively with American students of color. Lastly, the popularity of relying on Chinese as a bridging tool slightly decreased, with some participants becoming critical and more selective about adopting this method.

During this time frame, three themes emerged. Firstly, compared with the earlier time point, higher linguistic demands on academic English writing could be observed across disciplines. Based on a text analysis informed by genre-based pedagogy (Brisk, 2015), the participants showed a general tendency to struggle in areas where severe cultural and linguistic incongruences were identified. To be specific, the two most challenging aspects were found to be thesis statement in argument writing and verb tense consistency; both areas featured considerably different expectations across Chinese and American cultures. Secondly, while the tensions between the *regular high* and *American high* students continued, it seemed that the conflicts between the two groups were less intense compared to the earlier time point. Several *regular high* students started reaching out to their *American high* peers for occasional academic support. Thirdly, while participants held similar negative attitudes toward support received from the OISS and equally positive attitudes toward help from their Chinese peers, they revealed mixed feelings toward their professors. This was because while some of the instructors provided concrete support that was beneficial to their language and academic well-being, others merely demonstrated sympathy without further action, and this help was considered 'superficial' and 'ineffective'.

Languaging experiences toward the end of the semester (Weeks 10–15)

As the semester approached its end, the *American high* participants continued to be able to function linguistically across contexts, and the *regular high* participants grew more accustomed to American higher education and were faced with relatively fewer linguistic barriers compared with earlier in the semester. Not only were all *regular high* students, except Matthew, comfortable with seeking support from their professors, but they also reported increasing contact with domestic students. Owing to their increased linguistic acculturation, the *regular high* participants were aware of the shortcomings of relying too heavily on Chinese as a bridging tool; this coping strategy gradually lost its popularity toward the end of the semester. While cultural and linguistic congruences continued to affect the participants' academic experiences, the tensions between the two groups of students were somewhat alleviated, as more *regular high* students reported seeking help from their *American high* peers.

Compared with earlier in the semester, the participants' perceptions of the effectiveness of the support from various sources remained unchanged. While they continued to appreciate support from their teaching assistants (TAs), tutors and Chinese peers, most of the Chinese international students held negative attitudes toward the support from the OISS. Professors continued to be perceived as a controversial source of support, toward whom the participants held mixed feelings.

Changes observed during participants' first-semester languaging journeys

In general, the *American high* students' language and academic experiences remained similar throughout the semester, which was likely due to their already high ability to function linguistically and their familiarity with US high school curricula and English-medium instruction. The only major change occurred in the case of Hugo, whose high English proficiency gradually led to his concerns about losing his heritage language and culture. To address his concerns, Hugo adjusted his socialization and languaging preferences to maintain his cultural and linguistic roots.

On the contrary, *regular high* students' journeys went through multiple important changes, especially in the following three areas: linguistic functioning in academic and social settings, coping strategies initiated and the perceived effectiveness of support received from others. In terms of *regular high* students' changes in linguistic functioning across contexts, a general pattern was that despite their substantial linguistic challenges at the beginning of the semester, with the passage of time the degree of their reported language struggles gradually declined. Throughout the semester, the *regular high* participants demonstrated increased frequencies in their communication with native speakers of English, and their major sources of contact also expanded from only professors and American peers to include tutors and TAs. Regarding changes in the participants' coping strategies throughout the semester, although the *regular high* participants frequently used their heritage language, Mandarin Chinese, at the very beginning of the semester as a popular bridging tool to facilitate their linguistic functioning in English in academic and social settings, the frequency of their Chinese usage gradually decreased over time. Toward the end of the semester, Chinese was no longer favored or popular as a bridging tool among all the participants. Moreover, while *regular high* students had almost exclusively relied on their Chinese peers at the beginning of the semester, the frequency of their support-seeking from professors, tutors and TAs increased substantially over time. Finally, regarding changes in participants' perceived effectiveness of the support they received, different from their overwhelmingly positive attitudes toward support from their professors at the beginning of their college life, more and more participants demonstrated mixed feelings toward their professors' help as the semester progressed. Toward the end of the semester, the participants concluded that the effectiveness of the support from their instructors should be considered on a case-by-case basis.

Myths and Realities about Chinese International Students

So far, I have provided a brief overview of the answers to the research questions. The findings of the study will be presented in detail in Chapters 9–13. Instead of reporting the findings in chronological order, I have intentionally chosen to engage readers by organizing key results into close examinations of five commonly held myths regarding Chinese international students' overseas experiences, including:

- **Myth 1**: TOEFL results accurately predict international students' abilities to function linguistically on college entry
- **Myth 2**: An English-only policy is necessary in college classrooms to help international students improve their linguistic functioning in English
- **Myth 3**: *First Year Writing* guarantees international students' successful writing performances in content-area courses
- **Myth 4**: English is responsible for all the challenges facing Chinese international students
- **Myth 5**: Chinese international students are well supported in American higher education, both linguistically and academically

The five myths were identified based on my participants' experiences throughout the aforementioned three stages during their first semester in college. The first stage ranged from orientation week (Week 0) to the end of the first month and marked the start of the participants' languaging journeys in college. During this stage, the participants experienced their initial challenges (see **Myth 4** on challenges) in social and academic linguistic functioning at the college level and devised their coping strategies to leverage their home language resources (see **Myth 2** on Chinese usage vs English-only). For those *regular high* students in particular, this phase also featured their realization of a gap between their high TOEFL achievements and the reality (see **Myth 1** on TOEFL). At the second stage (Weeks 5–9), ranging from slightly before to immediately after the midterm examinations, most participants started to experience increased academic stress, especially due to the higher written linguistic demands across the disciplines (see **Myth 3** on *First Year Writing for Multilingual Writers*). In response to the challenges, they started to adjust their initial coping strategies and sought support from the university support system accordingly (see **Myth 5** on support system). At the last stage, from the latter half till the end of the semester (Weeks 10–15), the Chinese international students gradually became more familiar with their overseas studies in an American higher educational institution, as they continued making adjustments to facilitate their linguistic functioning across academic and social settings.

To discuss the five myths, I drew on data collected from various sources, including semi-structured interviews, students' writing samples, talks-around-texts interviews, bilingual language logs, informal communication, *WeChat* observations and ongoing research memos (see Chapter 3). As summarized in Table 8.1, in tackling each myth, I may not have utilized data from all seven sources. Yet, by triangulating the data collected from various sources using multilingual and multimodal means, I strived to capture the myths and realities regarding the 12 Chinese international students' first-semester languaging journeys in an American higher education institution.

Table 8.1   Overview of data sources in each myth chapter

Data sources	Myth 1	Myth 2	Myth 3	Myth 4	Myth 5
Semi-structured interviews	X	X	X	X	X
Students' writing samples		X	X		
Talks-around-texts interviews			X		
Bilingual language logs				X	X
Informal communication	X				X
WeChat observations	X	X	X	X	X
Ongoing research memos		X	X		X

Following the five myths, in Chapter 14, I reflect on the research findings to draw pedagogical implications on (1) how the university support system could better help newly arrived Chinese international students during their initial transnational, transcultural and translingual experiences; and (2) how these students could better strategize to take advantage of the support system to facilitate their initial overseas studies experiences. Finally, I wrap up the book with a discussion of research methodology innovation integrating WeChat observations informed by digital ethnography (Pink et al., 2016) as a non-intrusive data collection approach and point to future research directions.

Concluding Remarks

By bringing the readers' attention on five focal cases back to the 12 participants, Part 3 presents a series of discussions, reflections and re-examinations of commonly held myths and misconceptions regarding Chinese international students' initial college journeys. While fully aware that the findings in Part 3 are based on a rather contextualized in-depth qualitative study with a small sample size, my intention to dive deeper into the first-semester journeys of the 12 participants has never been to (over)generalize. Instead, drawing on the findings, I hope to push the readers to re-examine and think beyond the commonly held stereotypes about Chinese international students in order to make sense of the contextualized research findings in their own educational settings.

9 Myth 1: TOEFL Results Accurately Predict International Students' Ability to Function Linguistically on College Entry

Introduction

The test of English as a foreign language (TOEFL) is a standardized assessment of non-native speakers' English proficiency. Administered by the Educational Testing Service (ETS) since the 1970s, TOEFL has been used as a high-stakes gatekeeping tool by many English-medium educational institutions around the world. Currently, as one of the most widely adopted English-language proficiency test in the world, the TOEFL is acknowledged and accepted in over 10,000 higher education institutes in more than 150 countries (ETS, 2020a). In the United States, where this standardized assessment originated from, almost all tertiary education institutions require non-native-speaking international students to pass certain threshold scores on TOEFL before granting admission.

Yet, the popularity of the TOEFL extends far beyond the college admissions process. In the past several decades, significant numbers of research studies have relied on TOEFL scores as a key indicator for their participants' English proficiency levels (Hill *et al.*, 1999; Huong, 2001; Johnson, 1988; Kerstijens & Nery, 2000; Krausz *et al.*, 2005; Light *et al.*, 1987, 1991; Martirosyan *et al.*, 2015; Woodrow, 2006). Given the influences of the TOEFL on higher education administration and research, a commonly held assumption is that multilingual international students' performances on this standardized assessment is an accurate predictor of their ability to function linguistically in college. However, is this really the case?

The purpose of this chapter is to challenge the commonly held myth equating TOEFL results to an accurate indicator of multilingual international students' ability to function linguistically on arriving in college in an Anglophone country. After reviewing the nature and design of the TOEFL as well as its corresponding preparation practices in China, I draw on empirical data to demonstrate the mismatches between my participants' TOEFL results and their actual ability to function linguistically in college on arrival. Drawing on data collected from semi-structured interviews, *WeChat* observations and ongoing informal communications, the findings of my study indicate that Chinese international students' victory on the TOEFL did not necessarily translate into their successful linguistic functioning during their initial overseas college experiences. This chapter ends with a brief discussion about some implications regarding educational research and college admission.

The Nature of the TOEFL

The TOEFL is an internationally recognized, standardized language proficiency assessment with high validity and reliability (Liu *et al.*, 2009). Integrating the four language skills including reading, writing, listening and speaking, the TOEFL is designed to reflect the authentic linguistic demands of college-level academic settings (ETS, 2020b). As the ETS (2019b) official website declares, '[t]he language used in the TOEFL iBT test [internet-based test] closely reflects what is used in everyday academic settings.... Students who score well on the TOEFL iBT test are prepared for success' in academic and professional settings.

Yet, regardless of the proud announcement on the ETS official website claiming that '[o]nly the TOEFL test prepares you for the academic English requirements of a university' (ETS, 2020b), the TOEFL is a decontextualized proficiency test focusing on discrete features of the English language. While the four skills of speaking, reading, listening and writing as assessed in the TOEFL are indeed important components in all English-speaking educational settings, a mastery of these skills alone may not guarantee that non-native English-speaking students function linguistically, or successfully meet 'the academic English requirements of a university' as its website claims (ETS, 2020b).

To fully function linguistically in tertiary educational contexts, students are expected to not only demonstrate their abilities in the four skills of English, but also actively adapt those skills to meet the linguistic demands in disciplinary areas, to follow course requirements and to meet the specific expectations of their professors. From this viewpoint, despite its many strengths, the TOEFL is likely to fall short in measuring all the linguistic needs for academic success. Similarly, from a functional linguistics perspective (Eggins, 2004; Halliday, 1984, 1985, 1994), in order to achieve overall academic success, college students need to be equipped with not only those decontextualized language skills (as assessed in the TOEFL), but also the ability to apply language resources in situational contexts as well as to adapt to the instructional and learning styles within specific disciplinary areas. Since the TOEFL only taps into one of the many dimensions of successful linguistic functioning in college, even if multilingual international students have achieved successful TOEFL scores, they may not be sufficient to predict their overall ability to meet the linguistic demands for college success, a strength claimed by the ETS.

TOEFL Preparation in China

In addition to the nature of the TOEFL as a rather decontextualized language proficiency assessment, the test preparation culture in China, which is mainly 'built upon recitation and regurgitation of the correct knowledge—from the text or the teacher—at the expense of problem solving, abstract thought and creativity' (Neuby, 2012: 684), has added another layer to the challenges that many Chinese international students may encounter during their linguistic functioning in American higher education.

With the growing popularity of pursuing tertiary education overseas, China's private English standardized test preparation companies have flourished over the past three decades. Among them, the New Oriental Education & Technology Group Inc., founded in 1993, is considered the 'most prestigious overseas English exam training school' in China (Zi, 2004). As the most dominant English language proficiency test preparation institution in China, New Oriental has been listed on the New York Stock Exchange with a total stock market capitalization of over $6.6 billion (Stecklow & Harney, 2016).

New Oriental has established an international reputation for its test preparation programs, TOEFL training in particular. Acknowledged by the ETS (2012) as 'the largest provider of private educational services in China', it is recognized as the only official provider of TOEFL online practice tests in China (Stecklow & Harney, 2016). Despite its popularity and success, however, the test preparation courses provided by New Oriental echo the heavily result-focused test preparation culture in China. In other words, New Oriental has the tendency to prioritize the improvement of students' test scores over the enhancement of their actual ability to function linguistically in English.

On its official website, New Oriental proudly announces teaching 'test-taking techniques designed to help students achieve high scores' as a key instructional focus of their test preparation courses (New Oriental Education & Technology Group, 2020). Echoing the aforementioned philosophy of education highlighted on its official website, the TOEFL preparation courses provided by New Oriental are widely known for their substantial emphasis on training students to memorize numerous templates for answers and to depend on test-wiseness or tricks to pick the correct answers in multiple-choice questions. Such strong examination-oriented instructional practices have led to some legal consequences. In fact, since the early 2000s, New Oriental has been involved in multiple lawsuits and scandals with the ETS due to copyright infringement and mishandling of test information (Stecklow & Harney, 2016). In particular, since the TOEFL in other countries sometimes precedes those administered in China, New Oriental has been accused of gathering test information from abroad and leaking keys to students before they attend TOEFL exams in China (Stecklow & Harney, 2016).

Considering the heavily examination-oriented TOEFL preparation training provided by agencies such as New Oriental as well as the popularity of such courses throughout China, it is reasonable to assume that a significant number of Chinese international students' TOEFL results may be somewhat inflated. Consequently, those students who are good at memorizing templates and have mastered the guessing tricks may achieve high scores in the TOEFL exams, putting them at an advantage in the college admissions process. Nevertheless, not equipped with proper linguistic abilities to function in authentic English-speaking higher education settings, these students are likely to encounter substantial challenges once immersed in Anglophone academic contexts.

An Empirical Investigation: Problematizing Unproblematic TOEFL Results

While the TOEFL is used as a high-stakes gatekeeping English language proficiency assessment by almost all US higher education institutions, it is up to individual universities to determine the specific threshold scores for their own admission. At Hillside University where my research project took place, the bottom-line requirement for the TOEFL was a score of 100 out of 120, which indicates high English proficiency based on the descriptors in the ETS official website. To be specific, in order to achieve 100 or above on the TOEFL, students need to have at least an average of 25 out of 30 in each of the four discrete areas of examination including listening, speaking, reading and writing. Based on the score interpretation guidelines provided on the ETS official website, scoring 22 or above in reading and speaking, 24 or above in writing and 26 or above in listening (totaling 94) is considered achieving 'high performance levels' in English proficiency (ETS, 2019b). Students at this level are expected to be able to demonstrate 'excellent' and 'solid' skills in listening and reading (ETS, 2019a), and should be able to conduct conversations on academic and social topics and write effectively not only in response to reading and listening, but also based on knowledge and experiences (ETS, 2019b).

Except for Hugo, who was exempt from the TOEFL requirement based on Hillside's admissions policy due to his four years of studies in an American high school, all the remaining participants had taken the

Table 9.1   Language and education backgrounds of participants

Pseudonym	Major	TOEFL experiences	Types of high school attended
Pat	Psychology	• Highest score: 110 (S 24, L 29, R 29, W 28) • Times tried: 3 • Score range: 94–110	• Traditional *regular high school*
Larry	Psychology and chemistry	• Highest score: 107 (S 20, L 30, R 30, W 27) • Times tried: 4 • Score range: 90–107	• Traditional *regular high school*
Bill	Psychology	• Highest score: 103 (S 20, L 26, R 30, W 27) • Times tried: 2 • Score range: 96–103	• International department within traditional *regular high school*
Hugo	Mathematics	• N/A (no TOEFL experiences; for details see Chapter 4)	• 4 years of *American high school*
Shawn	Computer science	• Highest score: 107 (S 22, L 30, R 28, W 27) • Times tried: 2 • Score range: 74–107	• 1 year of regular high; 3 years of *American high school*
William	Marketing	• Highest score: 108 (S 26, L 29, R 30, W 23) • Times tried: 5 • Score range: 56–108	• Traditional *regular high school*
Matthew	Economics	• Highest score: 103 (S 25, L 27, R 28, W 23) • Times tried: 3 • Score range: 99–103	• Foreign language *regular high school*
Sarah	Psychology	• Highest score: 107 (S 26, L 23, R 30, W 28) • Times tried: 5 • Score range: 90–107	• International department within traditional *regular high school*
Rebecca	Chemistry and biology	• Highest score: 117 (S 27, L 30, R 30, W 30) • Times tried: 4 • Score range: 60–117	• 1 year of *regular high*; 3 years of *American high school*
Kristin	Economics	• Highest score: 110 (S 23, L 29, R 29, W 29) • Times tried: 4 • Score range: 90–110	• International department within traditional *regular high school*
Lily	Psychology	• Highest score: 106 (S 22, L 26, R 24, W 24) • Times tried: 3 • Score range: 86–106	• International department within traditional *regular high school*
Eva	English	• Highest score: 115 (S 27, L 30, R 30, W 28) • Times tried: 2 • Score range: 99–115	• Traditional *regular high school*

TOEFL prior to college entry. Their scores ranged from 103 to 117, with an average total of just under 109 out of 120 and a subtest average above 27 out of 30 (Table 9.1). Based on descriptions on the ETS official website, my participants' overall successful TOEFL results served as a strong indicator of their high ability to function linguistically in overseas studies. It was noteworthy, however, that despite the 11 Chinese international students' overall high TOEFL performance, they all reported having had between two and five trials before yielding successful results in the standardized assessment (see Table 9.1). Additionally, all these Chinese international students reported that they had taken at least one semester of intensive TOEFL preparation courses offered by private, for-profit educational organizations or companies, especially the New Oriental School. These preparation courses were said to place heavy emphasis on the rote memorization of language patterns and answers to previous exam questions, as well as tricks to score the correct answer (Interview, 8.30.18).

With the assistance of the test preparation courses and repeated trials of the standardized assessment, my participants witnessed significant improvement in their TOEFL scores, increasing from an initial average score of slightly under 85 to their final average total of over 108. In one extreme case (William), the participant's score almost doubled from 56 to 108 after five repeated trials within a short period of time. An achiever of 108 in the TOEFL, William concluded that the whole meaning for the existence of the TOEFL was 'nothing but to 教会我们如何应试' (nothing but to teach us how to do well in standardized assessment) (Interview, 8.30.18). Considering that language acquisition and improvement is usually a prolonged process, the true indication of English language proficiency behind such sharp score increases as measured by the TOEFL remains under question. Therefore, it may not be too surprising that despite their similarly satisfactory TOEFL results for college entry, Chinese international students tend to demonstrate varying degrees of English proficiency levels on arrival in American higher education institutions.

An Empirical Investigation: TOEFL Results vs Ability in Linguistic Functioning

The participants in my study reported that they had originally expected the TOEFL to be an accurate indication of their linguistic functioning in college. To put it another way, receiving successful scores on the TOEFL made them feel positive about their upcoming international studying experience in an English-speaking environment. However, on starting their overseas journeys, these Chinese international students were shocked to realize that despite their successful TOEFL performance and high hopes for a smooth linguistic start on entering the US higher education system, many of them found their initial linguistic functioning at college 'struggling' and 'unsuccessful' (Interviews, 8.30.18.9.4.18, 9.6.18).

Echoing the many challenges described in the individual portraits of William, Matthew and Sarah (see Chapter 5), all *regular high* students in my study voiced their concerns regarding their initial abilities to function linguistically in college despite their successful TOEFL performances. This led to their academic stress and frustration at the beginning of their overseas college experiences, referring to the standardized assessment as '不靠谱' (unreliable), '没用' (unhelpful), '假' (inauthentic) and 'misleading' (Informal Communication, 8.29.18; Interviews, 8.30.18, 9.4.18, 9.6.18). Having yielded a very competitive TOEFL score of 107, Sarah sighed, '连我这种托福高分的人都这么吃力，很难想象那些划着100线过来的人怎么才能熬过。。。' (Even people like me who yielded a high score in the TOEFL were so struggling, it was really hard to imagine how those people right at the admission threshold of 100 could survive...) (Interview, 9.6.18). Blaming the TOEFL for the many language difficulties they encountered in their linguistic functioning on arriving at Hillside University, the Chinese international students raised concerns about TOEFL's strong tendency to misrepresent and underestimate authentic linguistic demands, especially in the domains of English reading and speaking.

TOEFL reading subtest vs college linguistic demands in reading

The participants described the TOEFL reading subtest as the least authentic assessment due to its failure to represent three key aspects of actual college-level linguistic demands in reading. The Chinese international students cast doubt on the authenticity of this standardized language proficiency test by pointing out their concerns regarding its length, format and content.

Firstly, the length of the articles in the TOEFL reading subtest is far shorter than most college-level reading assignments. While each article in the TOEFL reading subtest usually consists of just a few short paragraphs, college-level content-subject courses such as philosophy and history often require students to tackle more than 50 pages of reading every week. Describing philosophy as 'an art of dying', Matthew's struggles with the heavy reading load he encountered in his philosophy class vividly reflected the substantial challenges international students faced in academic English reading, and how their overseas academic experiences could be negatively influenced when the TOEFL reading subtest failed to tap into this aspect.

Secondly, the skills assessed in the TOEFL reading subtest fall short in reflecting the actual linguistic demands in reading that students experience in college-level courses due to its format and the medium of this standardized assessment. To successfully meet the reading linguistic demands of college, students are expected to draw on holistic reading skills in properly conducting annotation, comprehension and critical thinking in order to be prepared for class discussions and written reflections. In contrast, given the computer-based nature of the TOEFL, students were not given the opportunity to annotate while reading. Moreover, due to the short length of the readings in the exam, annotation was not an essential element to yield the correct answer. Nevertheless, the lack of exposure and practice in reading annotation put international students at a disadvantage at the beginning their overseas college studies. For instance, Bill, who achieved a perfect score in the TOEFL reading subtest prior to college admission, found it extremely difficult to comprehend course readings and meet course requirements without proper annotation skills:

> 我除了划线之外都不知道怎么做笔记。这些文章很多都特别长，而且一篇文章说了很多人的观点，每个人观点还不同，读的时候我勉强知道谁大概在说什么，可是到后面*discussion*的时候就完全搞不清楚谁提了什么观点。但是老师，特别是我们哲学老师，偏偏喜欢在课上让我们用一个词还概括某个人的观点。。。真是很难。

> Other than underlining, I have no idea about how to annotate. The course readings are usually a lot and the articles are also super long. To make things worse, each reading contains the opinions of many people. Since everybody holds a different opinion, initially I was only able to vaguely understand the gist of each individual's ideas. However, as I approached the discussion section of the paper, I usually had no idea about who raised what opinion. Unfortunately, my professors, especially the *Philosophy* professor, very often asked us to use one word to summarize one particular person's opinion mentioned in the readings... This is very hard for me. (Informal Communication, 9.11.18)

Additionally, in the TOEFL, multilingual students' reading proficiency is assessed exclusively by their performance on a set of multiple-choice questions at the end of each passage, which makes it possible for test takers to draw on their test-wiseness to solve the problems without thoroughly comprehending the text. For example, the first question in the reading section of the official TOEFL practice test available on the ETS website is 'According to paragraph 1, why do researchers doubt that agriculture developed independently in Africa?' (ETS, 2019c). Test takers are requested to answer this multiple-choice question by selecting one of four choices provided. Nevertheless, even without fully reading or understanding the designated paragraph, students are very likely to be able to eliminate Option A by following their common sense, which says 'African lakes and rivers already provided enough food for people to survive without agriculture' (ETS, 2019c). Although tactics like test-wiseness could be useful in increasing the likelihood of students achieving high scores on this standardized assessment which ultimately helps them gain admission to better colleges, it is extremely rare for them to rely on such strategies to function linguistically on arriving into an authentic English-speaking academic environment. Therefore, the TOEFL reading subtest again falls short as a truthful reflection of the linguistic demands required to be successful in real-world college-level reading where students are asked not only to conduct critical reflections based on the course readings, but also to communicate their thoughts in oral or written form. Neither of these expectations could be met without students' ability to comprehend the main ideas of the readings, which may not always be a prerequisite for their successful TOEFL performances.

Last but not least, passages in the TOEFL reading subtest are often likely to entail relatively fewer technical terms and comparatively less complex sentence structures as they tend to be general academic readings that target prospective international students from various disciplinary areas across all age groups. On the contrary, in many cases, actual college readings contain denser vocabulary and more complicated sentence structures. For instance, in her *WeChat* post, Eva complained that a philosophy reading assignment was 'dEEp' (see Figure 9.1, *WeChat* Observation, 10.1.18). She intentionally spelled 'deep' as 'dEEp' to show her desperation and frustration (Informal Communication, 10.2.18). The following is one of the sentences that Eva marked:

> The difference between the sage and the ordinary person is that the former can feel unconditional love for those who suffer and do everything in his power to attenuate their pain without allowing his lucid vision of existence to be shaken. (*WeChat* Observation, 10.1.18)

This sentence was indeed very dense and difficult to digest, especially for those newly arrived Chinese international students. The first challenge was its length. Consisting of 41 words, this sentence appeared visually intimidating to most readers. Additionally, it was easy to identify that in this paragraph-long sentence, the only punctuation mark was the period used at the end of the sentence, making it challenging for readers to digest the meaning in chunks. Thirdly, the usage of the passive voice (e.g. to be shaken) added an additional layer to the comprehension of the sentence. Additionally, the vocabulary in the sentence was found to be very dense, featuring nominalization of verbs (e.g. existence), words with multiple meanings (e.g. sage, vision) and formal, academic expressions (e.g. attenuate, lucid). Lastly, this sentence was made up of multiple layers of modifiers and subordinate clauses. For instance, in 'the former can feel unconditional love for those who suffer and do everything in his power', a small chunk extracted from this long sentence, the word 'love' was modified by the premodifier 'unconditional' and followed by the postmodifier 'for those who suffer and do everything in his power'. Within the aforementioned postmodifier was a subordinate clause 'who suffer and do everything in his power'

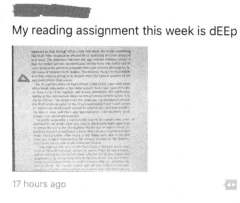

Figure 9.1   An example of difficult language in philosophy readings, 10/1/18

functioning as a sub-postmodifier to modify 'those'. Such a complex sentence structure posed challenges for international students' comprehension; without the ability to distinguish the layers of modifiers from the stem of the sentence, it seemed almost impossible to grasp the main idea of the reading.

TOEFL speaking subtest vs college linguistic demands in speaking

Similar to the reading part, the TOEFL speaking subtest was also criticized by the Chinese international students for its lack of authenticity. The test requires students to express their opinions on a given topic. In the process, test takers are expected to talk to computers in a monologue style, with their oral production automatically recorded and strictly timed (usually with a 45 or 60 second limit). In contrast, to fulfill the oral linguistic demands of college, not only are there no strict time restraints on one's oral production, but also very often the emphasis is placed on students' ability to contribute to dialogues rather than their fluency, pronunciation and intonation during their production of scripted monologues in English. In authentic college settings, students are often required to have engaging interactions with their interlocutors through questioning, responding, explaining and clarifying, during which proper turn-taking skills are also necessary. As these important aspects are not fully assessed in the TOEFL speaking subtest, the results of this standardized assessment may fall short in accurately predicting multilingual international students' ability to meet the oral linguistic demands on college entry.

For instance, William and Sarah both received a score of 26 on their TOEFL speaking subtest, which according to the ETS official website indicated their high oral English proficiency and strong likelihood to have a smooth adjustment in their oral communication upon college entry. However, as detailed in their first-semester journeys (see Chapter 5), both students were shocked to experience significant struggles with their English speaking in various academic and social settings especially at the beginning of their overseas studies at Hillside University. Based on their experiences, it turned out that the lack of turn-taking between interlocutors due to the talking-to-the-computer-style TOEFL speaking subtest failed to prepare them for the highly interactive nature of oral communication in authentic English-speaking environments. Moreover, despite their high test performances, since the TOEFL speaking subtest did not require any personal contact with native speakers of English, both students were anxious during their initial conversations with their native-English-speaking professors and peers, and because of this negative emotion, their actual ability in oral linguistic functioning was further compromised.

Concluding Remarks

Through a brief overview of TOEFL's popularity, nature and test preparation practices and a discussion of my research findings, this chapter attempted to challenge the commonly held myth that multilingual international students' TOEFL results accurately reflect their actual ability to function linguistically in college. Despite its international popularity in college admissions, the TOEFL is a somewhat decontextualized language assessment that gauges students' language proficiency in four discrete areas; it falls short in predicting students' actual ability to function linguistically in college. In China, the world's largest international student exporting country (Institute of International Education, 2019), the examination-oriented test preparation culture and practices has further complicated the issue. As shown in the findings of my study, one clear consequence of mistakenly equating a successful TOEFL performance to students' actual ability in linguistic functioning has been that the Chinese international students were likely to overestimate their true ability to meet the linguistic demands of college. Once students encountered unexpected language difficulties, they became overwhelmed at the initial stage of their overseas studies, which may lead to increased mental stress (see Sarah's case) and demotivate them (see Matthew's case) in the long run .

From a research perspective, the myth challenged above can be somewhat disturbing. For decades, it has been common practice in educational research to equate students' TOEFL results to their English proficiency. Correlational analysis has been conducted to analyze the relationship between students' English proficiency and their academic performance (e.g. Cho & Bridgeman, 2012; Ginther & Yan, 2018; Wait & Gressel, 2009). Yet, if the TOEFL results themselves are not accurate indicators of students' actual ability to function linguistically, how do we interpret the findings of those correlational studies that have used TOEFL to predict students' academic achievements?

Likewise, from the standpoint of college admission, a series of questions remain to be answered. If TOEFL preparation has become a highly profitable industry and international students' repeated efforts to boost their TOEFL results have become common practice, how do we interpret their TOEFL scores submitted for college admission? If the TOEFL fails to accurately predict prospective multilingual students' ability to function linguistically in college, should we still use this standardized assessment as a high-stakes gatekeeping tool for college admission? Yet, without such a standardized language assessment, how can we effectively recruit multilingual international students who are qualified for college studies and screen out those who may need additional language training before their overseas studies?

Given the TOEFL's inaccurate measure of multilingual international students' actual ability in linguistic functioning, pairing the TOEFL with some student-centered alternative assessments may provide promising solutions to the aforementioned concerns on research and administration. For example, instead of solely making placement decisions based on students' performances on the TOEFL writing subtest, my home institution, Northeastern University, has adopted a guided self-placement process to help newly arrived college freshmen place themselves into different types of composition classes (https://cssh.northeastern.edu/writing/first-year-writing/guided-self-placement/). This guided self-placement was inspired by what Royer and Gilles (1998, 2003) referred to as *directed self-placement*. Students are asked to write short essays reflecting on their successful and unsuccessful languaging and literacy experiences before making their self-placement decisions. Approaches like this de-centralize the heavy emphasis on students' standardized test performances on the TOEFL and provide them with opportunities to engage in authentic college writing experiences. Meanwhile, college composition professors can access rich information through these short essays to (1) learn more about the language and educational experiences of multilingual students and (2) get a sense of students' ability to meet the written linguistic demands of college. This could eventually help them make recommendations for students' course selection if necessary.

10 Myth 2: An English-Only Policy is Necessary in College Classrooms to Help International Students Improve Their Linguistic Functioning in English

Introduction

Despite the rising popularity of World Englishes (e.g. Canagarajah, 2006, 2012; Kachru & Nelson, 1996; Lee, 2014) and the widely agreed benefits of multilingualism, English-only attitudes still prevail in society (e.g. Macedo, 2000; White, 2012; Wright, 2004; Zhang-Wu, 2021a). For example, a recent anti-bilingual comment by Duke University Professor Megan Neely about whether to reinforce an English-only policy caused controversy and brought the issue back to public attention. As the director of graduate studies in biostatistics at Duke University, Professor Neely sent out a group email, urging all international students to avoid heritage language usage both inside and beyond classroom settings to 'commit to using English 100% of the time' (Mervosh, 2019). In the email, the professor explicitly pointed out that those students who resorted to their home language in college 'were not taking the opportunity to improve their English and were being so impolite as to have a conversation that not everyone on the floor could understand' (Mervosh, 2019). Targeting Chinese international students, the largest international student group at Duke, she further emphasized 'PLEASE[1] PLEASE PLEASE keep these unintended consequences in mind when you choose to speak Chinese in the building...' (Mervosh, 2019).

The Duke professor's comment echoed a commonly held myth in American higher education and beyond, believing that in order to improve their English, bilingual students need to be immersed in an English-speaking environment as much as possible; the usage of their heritage language is therefore nothing but a distraction. Nevertheless, the findings of my research project have cast doubt on such a myth, putting the necessity of an English-only policy in American higher education into question.

This chapter draws on data collected from semi-structured interviews, students' writing samples, ongoing research memos and *WeChat* observations. I begin by discussing the negative impacts of an English-only policy mandated in their *First Year Writing for Multilingual Writers* classrooms and how a pro-multilingual classroom environment created by a history professor could benefit native and non-native English-speaking students alike. After presenting the distinct language policies in these two classes and their consequences, I describe how international students' home languages (in this case Mandarin) can be used as a bridging tool to support students' academic studies and social adjustments at the initial stage of their overseas college studies. Without any intervention, the participants gradually reduced their reliance on Chinese over time, and became increasingly accustomed to utilizing English to navigate their overseas college studies. Based on the experiences of my participants, I question the necessity of adopting an English-only policy in higher education contexts and argue that a pro-multilingual environment in college classrooms could benefit both international and domestic students alike in the long run.

Negative Influences of a Classroom-Level English-Only Policy

An English-only policy has been present throughout all sections of *First Year Writing for Multilingual Writers* at Hillside, an introductory writing course exclusively designed for non-native speakers of English who need additional language support. According to one veteran instructor of *First Year Writing for Multilingual Writers*, the rationale behind banning students' home language usage in these writing classes was to create an English immersion learning environment so that multilingual international students could have ample opportunities to practice English and enhance their language proficiency. Despite the good intention behind such a classroom-level language policy, however, the program-wide English-only policy in these introductory writing classes led to confusion among many Chinese international freshmen. Although Hillside University did not have any institution-wide language policies, the lack of clarification from writing professors about the rationales behind such a classroom-level policy in *First Year Writing for Multilingual Writers* misled many multilingual international students. They ended up holding the misconception that an English-only policy was an institution-wide language regulation at Hillside University and an unspoken rule across all higher education institutions in Anglophone countries. Such a misconception consequently exerted negative influences on their linguistic adaptation and content-subject learning.

On the one hand, due to the English-only policy mandated in *First Year Writing for Multilingual Writers*, many participants developed negative perceptions toward their heritage language. For instance, multiple participants described Mandarin Chinese as 'not important', 'less useful' and 'too silly' compared with the English language (Interview, 8.30.18). Additionally, some revealed concerns about whether they would be discriminated against or punished for talking Chinese in non-classroom settings on campus (e.g. in the hallway, in student lounge). As a result, these negative perceptions toward their mother tongue and the English-superiority fallacy that developed along the way further aggravated the tensions between *regular high* and *American high* students. As vividly demonstrated in William's painful experience of being bullied by his *American high* peer (see Chapter 5) and Rebecca's harsh comments about her *regular high* peers (see Chapter 6), instead of establishing a supportive network and bonding with one another based on their shared home language, soon after arriving at Hillside, Chinese international students were divided into two opposing camps based on their English proficiency levels and degree of exposure to American culture and education.

On the other hand, misinterpreting this classroom-level language policy as an institutional norm posed threats to Chinese international students' content-subject learning, which may jeopardize their overall academic well-being in the long run. My participants' fear of violating the English-only rule led to their hesitation to draw on Mandarin Chinese to make quick clarifications with their Chinese peers about course content during lectures (Research Memo, 9.18.18). Since their English was often not good enough to make quick clarifications with peers, some international students ended up letting go of those learning moments by staying quiet. Furthermore, because often the questions and confusion that Chinese international students faced in class were in fact related to their language barriers, it was almost impossible for them to digest certain knowledge points without support from their first language as a medium of communication between peers.

Positive Influences of a Pro-Multilingual Classroom Environment

Contrasting with the potential harm of a monolingualist local policy, a pro-multilingual classroom environment was found to be beneficial for all students, international and domestic learners alike. To create such a learning environment, it is important to disrupt English-only by explicitly promoting cultural and linguistic diversity.

For example, *Asia in the World* is an elective history course open to all Hillside undergraduate students. Similar to *First Year Writing*, this course is also among the very few classes that have a mandated classroom-level language policy. However, contrary to the introductory writing course which embraces an English-only policy, the instructor of

Asia in the World, Professor Zhao, made it clear that students' diverse cultural and linguistic backgrounds were always highly valued in class. Originally from China, Professor Zhao is bilingual in Mandarin Chinese and English. To create a pro-multilingual classroom environment, Professor Zhao frequently drew on her own bilingual linguistic repertoire in class. Her usage of Mandarin during instruction not only empowered multilingual non-native English-speaking students but also benefited all learners in her class, native and non-native English speakers alike, by engaging them in a welcoming and diverse learning atmosphere.

One *American high* student Shawn recalled that at the very beginning of the first lecture, the history professor announced to her 200 students that she preferred to be called '赵老师' (pronounced as 'Zhao Laoshi', direct translation: Teacher Zhao) instead of 'Professor or Doctor Zhao' (Interview, 8.30.18). Requesting students to address their instructors in a preferred way at the very beginning of the semester is a common practice in almost all educational settings. Yet, Professor Zhao drew on this routine as a teachable moment to raise students' cross-cultural awareness. She took advantage of this opportunity and created a culturally and linguistically inclusive classroom environment by engaging students in discussions about the differences between Western and Eastern perceptions of the word 'teacher' (Interview, 8.30.18). She explained that in Western culture, university teachers were often considered somewhat 'fancier' than their elementary and secondary counterparts, because of which honorifics such 'Doctor' and 'Professor' have often been used exclusively to address college instructors. Yet, this was not the case in Eastern culture. In the histories of Asian countries such as China, Japan and Korea, teaching has always been viewed as a noble profession. In fact, teachers are so respected in Eastern society that the term 'teacher' (Chinese equivalent of 'laoshi') has been used as an honorific for centuries to refer to all educators as well as experts in various fields (e.g. scientists, artists, writers, engineers, politicians).

According to Shawn, Professor Zhao's welcoming attitude to cultural and linguistic diversity not only raised her students' awareness of cultural differences and encouraged them to view matters from various perspectives, but also aroused their interest in the course subject – Asian history and culture. Reflecting on his American classmates' integration of 'Laoshi' as part of their linguistic repertoire, Shawn commented 'I think it's really cool, cuz right after that class, I overheard a couple American students gossiping about another professor. They called him Johnson Laoshi! Obviously, those Whites have internalized some Asian culture right away hahaha...' (Interview, 8.30.18).

The pro-multilingual, culturally responsive learning environment created by Professor Zhao also empowered students from minoritized cultural and linguistic backgrounds. Shawn perceived it an empowering moment when Professor Zhao modeled the Chinese pronunciation of 'Zhao Laoshi' and requested all students to practice after her. This moment allowed multilingual international students to rethink about themselves – they were not simply English language learners but capable multilingual beings whose home language and culture were incredibly valuable. Meanwhile, domestic students were pushed to experience a snapshot of the everyday challenges of multilingual international students studying in an unfamiliar language environment. Shawn was amused to find that Mandarin, which Chinese students considered so easy and effortless, turned out to be a huge challenge to their American classmates:

> 她说 '*In the future, please call me Zhao Laoshi. Now, repeat after me: Zhao-Lao-Shi...*' 太搞笑了，你不知道那些美国人念她名字有多挣扎！哈哈哈，笑死我了。我们在场的中国人好多都笑出声了。。。 *I really LOVE this... You know, it's great to put them [the American peers] in our shoes...*

> She said 'In the future, please call me Zhao Laoshi. Now, repeat after me: Zhao-Lao-Shi...' This was so funny. You can't imagine how those Americans struggled to pronounce her name! Hahaha, this really amused me to death. At that moment, many of the Chinese student burst into laughter in class... I really LOVE this... You know, it's great to put them [the American peers] in our shoes... (Interview, 8.30.18)

Echoing Shawn's observations, favorable attitudes toward the multilingual space created by Professor Zhao could also be observed in my other participants' public *WeChat* posts. For instance, when the professor used an online live poll to get her students' perception about the course subject at the beginning of the semester, she specifically asked students to draw on all languages in their linguistic repertoires and '[u]se one to three words to describe history, studies of history, and history courses' (*WeChat* Observation, 8.29.18; see Figure 10.1). The participants were thrilled when invited to use their home languages in academic settings. Bill expressed his excitement at Professor Zhao's pro-multilingual stance by posting the result of the poll on his *WeChat* and commenting 'Hahahahaha, the lecture by Zhao Laoshi'. As shown in Figure 10.1, the results of the poll contained students' answers in various languages and forms, such as English, Simplified Chinese, Traditional Chinese, Korean, Swahili and even onomatopoeic words to express emotions (e.g. hmm, yerrr, nooo, yeet).

The Evolvement of Home Language as a Bridging Tool throughout the Semester

On arriving at Hillside University, the Chinese international students in my study started to rely on their home language, Mandarin

哈哈哈哈哈哈哈██老师的lecture

8 day(s) ago

[Translation]
Bill's post content:
Hahahahaha, the lecture by
Zhao Laoshi

[The picture showed one of
the slides in Zhao Laoshi's
history class. In this picture,
students' responses to a live
poll asking them to
"describe history, studies of
history and history courses"
were documented.]

[The post was liked by a
few other students]

Figure 10.1   Screenshot from Bill's public *WeChat* post, 8/29/2018

Chinese, as a bridging tool to enhance their linguistic functioning in the English-speaking environment and facilitate their academic success in content-subject learning. While the home language was frequently and heavily drawn on as a bridging tool among newly arrived Chinese international students at the very beginning of the semester, its popularity gradually declined with the passing of time. Over the course of their first semester in college, even without any institutional-level intervention emphasizing an English-only policy, my participants naturally reduced their dependence on Chinese as a bridging tool as they were increasingly acculturated into the English-speaking environment. This demonstrated the dynamic nature of multilingual individuals' languaging practices in which they drew on all the available linguistic resources to facilitate their communication purposes (e.g. Canagarajah, 2011; Creese & Blackledge, 2015; García & Kleifgen, 2020; Jørgensen, 2008). Since a strategic reliance on the home language is a natural languaging practice among multilingual communicators, the findings have again questioned the myth that an English-only policy at the institutional level is needed to enhance multilingual international students' academic well-being and linguistic adjustment.

The first month in college: 'Chinese is the key to success'

Echoing what has been illustrated in the stories of William, Matthew and Sarah (see Chapter 5) during their first month in a US university, all nine *regular high* Chinese international students claimed that they frequently resorted to Mandarin Chinese as a bridging tool to cope with their linguistic and academic challenges. The most common practice was the usage of English-Chinese bilingual dictionaries, which included not only traditional dictionaries but also popular online translation applications such as ICIBA, Youdao Dictionary and Google Translate. Regardless of their awareness of the many advantages of English-English dictionaries that would allow them to practice thinking in English and get more target language exposure, the Chinese international students still preferred to use English-Chinese bilingual dictionaries, which made it possible for them to grasp the meaning of the vocabulary much more quickly (Interviews, 8.30.18, 9.4.18, 9.6.18). As William explained:

> 很多时候，特别是听老师讲课的时候，我必须在最快的时间里了解它的意思，因为如果我花太久在查单词上，老师的知识点我就听不到，这样恶性循环。英英解释要看半天，还是英中来的快！

> Many times, especially when I'm listening to the professor's lecture, I need to get the meaning of the vocabulary in the shortest time possible. Because if I spend too long with the dictionary, then I will miss the points of the lecture, which could lead to a vicious spiral. It takes too long to read the English explanation of the words, so I prefer English-Chinese dictionaries! (Interview, 8.30.18)

In addition to bilingual dictionaries, another commonly adopted approach across all *regular high* participants at the beginning of the semester was to resort to Chinese online resources. My participants used Chinese online resources mainly for three purposes. Firstly, in order to manage the heavy reading load and meet the reading linguistic demands of college courses, they often tried to look for the Chinese version of the corresponding literature to grasp the main idea. Depending on their academic load, they may or may not have had time to read the English version afterwards. Secondly, to facilitate their understanding of certain unfamiliar concepts in class, around half of the *regular high* students reported quickly browsing through some background information online in Chinese in order to keep up with the lecture. Lastly, one participant mentioned that he resorted to literature published in local Chinese journals as a trick to avoid in-text citations required in academic English writing:

> 如果你先找中文论文，再用自己的话把相关知识点翻译成英文，再写进你的*essay*里，你就不用管烦人的*in-text citation*了。因为美国教授的放抄袭软件无论如何不可能发现你其实引用了中国论文的句子，因为在你*essay*里的出现的只有你的翻译.

> You don't have to worry about the annoying formats of in-text citation if you first find literature in Chinese, then translate relevant key information into English using your own words, and finally integrate it into your essay. There is no way for American professors' anti-plagiarism software to figure out that you actually cited something from literature published in Chinese, because the only thing that shows up in your essay is going to be your own translation. (Interview, 8.30.18)

Something worth noting is that while none of the *American high* participants adopted Chinese as a bridge in college, all had resorted to this strategy when they first started high school in the United States, be it using English-Chinese dictionaries or browsing for information in Chinese (Interviews, 8.30.18, 9.6.18). However, they reported abandoning this strategy later in high school because it was found to be 'not as helpful' and 'time-consuming' (Interviews, 8.30.18, 9.6.18).

Around midterm: 'Using Chinese can cause some problems'

Two months into their freshmen year, Chinese continued to be a popular bridging tool among *regular high* students. On the one hand, Chinese-English bilingual dictionaries were still considered essential in facilitating their academic studies, especially when the participants were faced with increasing academic stress from the midterm examinations during their second month in college (Research Memo, 10.28.18). On the other hand, the participants continued to rely on Chinese online resources to facilitate their academic studies in content-subject learning. For instance, as illustrated in Matthew's story (see Chapter 5), philosophy was particularly challenging to Chinese international students due to its heavy reading load and its Western-centered content. To cope with these challenges, the participants frequently resorted to online Chinese materials to establish their background knowledge and facilitate their understanding of subject contents. For instance, as illustrated in Figure 10.2, Eva utilized Chinese Wikipedia as a resource to facilitate her understanding of *The Republic* by Plato (*WeChat* Observation, 10.15.18).

Despite its popularity, the participants started to realize that excessive reliance on Chinese may have some potential drawbacks and thus became more selective in adopting this strategy. While most of them continued to adopt this strategy, some started to move away from their dependence on Chinese as a bridging tool.

Firstly, the dependence on a Chinese-English dictionary in reading was said to be ineffective and time-consuming. For instance, Sarah, who had 'zero tolerance' for unknown vocabulary in English readings, claimed that whenever she encountered a new word, she could not resist the temptation to figure out its meaning by looking it up in the bilingual dictionary (Interview, 11.20.18). Nevertheless, since there were various discipline-specific jargons in each academic reading, it usually took her several hours to read while looking up each unfamiliar word (Interview, 11.20.18). Because of this academic burden, very often she had to stay up late in order to finish her assignments. To make matters worse, her frequent bilingual dictionary usage also impeded her overall reading comprehension, as Sarah was forced to 'jump back and forth' between the two languages during reading (Interview, 11.20.18). Reflecting on her experience, Sarah decided to prioritize the holistic comprehension of the

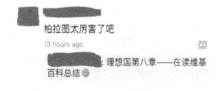

柏拉图太厉害了吧

13 hours ago

理想国第八章——在读维基

百科总结 😊

[Translation]

Eva's post content: Plato is too cool to believe

Eva's additional comment: I am currently reading the summary of Chapter 8 in *The Republic* on Chinese Wikipedia [smiling face emoji]

Figure 10.2 An example of the usage of online Chinese materials, 10/15/18

article and be more selective in the words she chose to look up (Interview, 11.20.18).

Secondly, the reliance on bilingual dictionaries in writing was likely to result in awkward wording. These strange wordings likely confused professors and consequently resulted in low grades (Research Memo, 11.28.18). For instance, in one of her essays, bilingual dictionary user Eva wrote 'Painting at Eastside *induced a more layered pleasure...*' in order to express that she was very happy painting at Eastside (Eva's Writing Sample, 9.30.18). Similarly, wanting to convey that college students pushed themselves out of their comfort zones to make friends with one another, Lily drew on translations provided by her bilingual dictionary and wrote '*they lower their invisible fence* and accept each other as a potential acquaintance' (Lily's Writing Sample, 9.28.18).

Lastly, while resorting to Chinese online resources and summaries facilitated their understanding of course readings, this strategy could negatively impact Chinese international students' academic well-being in the long run. Due to its convenience, many participants reported having occasionally skipped the English version and depended solely on Chinese resources. This occurred more frequently when they were facing increasing academic stress around the midterm exams. Without reading the English version, however, the participants were not exposed to some content-specific technical terms, which further reduced their capacity to fully participate in oral discussions in class. Consequently, despite their general knowledge of the course readings, the students reported difficulties functioning linguistically in class (Interviews, 11.19.18, 11.21.18).

Towards the end of the semester: 'Chinese is my last resort'

Approximately three months into the semester, the popularity of using Chinese as a bridging tool decreased significantly among the participants because of its many disadvantages. While some students became more selective and stringent in adopting this strategy, others gave up completely their reliance on Chinese as a bridging tool.

On the one hand, the final examinations of many courses were said to include short answers questions, which not only required the students to be familiar with the contents of the course readings, but also tested their mastery of the discipline-specific vocabulary and expressions. Therefore, in preparation for their upcoming final exams, directly resorting to the English version would be more effective and efficient for international students to get familiar with disciplinary vocabulary compared with reading Chinese translations of the course readings.

On the other hand, multiple participants mentioned that they grew cautious about using bilingual translation tools because of their potential to create awkward expressions in writing. Pat, who preferred English-English dictionaries, referred to the usage of bilingual dictionaries as his 'last resort' (Interview, 11.19.18). Being aware that relying on bilingual translations tools may lead to awkward wording in academic English writing, Pat tried to minimize his usage of Chinese-English dictionaries as much as possible. For situations where he had to depend on bilingual translation tools, he would always double check the results provided by Chinese-English translation software by verifying them with an English-English dictionary before including them in his academic essays (Interview, 11.19.18).

Concluding Remarks

As leading translingual scholar Canagarajah (2006: 592) points out, 'Classes based on monolingual pedagogies disable students in contexts of linguistic pluralism'. Drawing on data from interviews, *WeChat* observations, students' writing samples and research memos, this chapter challenged the myth regarding the need for an institution-level English-only policy in order to facilitate multilingual international students' language development and academic success. The findings presented in this chapter not only questioned the myth regarding the necessity of a local-level English-only policy but also highlighted the importance of acknowledging the rich and dynamic nature of multilingual students' languaging practices.

While a monolingualist classroom environment exerts negative influences on multilingual students, a pro-multilingual learning context is beneficial to all learners' academic and psychological well-being. As illustrated in the case of the *First Year Writing for Multilingual Writers* course, a classroom-level English-only policy may not only confuse multilingual international students but also lower their self-esteem by creating negative associations toward their home languages. Consequently, such a classroom-level language policy, despite its good intentions to empower international students and facilitate their academic success by maximizing their English exposure, has disadvantaged these students by posing additional psychological, emotional and academic challenges (Smith & Khawaja, 2011; Yan & Berliner, 2011). In contrast, when a pro-multilingual language policy and classroom environment is created, all learners regardless of their culture and language backgrounds are likely to benefit in the process. The case of Professor Zhao vividly illustrated how an inclusive classroom environment not only empowers non-native English-speaking international students, but also raises cross-cultural awareness especially among domestic students. Furthermore, Professor Zhao's engaging and learner-centered way of advocating for cultural and linguistic diversity further aroused her students' interest in the course content.

Multilinguals are by no means multiple monolinguals in one body but instead they are active decision makers who strategically deploy resources from their linguistic repertoire to fulfill communicative purposes (e.g. Canagarajah, 2011; Creese & Blackledge, 2015; García & Kleifgen, 2020; Jørgensen, 2008). In academic contexts where the goal is to master content-subject knowledge to advance students' college studies, keeping international students' home language outside of the classroom is both a violation of their basic linguistic rights and a denial of their identities as multilingual and multicultural beings. Based on the findings of the study, the usage of multilingual international students' home language, Chinese, as a bridging tool played a positive role in facilitating their academic, language and cultural transition especially at the very beginning stage of their first semester in college. With the initial support of drawing on their heritage language as a bridging tool, Chinese international students were able to gradually function linguistically in English; their increased linguistic adjustment in the process, in turn, led to their decreased reliance on Chinese. To put it another way, rather than remaining as a hurdle and minimizing their opportunities to use English, the participants' dependence on Chinese naturally decreased over time with their improving ability to function linguistically in English as well as their active response to the linguistic demands and communicative purposes of college courses. Since strategically drawing on all resources in their linguistic repertoire to fulfill communication purposes is the lived reality of multilingual languagers (Zhang-Wu, 2021a), it is unnecessary to adopt an English-only policy be it at the classroom level or beyond.

Note

(1) Text capitalized and emphasized in Neely's original email correspondence.

11 Myth 3: *First Year Writing* Guarantees International Students' Successful Writing Performances in Content-Area Courses

Introduction

In his recent blog entry in *Inside Higher Ed*,[1] John Warner (2018), the author of multiple books on writing pedagogy and a veteran college composition professor, has referred to the *First Year Writing* course as 'a chore, rather than a choice'. The reason behind Warner's claim is simple – for years, *First Year Writing* has been one of the institutional core courses in almost every university across the US. Designed specifically to improve the academic writing ability of college freshmen, *First Year Writing* is open to native and non-native English-speaking students alike across the disciplines. Regardless of their preferences, students have little choice but to take this course as part of their initial college experiences. An underlying assumption frequently associated with this mandatory composition course is that *First Year Writing* is simply designed to prepare international college freshmen for their academic writing in other courses. This assumption indicates that (1) with the writing support received in *First Year Writing*, multilingual students will be able to function linguistically and meet the writing demands of content-subject courses, and (2) due to the existence of *First Year Writing* as an institutional core, it is never content-subject faculty members' responsibility to support the academic writing development of multilingual college students. However, is this really the case?

The purpose of this chapter is to investigate this commonly held misconception regarding *First Year Writing*. To facilitate my discussion, I start the chapter with a brief overview of how this introductory writing course is contextualized and operationalized at Hillside University. Drawing on empirical data collected from semi-structured interviews, talks around texts, students' writing samples, ongoing research memos and *WeChat* observations, I present my participants' contrasting experiences and academic performances in meeting the writing demands of their composition classrooms and other content-subject courses. While my participants were able to meet the writing demands and demonstrate overall positive attitudes toward their performances in their multilingual composition classes, their ability to function linguistically and write effectively in content-subject courses varied. By analyzing these Chinese international students' writing samples across disciplines using genre-based rubrics informed by systemic functional linguistics (Brisk, 2015), I draw attention to the challenges facing multilingual international students and the support needed in their effort to meet the written linguistic demands in academic contexts. Based on the findings, I end the chapter with a discussion on the implications of the study and call for content-subject professors to incorporate culturally and linguistically responsive pedagogy in their instruction and course design in order to support the linguistic acculturation, language development and academic well-being of an increasingly diverse student population.

First Year Writing at Hillside University: A Brief Overview

At Hillside University, *First Year Writing* has been an institutional core for more than three decades. To provide customized linguistic support for multilingual writers and in response to the growing diversity of its student body, Hillside University has provided two variations of the freshmen composition course, namely, regular *First Year Writing* and *First Year Writing for Multilingual Writers*. The two variations carry exactly the same course credits, and they both fulfill freshmen students' curriculum requirement in *First Year Writing*. Yet, as indicated by its name, *First Year Writing for Multilingual Writers* is designed specifically for non-native English-speaking international students, and it is taught by instructors with knowledge and credentials working with learners from culturally and linguistically diverse backgrounds. Given the large numbers of Chinese international students enrolled at Hillside, each year a significant proportion of the students in *First Year Writing for Multilingual Writers* are from China. Each semester, Hillside University provides approximately eight sections of *First Year Writing for Multilingual Writers*, with an enrollment cap of 15 students per class. As mentioned earlier in the book, across all these sections an English-only policy is mandated in the hope of maximizing students' English exposure and enhancing their English proficiency.

Although *First Year Writing for Multilingual Writers* is composed exclusively of multilingual international students, this does not necessarily mean that all non-native English-speaking students are automatically placed into this course on college entry. Placement in *First Year Writing* is primarily based on students' performance in a writing assessment designed and later graded by one professor from the English department who has considerable expertise educating non-native speakers of English. This hour-long test consists of two parts: reading a preselected news article and responding to the prompts about the news article in writing. The news article is usually about a recent event or topic that is relevant to college students. No absolute word limit is required by the test, and students are evaluated based mainly on the rater's holistic impression of their writing ability, accuracy of grammar and complexity of sentence structures. On average, around two thirds of the international students who take the placement test are often found to need extra academic writing support and are assigned to *First Year Writing for Multilingual Writers* classes. The rest are recommended to be placed in *First Year Writing* along with their native English-speaking peers.

Among the Chinese international students in my study, 10 were enrolled in *First Year Writing for Multilingual Writers*, one in *Literature* (Kristin) and another in regular *First Year Writing* (Eva). Indeed, an overwhelmingly high proportion of my participants were enrolled in the multilingual composition course during their first semester at Hillside University. Nevertheless, it is worth noting that based on their performances in the placement writing assessment, only approximately half of the students were initially diagnosed as in need of additional language support and placed in *First Year Writing for Multilingual Writers*. In fact, five participants, including two *regular high* students (Kristin, Eva) and three *American high* students (Rebecca, Shawn, Hugo) had all been given permission to join the non-multilingual section. Yet, toward the end, English major Eva ended up the only student who chose to join *First Year Writing*, with the other four students all giving up their opportunity to study with native speakers of English. Rebecca, Hugo, Shawn and Kristin provided their reasons for their preference to join *First Year Writing for Multilingual Writers*. On the one hand, owing to their high English proficiency, the four students believed that they would have a higher chance of receiving an 'A' in this sheltered writing course since the vast majority of their classmates were likely to be those who needed additional language support (Interviews, 8.30.18, 9.4.18, 9.6.18). On the other hand, the three *American high* students, Rebecca, Hugo and Shawn, claimed that they preferred 'a course specifically designed for second language learners' so as to improve their academic English writing systematically, an area that had been given very little attention during their US high school education experiences (Interviews, 8.30.18, 9.4.18, 9.6.18).

To take their preferred writing course, while Rebecca and Shawn had left notes on the anchor writing assessment expressing their desire to join the multilingual writing sections, Hugo intentionally skipped the test and directly requested the English department to place him into one of the sheltered writing sections. Consequently, the three *American high* students managed to be reassigned into *First Year Writing for Multilingual Writers*. On the contrary, despite her desire to join a multilingual class, Kristin was told that since all sections were already full, she could either stay in regular *First Year Writing* or take *Literature*, another required undergraduate core course provided by the English department, in the fall before taking the multilingual writing course during the following spring semester. Determined to join *First Year Writing for Multilingual Writers*, Kristin decided to take *Literature* in her first semester instead.

Success in *First Year Writing for Multilingual Writers*: 'I can be a good writer!'

The 10 participants who ended up in *First Year Writing for Multilingual Writers* unanimously expressed overall positive attitudes toward their experiences in this course. Firstly, since the English language has always been treated as a main subject rather than simply a medium of education in *First Year Writing for Multilingual Writers*, my participants were motivated to engage in the course in order to set the foundation for their linguistic functioning in their future college studies (Interviews, 8.30.18, 9.6.18). Furthermore, in response to many international students' needs for additional language support, they were assigned graduate students at the Department of English as peer tutors. This peer-to-peer support network provides multilingual students with additional opportunities to receive feedback on their writing. Such a resource, when utilized strategically, could help students maximize their office hour consultation with professors to receive holistic and structural-level feedback to enhance their writing, while leaving the mechanical language problems to peer tutors. As illustrated in Sarah's story (see Chapter 5), her writing professor and peer tutor could support her in different ways: '老师可以帮我的文章搭框架，*tutor*可以帮我改语法' (my professor can help me build the structure of my papers, while tutors can edit my papers to eliminate grammatical errors) (Interview, 11.20.18).

Additionally, multiple participants claimed that, compared with their experiences in other courses, they felt more comfortable in *First Year Writing for Multilingual Writers*. The reason given was that their writing professors were very well-trained language educators who were more understanding and less judgmental about their grammatical mistakes and language difficulties. For instance, as illustrated in a *WeChat* screenshot in Chapter 5 (see Figure 5.5), when William was stressed about his failure to function linguistically on arriving at Hillside, his writing professor sent him an email to show her deep empathy and strong commitment to supporting him to meet the linguistic demands of college. Rather than advise William to seek support from the university writing center or the international tutoring center to enhance his English proficiency, the writing professor wrote in her email: 'You are always welcome in my office hours... You could come every day in you wanted! I'm here to help you however I can' (*WeChat* Observation, 9.30.18). Similarly, instead of blaming William for his inability to meet the oral linguistic demands in class, the professor offered to provide clarification whenever needed: 'Please ask questions if you have them and ask me to repeat myself or rephrase what I said if you need to' (*WeChat* Observation, 9.30.18). Finally, to comfort William and encourage him to seek additional support whenever needed, the professor added '[I]t would never be a "trouble", like you mentioned... You will never bother me' (*WeChat* Observation, 9.30.18).

Furthermore, since the primary goal of *First Year Writing for Multilingual Writers* is to familiarize students with common genres in college and basic skills in academic writing, students were encouraged to draw on their personal experiences and choose their preferred topics to contextualize their learning of target genres and writing techniques. In this process, my participants reported being empowered and feeling comfortable, confident and motivated in writing (Interviews, 9.4.18, 9.6.18). For example, business major William chose to draw on his area of expertise – hotel management and hospitality – as the topic of his narrative essay. Since his writing professor had extensive knowledge in applied linguistics and writing, yet had little prior knowledge of William's topic, the traditional expert/authority vs apprentice power relationship between faculty and students was substantially disrupted; instead, it transformed into a less unbalanced power relation in which both parties were experts and apprentices simultaneously. In other words, William assumed the role of content expert and apprentice in writing, while his professor worked as a writing expert with limited knowledge of content. Consequently, the more balanced power relationship between faculty and students resulting from learners' free topic choice was beneficial in reducing second language learner anxiety, which could in turn enhance their writing performances.

Finally, providing students with the autonomy and agency to choose their own topics of writing, *First Year Writing for Multilingual Writers* could motivate students by engaging them in exploring their true passion. For instance, computer science major Shawn determined his areas of study due to pressure from his parents, both of whom have achieved advanced degrees in engineering. Nevertheless, despite his ability to do well in computer science courses because he has always been 'a super hardworking student', Shawn had little passion for his major and felt demotivated in his college studies (Interview, 8.30.18). It was not until Shawn wrote an expository essay in *First Year Writing for Multilingual Writers* about the differences between Eastern and Western traditions that he discovered his passion for East Asian Studies. To further explore the ancient Chinese Taoism concept of Yin and Yang, Shawn's writing professor connected him with another faculty member at the Asian Studies department to further his research interest.

It is worth noting that despite my participants' overall positive experiences in *First Year Writing for Multilingual Writers*, there were two areas where they reported mixed feelings. For one thing, as discussed in an earlier chapter, due to a lack of clarity and explanation when the English-only policy was introduced, many Chinese international students misunderstood this classroom-level language policy as an institutional demand, which could exert negative impacts on their academic and psychological well-being in the long run. For another, given the large number of Chinese international students enrolled in *First Year Writing for Multilingual Writers*, my participants held contrasting opinions toward the student demographics and its consequent linguistic environment. Most viewed the high percentage of Chinese international student enrollment positively, claiming that due to the presence of many students from the same linguistic and cultural backgrounds, they felt safer and more confident when participating orally in class. As Lily concluded, '大家都是中国人，而且基本都认识，说起话来也不会紧张' (Since we are all Chinese and we pretty much know each other well, I don't feel nervous while speaking up in class) (Interview, 9.6.18). On the contrary, some held negative attitudes toward such a student demographics. For example, as illustrated in Sarah's story (see Chapter 5), compared with all other classes at Hillside where native and non-native speakers were mixed together, the high percentage of Chinese international students enrolled in this sheltered course designed exclusively for multilingual learners made her feel more anxiety about peer pressure. According to Sarah, it was much more stressful to when she had difficulties meeting the oral linguistic demands in a class dominated by Chinese students than that consisting mostly of domestic students. From a slightly different perspective, *American high* student Rebecca was also concerned about the linguistic environment created as a result of the large number of Chinese student enrollment. She argued that because all her Chinese peers frequently engaged in conversations in Chinese before and after the writing class, non-Mandarin-speaking international students with different cultural backgrounds were often isolated and marginalized (see Chapter 6).

While my participants indeed expressed mixed feelings regarding the two aforementioned aspects, neither was directly related to their academic writing development and general college writing experiences. Therefore, it is reasonable to conclude that, overall, Chinese international students had very positive experiences in their introductory writing course, where they were able to resume writer agency in topic choice, gain confidence as content experts and explore their disciplinary passion through written communication.

Challenges in Disciplinary Writing: 'I don't know how to write...'

Although the Chinese international students in my study reported very positive experiences in their composition course, their success in meeting the written linguistic demands of *First Year Writing* did not seem to naturally translate into high performances in content-subject writing. In other words, although *First Year Writing* was highly effective in preparing the international students to meet the writing demands within that course, its positive influences were likely to fall short in transitioning into students' successful written communication across the disciplines.

Genre-based analysis of students' writing: Imbalanced performances

While the students did not have many writing assignments in content-subject courses during their first several weeks in college, the second month of the semester witnessed increasing linguistic demands in academic English writing across disciplinary subjects. By Week 5, all participants had been given at least one writing assignment from their content-subject professors (Research Memo, 10.5.18). To understand my participants' academic writing performances, I collected their writing samples shortly before the midterm. Every participant was instructed to send me at least two writing samples, one from their writing class and the other from any content-area courses (e.g. history, philosophy, psychology). There were two exceptions – Kristin and Hugo – who received special arrangements in the process. For Kristin, who was not enrolled in *First Year Writing* but took *Literature* instead, I requested two essays from different content-area classes. For Hugo, whose *First Year Writing* essay focused on a very private issue that he only felt comfortable sharing with his composition professor, I allowed him to submit one writing sample from a content-subject course.

My participants were told that if they would like to share more than two essays, they were free to do so as long as they submitted at least one from their composition course and one from a disciplinary class. By Week 7, I had received 29 pieces of essays, covering four genres: argument (*n* = 12), recount (*n* = 15), one explanation sample from Hugo and one report sample from Eva. Among them, all the recount essays were from *First Year Writing*, while the remaining three genres were from my participants' disciplinary classes. Tables 11.1 and 11.2 summarize the students' performances in argument and recount, the two genres that yielded the most writing samples. As introduced in the methodology section (see Chapter 3), students' writing performance was evaluated based on a scale from 1 to 4 using Brisk's (2015) rubrics. While a score of 3 or more shows that the writer has generally met the genre and language expectations, scores 1 and 2 indicate that substantial support is needed for students to meet the genre-specific written linguistic demands. For demonstration

Table 11.1 Comparative grading of students' argument writing samples in the disciplines

	Student samples											
	Kristin 2	Matthew 2	Kristin 1	Shawn	Matthew 1	Eva	Pat	Bill	Sarah 2	Lily 1	Lily 2	Sarah 1
Argument: Purpose and stages	4	4	4	4	4	3	3	3	3	–	4	3
Verb tense	4	3	4	3	4	4	4	3	3	3	1	2
Title	4	4	4	4	4	4	4	4	4	4	4	4
Thesis statement or claim	4	4	4	4	4	1	4	4	3	1	4	1
Reasons supported by evidence	4	4	4	3	4	4	4	4	4	4	4	4
Reinforcement of statement of	4	4	4	3	1	4	1	1	1	4	4	1
Cohesive text	4	4	4	4	4	4	4	4	4	3	1	2
Argument: Language												
Generalized participants	4	4	3	4	4	4	4	4	4	4	2	2
Language choices	4	4	3	4	4	4	4	4	4	4	4	3
Use of technical vocab	4	4	4	4	4	4	4	4	4	4	4	4
Types of sentences – statements	4	4	4	4	4	4	4	4	4	4	4	4
Use of person	4	4	4	4		4	4		3	4	4	4
Modality	4	4	4	4	3	4	4	4	4	4	4	
Evaluative Vocab	4	4	4	4	4	4	4	4	4	4	4	4
Grading	4	4	4	4	4	4	4	4	4	4	4	4
Text connectives	4	4	4	4	4	2	4	4	4	4	4	3
Cohesive paragraphs	4	4	4	4	4	4	4	4	4	4	2	4
Total points	68	67	66	65	62	62	61	61	61	60	58	50

Table 11.2 Comparative grading of students' recount writing samples in *First Year Writing*

	Matthew	Rebecca 1	Rebecca 2	Patl	Shawn	Eva	Sarah	Lily	Larry 1	Larry 2	Bill 1	Pat 2	William 1	Bill 2	William 2
Recount – Analysis of student work: Purpose and stages															
Purpose	4	4	4	4	4	4	4	4	4	4	4	4	4	4	4
Verb tense	4	4	4	4	4	4	3	1	3	4	2	2	1	1	2
Title	4	4	4	4	2	4	4	4	4	4	4	4	4	NA	3
Orientation	4	4	4	4	4	4	4	4	4	4	4	4	4	4	4
Sequence of events	4	4	4	4	4	4	4	4	4	4	4	2	4	4	2
Conclusion	4	4	4	4	4	4	4	4	4	4	4	4	4	4	1
Coherent text	4	4	4	4	4	4	4	3	4	3	3	4	2	2	2
Paragraph formation	4	4	4	4	4	4	4	4	4	4	4	4	4	4	3
Recount – Analysis of student work: Language															
Verb groups	4	4	4	4	4	4	4	4	4	4	4	4	4	4	4
Noun groups – adjectivals	4	4	4	4	4	4	3	4	4	4	4	4	4	4	3
Packs of noun groups	4	4	4	4	4	4	4	4	4	4	4	4	4	4	4
Adverbials	4	4	4	4	4	2	4	4	4	3	4	4	4	3	2
Use of clause complexes	4	4	4	4	4	4	4	4	4	4	4	4	4	4	2
Use of dialogue	4	4	4	4	4	4	4	4	1	1	4	1	4	1	4
Audience	4	4	4	4	4	4	4	4	4	4	4	4	4	4	3
Voice	4	4	4	4	4	4	4	4	4	4	4	4	4	4	4
Text connectives	4	4	4	4	4	4	4	4	4	4	4	4	4	4	4
Reference ties	4	4	4	3	4	4	4	4	3	3	3	3	4	4	4
Total points	72	72	72	71	70	70	70	68	68	68	68	66	64	60	57

purposes, I have filled all cells with a score of one in red and all with a score of two in orange (see Tables 11.1 and 11.2).

By comparing the numerical scores of samples collected within and beyond *First Year Writing*, it was evident that, overall, Chinese international students demonstrated a higher tendency to perform better in meeting the written linguistic demands of their writing classes than content-subject courses. As shown in Table 11.1, in content-subject writings, 6 of the 12 samples scored 90% or higher (total points 62 or higher) based on the rubric, while a third of the samples achieved scores equal to or greater than 95% (total points 65 or higher). Only one sample from Kristin achieved full marks. Yet, it is worth noting that Kristin was the only student to take *Literature* instead of *First Year Writing* because there was no available spot in any of the multilingual sections. In contrast, among the writing samples collected from the freshmen writing course, more than two thirds of the essays (11 out of 15) achieved scores of around 95% or more. Among them, approximately half of the samples (7 out of 15) scored over 97%, and 20% yielded perfect scores. Additionally, by looking at the incidences where the writers were found to be in need of substantial writing support (i.e. scores '1' and '2'), it was also obvious that there were significantly more areas that required additional instructional support in disciplinary writing samples as compared with those in *First Year Writing*. Therefore, based on my participants' performances as assessed by the rubric, their positive experiences and high performances in *First Year Writing* did not fully translate into their successful linguistic functioning in disciplinary courses.

Interviews: Another look at students' writing samples

The general patterns reflected in the results from genre-based analysis indicated Chinese international students' overall tendency to perform better in *First Year Writing* than in content-subject writings. Yet, one may disagree that since samples collected from composition and disciplinary courses were written in completely different genres, the numerical results above have demonstrated nothing but my participants' superior mastery of the recount genre over argument writing. But is this really the case? To better understand Chinese international students' experiences in meeting the written linguistic demands of their disciplinary classes, in this section I present findings from talks around texts as well as semi-structured interviews to provide a more in-depth examination of my participants' experiences beyond numerical scores.

During the interviews, the participants voiced three unique challenges in disciplinary writing that hindered them from translating their high performances and positive experiences in their writing classes into successful linguistic functioning in content-subject courses. Firstly, while they were always encouraged to write about their topics of interest in *First*

Year Writing, the participants were rarely given the agency to determine their topics in disciplinary writing. Additional, while they were explicitly asked to draw on their personal experiences in *First Year Writing*, content-subject professors very often required students to connect with course readings and literature in the field and refrain from bringing their subjective opinions. Since the freedom of topic choice and connection with lived experiences are an important element to engage students in writing, my participants reported experiencing challenges in meeting the written linguistic demands of disciplinary courses. For example, Larry explained his contrasting experiences writing in composition and disciplinary courses:

> 我很喜欢写作课的写作，因为你只要跟着老师的文体走，想写什么都可以。像我回忆我爷爷的故事，就有很多真-情实感，所以写起来很顺。而其他课的*research paper*都规定我们要些什么内容了，你必须就一些课堂概念讨论。我之前也不是很了解这些专业课概念，也没有很多背景知识，所以很难写好。

> I have really enjoyed writing in *First Year Writing for Multilingual Students*. As long as you follow the genre expected by the professor, you can write about anything you like. For example, in one paper, I wrote about my grandpa's story, during which my real emotions were integrated. Including my emotions and stories has made it very easy to write. On the contrary, in content-subject essays, we are required to discuss about specific topics. You have to construct your essays based on some content-specific concepts. Due to my lack of understanding in those content-specific concepts, I have limited prior knowledge to draw upon. Therefore, I find it very hard to write essays for content courses. (Interview, 11.21.18)

Secondly, the participants reported that their disciplinary professors were likely to be 'stricter' and 'harsher' toward non-native English speakers' surface-level language problems, which raised some concerns about fairness in essay evaluation across disciplines (Interview, 11.20.18). The participants argued that compared with their native English-speaking classmates who were only evaluated based on their content knowledge, multilingual international students were also simultaneously judged on their ability to 'write like an American' (Interviews, 11.20.18, 11.21.18). Given this additional pressure, the participants were less motivated and more intimidated in their effort to fulfill the written linguistic demands of disciplinary courses (Interview, 11.20.18).

To be specific, as mentioned earlier, instructors of *First Year Writing for Multilingual Students* were often well-trained to work with students from culturally and linguistically diverse backgrounds and were likely to be very understanding, empathetic and supportive of multilingual students' small grammatical errors and their occasional deviation from

Western writing styles. Consequently, their grading and feedback tended to focus more on the overall quality and ideas in the essays as they regarded those imperfections as a normal phenomenon during second language learners' English development. Yet, this was rarely the case in disciplinary writing, where instructors were content experts who often had little training on how to support multilingual students. Despite their good intentions to support students from diverse cultural and linguistic backgrounds, those instructors were very likely to be distracted by multilingual students' surface language problems and deviation from Western norms of writing which could mask their over-ability in writing and led to unsuccessful grades (see Sarah's case). Consequently, multiple students reported that their grades in disciplinary essays suffered due to their occasional grammatical errors as well as their lack of knowledge of Western writing styles.

For instance, in the opening paragraph of her philosophy paper, Lily did not follow the Western argument writing convention to clarify her thesis statement; instead, she summarized some background information about the topic and posed a thesis-related question. Despite Lily's critical thinking, strong reasoning and the clear stance she presented in the concluding paragraph, her philosophy professor found her paper 'unclear and hard to follow' since she had not found the thesis statement in the expected location (Talks around Texts, 10.20.18). This resulted in an unsatisfactory grade for the assignment. Among the many in-text comments provided by Lily's philosophy professor, most of which focused on grammar correction, one cast doubt on her usage of questions in the opening paragraph: 'Your thesis should answer the question, not pose it, and then you use the body of the paper to defend your understanding of the text' (Talks around Texts, 10.20.18). Interestingly, this comment seemed to conflict with the common composition practice of posing a thesis-related question in the opening paragraph of an argumentative essay as an approach to engage readers. As Brenda Rinard (2011: 20), a veteran writing instructor and researcher at the University of California Davis and author of the book A *Student's Guide to Academic and Professional Writing in Education*, once pointed out 'Persuasion was accomplished through the use of directives and questions'. From this perspective, it is likely that despite their expertise in content-subjects, disciplinary instructors may not always be well-informed in their knowledge of composition studies, which may cause additional challenges for multilingual international students.

Lastly, different from writing in composition classes where students are evaluated mainly based on their English writing proficiency, disciplinary writing also requires students to demonstrate content knowledge. In other words, in order to meet the written linguistic demands of disciplinary courses, merely being a good writer is not enough. This further indicates that students' success in *First Year Writing* may not naturally translate into successful linguistic functioning in content-subject writing assignments.

For instance, Sarah had mistaken the concept of child maltreatment for a phenomenon that was particular to low-income families. As a result, in her argument about the importance of conducting research on child maltreatment in applied psychology, Sarah interchangeably referred to 'child maltreatment' as 'child maltreatment among low-income families', which caused confusion throughout her essay and weakened her argument (Talks around Texts, 11.2.18). Sarah started the article by providing lots of research-based evidence on how harmful child maltreatment was in general:

> The consequences of child maltreatment had been repeatedly shown to extend into and beyond childhood to affect educational and employment outcomes, mental and physical health, relationship quality, and antisocial and criminal behaviors (Phaedra, C.S., & Valerie, E.J., & Xiangming, F., PhD, and James, M.A., 2008). It demonstrated those children were at an increased risk to have failures in the future. To be more specific, they trapped into a vicious circle which made them be unable to get educational attainment and socioeconomic status to improve their lives... (Sarah 1, 10.24.18)

Later in her essay, Sarah suddenly shifted her topic by addressing how urgent it was for parents from low socioeconomic families to realize the detrimental consequences of child maltreatment. As she continued, 'For those poor families, parents should pay attention to such bad consequences. If they did not want to destroy their children's future developments, they needed to consider carefully before they abused their children...' (Sarah 1, 10.24.18). This transition was very abrupt and confusing because while the earlier evidence tapped into the general population, the later warning was suddenly targeted specifically at 'those poor families'. Throughout her essay, Sarah jumped back and forth between child maltreatment among the general population and poor families. Her lack of content knowledge consequently led to her severe violations in multiple areas such as cohesiveness, thesis and generalized participants as assessed in the genre-based rubric, which consequently resulted in a low grade (see Table 11.2).

Concluding Remarks

In this chapter, I challenged the commonly held misconception that *First Year Writing* guarantees international students' success in disciplinary writing. An analysis of students' writing performances based on the genre-based rubrics (Brisk, 2015) showed that my participants tended to perform better in *First Year Writing* than in disciplinary courses.

By comparing students' experiences in their composition and content-subject courses, I argued that success in *First Year Writing* may not translate into multilingual students' ability to meet the written linguistic demands of disciplinary courses. This was partially because, compared with students' experiences in *First Year Writing*, content-subject writing assignments across the disciplines were less likely to draw on students' personal, cultural and linguistic backgrounds. Furthermore, regardless of the quality of the writing itself, mastery of content knowledge was a prerequisite for successful writing in the disciplines. As shown in Sarah's case, her misinterpretation of the course concept jeopardized the cohesiveness of her writing. Since to function linguistically in content-subject courses requires more than good academic writing skills, *First Year Writing* alone cannot fully prepare multilingual international students to meet the written linguistic demands across the disciplines.

By making the statement above, I, as a writing program faculty member who has taught *First Year Writing*, am not blaming composition courses for failing to effectively prepare multilingual international students in their disciplinary writing. As a matter of fact, misconceiving that the introductory writing course is responsible for multilingual students' successful writing performances across disciplines reveals a very deficit mindset that only writing instructors should support multilingual students' languaging experiences in disciplinary courses. Sadly, such a deficit perspective has been found prevalent among content-subject educators (e.g. Gallagher & Haan, 2018; Lee & Oxelson, 2006) who tend to assume that because writing professors are language teachers by nature, it is simply not their responsibility to support students from culturally and linguistically diverse backgrounds to meet the linguistic demands in their classes.

As John Warner (2018) has correctly pointed out, writing and rhetorical studies itself should be seen as a legitimate discipline rather than a preparation course for other disciplinary subjects. In order to facilitate multilingual students' successful linguistic functioning across disciplines, it is not enough to merely depend on the support of their writing professors; content-subject faculty members should also take responsibility in this process. No content knowledge can be conveyed without language, because language is the underlying curriculum in every course (Brisk & Zhang-Wu, 2017; Zhang-Wu, 2021b). This is true for all areas of study, not only in terms of relatively language-heavy disciplines in the social sciences and humanities, but also for those fields that were traditionally viewed as number driven and less language dominant, such as mathematics. For instance, regardless of multilingual students' ability in calculation, if they are unclear about the differences between *three times more than* and *three times as many as*, it would be extremely challenging for them to perform well in class (Zhang-Wu, 2021b). Since language exists in contexts and academic language has always been a part of every content-subject matter, it is mandatory for all faculty members – both writing and disciplinary instructors – to resume their responsibility as language teachers (Brisk & Zhang-Wu, 2017; Zhang-Wu, 2021b).

The importance and urgency for content-subject educators to also be language teachers in order to fully support multilingual students' linguistic functioning across disciplines is clearly reflected in recent research in linguistically responsive pedagogy (Lucas & Villegas, 2013; Villegas & Lucas, 2002), which addresses the growing diversity in education settings and supports the academic success of linguistically diverse student population by providing language support in content-subject classrooms, especially those traditionally situated in monolingual norms. Yet, although substantial research attention has been paid to the adoption of a linguistically responsive pedagogy in elementary and secondary education (e.g. de Jong *et al.*, 2013; Echevarria *et al.*, 2013; Zhang-Wu, 2017), significantly less is known about how to implement such a pedagogical practice to support multilingual college students (Gallagher & Haan, 2018). Undergraduate international students, especially college freshmen, are in urgent need of such support, as they are simultaneously faced with the transitions from secondary to tertiary education and from their home language to an English-speaking environment. It is hoped that the findings presented in this chapter draw research attention to this unique population so that educators across disciplines work together to facilitate multilingual students' writing development (Zawacki & Cox, 2014) during their international college studies thousands of miles from home.

Note

(1) *Inside Higher Ed* is a popular online publication that disseminates news, stories, opinions and job information in relation to higher education. Founded in 2004, Inside Higher Ed is located in Washington, DC.

12 Myth 4: English is Responsible for All the Challenges Facing Chinese International Students

Introduction

What is the top challenge for Chinese international students studying in Anglophone countries? Most, if not all, may think it is their lack of proficiency in the English language. Holding the assumption that English is responsible for all the challenges facing Chinese international students, many higher education administrators believe that improving their English proficiency is the ultimate solution to their languaging challenges. For instance, James Dorsett, director of the Office for International Students and Scholars at Michigan State University, responded to the fast-growing Chinese international student population on campus by suggesting: 'For international students, the most helpful is oftentimes getting out of their comfortable zone and meeting people who are not like them, who do not speak Mandarin or Cantonese' (Zhu, 2017). In a journal article reviewing recent research on Chinese international students (Zhang-Wu, 2018), I found that the vast majority of previous research on this topic touched on English language difficulties as one of their key focuses (e.g. Jiang, 2014; Wang, 2016; Xue, 2013; Yeh & Inose, 2003), which further adds to the myth blaming English incompetency for Chinese international students' challenges during their overseas experiences.

Yet, such an overgeneralized conception equating all Chinese international students with limited English proficient learners not only perpetuates a deficit perspective on culturally and linguistically diverse student populations but also masks the many important culture-related challenges with which they are confronted. Understanding the influences from cultural factors could pave the way for the university support system to facilitate students' languaging success and overall academic well-being. In this chapter, drawing on data collected from students' bilingual language logs, semi-structured interviews and *WeChat* observations, I cast doubt on the commonly held myth blaming Chinese international students' lack of English proficiency for all the difficulties they encounter during their overseas studies. I start by pointing out the inaccuracy and overgeneralization in blaming the English language for all the challenges facing Chinese international students. Based on empirical data, I then discuss how culture played a role in the participants' languaging experiences as well as their ability to navigate the university support system. My findings indicate that when Chinese international students encountered culturally incongruent languaging experiences, their communication in academic and social contexts might be negatively influenced. When such cultural incongruency was accompanied by language difficulties, participants were likely to face even more challenges. On the contrary, when cultural congruency was present, Chinese international students often had positive languaging experiences. Thinking beyond language and paying attention to the role of culture, the findings of the study shed light on how the university support system could better support its international student populations.

Inaccurate Overgeneralization: Not Everybody Has English Difficulties

Academic English could pose significant challenges to multilingual students studying in Anglophone contexts who are simultaneously going through the transitions of trying to get familiar with English and learning all content-subjects through English (Brisk & Zhang-Wu, 2017). Chinese international students, especially those who are at the beginning stage of their overseas studies, are prone to many challenges related to the English language. As stated in Chapter 9, despite their high performances on the test of English as a foreign language (TOEFL), many Chinese international students, especially *regular high* students, have encountered substantial difficulties during their initial languaging journeys in college. Yet, this does not mean that all Chinese international college freshmen have encountered difficulties in English. Given the fact that Chinese international students represent a very diverse student population, it is inaccurate to come to the overgeneralization that all Chinese international students are struggling with English.

In Chapter 4, I touched on the within-group variability among Chinese international students pursuing higher education in America. Based on their previous language and educational backgrounds, I proposed a continuum of readiness for international studies in the US and categorized them into five sub-groups, including traditional *regular high* students, foreign language *regular high* students, international department *regular high* students, three-year *American high* students and four-year *American high* students (see Figure 4.1). In subsequent chapters, I illustrated the distinct college experiences of participants from different sub-groups. Although every student's languaging journey was unique, a pattern that could be seen was that *not* all Chinese international students were struggling with English. While *regular high* students like William, Matthew and Sarah were more likely to face challenges in linguistic functioning especially on arrival at Hillside, *American high* students such as Hugo and Rebecca encountered few language difficulties in college due to their previous exposure to English-medium instruction and US high school curricula. Therefore, although grouped under the same umbrella name of 'Chinese international students', not all the participants had difficulties in meeting the linguistic demands of college.

In spite of this, within-group variability has often been overlooked and the broad category of 'Chinese international students' has very often been mistakenly applied exclusively to refer to those *regular high* students who are more likely to face language difficulties (Zhang-Wu, 2018). Consequently, Chinese international students are frequently overgeneralized in educational research as having a language barrier (Wang, 2016), incompetent (Jiang, 2014), with language difficulties (Yeh & Inose, 2003) and deficient in English (Xue, 2013) among many other negative descriptions. Such an overgeneralization has not only oversimplified the rich diversity among Chinese international students, but it has also strongly reinforced a commonly held misconception blaming their lack of English proficiency for all the difficulties that Chinese international students have encountered during their overseas studies. Consequently, university support systems may not be able to look beyond addressing language difficulties among multilingual international students, leading to missed opportunities in addressing their various other needs.

Cultural Challenges of Chinese International Students' Communication in Academic Contexts

Beyond the potential difficulties in meeting the English demands across the disciplines, culture also serves as a key challenge during Chinese international students' initial college experiences. In this section, I present how three culturally incongruent aspects, namely Western-centered course content, distinct expectations on the same course across cultures and office hour consultations, could pose challenges to Chinese international students' initial languaging journeys in academic settings.

Cultural incongruence: Western-centered course content

Cultural incongruency caused by Western-centered course content has been found to contribute to languaging difficulties among Chinese international students, especially *regular high* graduates. According to my participants, philosophy, a mandatory undergraduate core course at Hillside University, was described as 'the most challenging' and 'GPA-unfriendly' course due to its extremely Western-centered content

(Interview, 8.30.18). During the initial interviews at the beginning of the semester, the *regular high* participants revealed their negative feelings about philosophy, describing it as a '死亡考验' (death challenge) (Interview, 8.30.18). While Pat and Larry dropped this course immediately after attending the first session, William decided not to register for philosophy until later in his undergraduate studies. Pat explained that despite his interest in philosophy in China, he decided to withdraw from the course for 'survival' purposes: '第一学期先保命要紧，还是等适应了再选哲学吧' (In the first semester, the priority is to survive. I'd better wait till later to choose philosophy) (Interview 8.30.18).

Although all Chinese international students experience taking philosophy classes as early as elementary school, the philosophical concepts taught in Chinese classrooms are quite different from those covered in American schools. While the philosophy they learned in China mainly focused on traditional Eastern schools of thought (e.g. Taoism, Confucianism) and concepts directly related to socialism such as Marxism, Leninism, Maosim and Deng Xiaoping Theory, philosophy education in the United States features Eurocentric content and Western wisdom. This has posed substantial challenges to Chinese international students' linguistic functioning in academic contexts. For instance, as vividly illustrated in Matthew's languaging journey (see Chapter 5), his lack of knowledge of the arguments of Aristotle and Plato put him at a disadvantage in contributing to oral discussions in class (Interview, 9.4.18).

When professors fail to take into consideration such a gap in students' culture-based funds of knowledge, Chinese international students could face additional academic stress. For instance, Matthew's philosophy professor had mistakenly assumed that all students were very familiar with *Confessions* prior to their college studies (see Chapter 5). Therefore, he assigned 7 out of the 13 books from *Confessions* for students to review after class, in addition to over 50 pages of regular course readings. While for most domestic students, reading the seven books was nothing more than a quick refresh of their memory, Matthew found this assignment extremely daunting and almost impossible to complete. As reflected in his bilingual language log, on average he spent over six hours on philosophy during a typical weekday. This triggered his negative attitudes toward this course, blaming his philosophy professor for being 'very unfair' and describing philosophy as 'an art of dying' (Interview, 11.21.18).

Cultural incongruence: Different expectations for the same course

Even when the course content itself may not be culturally incongruent, disciplines such as mathematics and music were found to be challenging to Chinese international students due their culturally incongruent course expectations.

Mathematics

All 12 students, regardless of their major, chose to take some form of mathematics classes during their first semester in college (e.g. *Calculus I*, *Calculus II*, *Business Statistics* and *Finance Probability*) as a means to '刷分' (boost their GPAs), '轻松拿A' (get an easy A) and '缓解其他课的压力' (balance off the stress from other courses) (Interviews, 8.30.18, 9.4.18, 9.6.18). According to my participants, there were two rationales behind their common interest in taking mathematics during the first semester. Firstly, compared with the situation in the United States, math education in China is widely known to be more intense and advanced; this naturally puts all Chinese international students at an advantage compared with their domestic peers. Secondly, echoing the widely held misconception regarding mathematics as a language-free discipline (Brisk & Zhang-Wu, 2017), my participants believed it would be easier for them to take a class 'full of numbers and calculations' where English skills were 'not important' (Interviews, 8.30.18, 9.4.18, 9.6.18).

In spite of their high hopes of having an easy time in mathematics, the Chinese international students were shocked to realize that different from math education in China, the same discipline had drastically different course expectations in the United States where simply getting the correct answers was by no means adequate (Interviews, 8.30.18, 9.4.18, 9.6.18). As described in Chapter 5, in addition to problem-solving skills, the ability to orally explain, discuss and persuade based on some given concepts or problem sets was also an indispensable part of the course expectation in American math classrooms. Having no experience in expressing their thought processes, the newly arrived Chinese international students were unable to persuasively articulate their problem-solving strategies in English. Due to the perceived cultural incongruence in mathematics, they were faced with significant challenges in their initial languaging journeys in college.

Music

Music education in China has been described as passive and receptive (Brand, 2004; Law & Ho, 2009). In Chinese K-12 education, the linguistic demands in music are relatively low, as students are rarely provided with the opportunity to critically examine the music and conduct appreciation and critiques in oral or written form. Instead, Chinese music classes are usually practice oriented, in which students are often expected to sing, dance or practice a certain musical instrument. Yet, contrasting with the situation in China, music education in the United States has remarkably higher linguistic demands. Based on the latest National Music Education Standards, in addition to those practice-oriented components as required in China, American students are also expected to 'identify', 'describe', 'demonstrate', 'interpret' and 'evaluate' musical ideas

(National Association for Music Education, 2014). In other words, while a certain music lesson in China and the United States may focus on the same song, their instructional focuses could be very different. Unaware of the distinct expectations and linguistic demands of the same disciplinary areas across the two cultures, Chinese international students are prone to additional academic challenges when taking music courses overseas.

For instance, believing that music was a practice-oriented course that could reduce her academic stress, Lily had confidently registered for the course long before the beginning of the semester: '这种水课就是让学生唱唱歌跳跳舞，既可以放松，还可以平衡其他课的读写压力' (such a super easy course that asks students to sing and dance will be relaxing and could balance the academic English reading and writing loads from my other courses) (Interview, 9.6.18). Nevertheless, on attending her first class, she was shocked by the very different expectations in Chinese and American music education. Intimidated by the heavy oral and written linguistic demands in music, Lily decided to immediately withdraw from the course due to its cultural incongruency:

> 吓死我了，老师一上来就让我们分析一首古典音乐，那些美国人都侃侃而谈，我超级懵逼。更夸张的是，他开学第三周就要交一篇1500字的论文！1500呀，比写作课还长！我选音乐是因为我喜欢跳舞唱歌，才不是来折磨自己写作文的呢！果断一下课就drop掉了。。。

> This has really scared me to death. Shortly after class started, the professor asked us to analyze some classical music. Those American students were all able to participate in the heated discussions, yet I was so confused. To make things worse, the professor asked us to submit a 1,500-word essay by the third week! It is 1500 words, longer than what's required from the *First Year Writing for Multilingual Students* course! I selected *Music* because I love singing and dancing. I am not here to torture myself by writing super long essays. Without any hesitation, I dropped that course right after the first class... (Interview, 9.6.18)

Cultural incongruence: Seeking support from office hour consultations

In academic contexts, the impacts of cultural factors on Chinese international students extend beyond their coursework experiences. Their support-seeking activities, especially getting help from their professors during office hour consultations, are also negatively influenced.

Office hour consultation is widely recommended as an important practice for college students to raise questions and receive feedback from their professors. While some research has been done focusing on factors that influence the frequency of students' office hour visits (Griffin *et al.*,

2014), others have examined the various benefits of office hour consultations on learners' academic performances (Schertzer et al., 2014). Since instructor–learner interaction beyond the classroom settings has been consistently found to be beneficial to students' academic well-being (Chickering & Gamson, 1986; Dika, 2012; Kuh et al., 2010), office hour consultations are usually perceived in an overwhelmingly positive light. As Chickering and Gamson (1986) summarized as the top element in their proposed *Seven Principles for Good Practice in Undergraduate Education*:

> Frequent student-faculty contact in and out of classes is the most important factor in student motivation and involvement. Faculty concern helps students get through rough times and keep on working. Knowing a few faculty members well enhances students' intellectual commitment and encourages them to think about their own values and future plans. (Chickering & Gamson, 1986: 3)

Despite the many benefits of office hour consultations, in order to take full advantage of this wonderful resource, students need to take the initiative to attend these meetings. Although this may sound easy, in reality seeking support from their professors during office hours has been found to be a daunting task to newly arrived Chinese international students due to its cultural incongruency. While initiating communication with professors during their office hours has been a common practice in US higher education, it is an extremely novel concept to newly arrived Chinese international freshmen. Their unfamiliarity with this Western-based support-seeking practice has challenged their ability to effectively navigate the university support systems.

Skeptical readers may argue that despite its popularity in American tertiary education, the concept of office hour consultation does not exist in K-12 education; thus, the challenges from initiating visits to professors' office hours is present among all college freshmen, regardless of their cultural backgrounds. Indeed, the actual action of visiting professors' office hour may be a new experience for domestic and international college students alike. Nevertheless, office hour consultation has long been present in US higher education and is widely promoted by popular mass media, university and high school counseling services, educational research and online forums among many other resources. These societal-level resources along with additional recommendations from family and friends based on their lived experiences have almost made office hour consultation an essential part of American culture. While not all domestic students have had first-hand experiences attending their professors' office hours, they are very likely to be familiar with the concept and have a good understanding of its purpose on arrival at college. Growing up in such a culture would therefore put American college students at a natural advantage in seeking support from professors compared with their international classmates.

On the contrary, newly arrived Chinese international students are very unlikely to have had any exposure or first-hand experiences with office hour consultation. On the one hand, in Chinese education, there has never been such a concept as office hours. Regardless of their grade levels, students are not expected to approach their instructors and initiate any personal connections beyond the classroom settings. Therefore, initiating a private conversation with their professors during office hours could be a daunting new task to most, if not all, Chinese international students, especially those facing additional language difficulties. On the other hand, as office hour consultation is a culturally incongruent concept that has never been part of the Chinese culture, newly arrived Chinese international students tend to be unclear about the definition and purpose of this instructional practice. Despite their need to be fully oriented when introduced to this common pedagogical practice, American higher education institutions may take it for granted given the popularity of office hour consultation in American culture. This could lead to inaccurate interpretations and misunderstandings about the concept, which may consequently exert negative influences on Chinese international students' academic well-being in the long run.

According to my participants, the importance of office hour visits was repeatedly emphasized at the freshmen orientation before the semester started; yet the exact definition and the purpose of office hour consultations were never clearly explained. While aware of its significance, most participants expressed confusion about the purpose and expectations of office hour visits at the beginning of the semester (Interviews, 8.30.18, 9.4.18, 9.6.18). Many guessed that office hours should be an opportunity for students to 'ask long and hard questions' which could not be solved by briefly communicating with professors before or after class (Interview 9.6.18). Matthew believed that office hour consultation was only necessary for struggling students and 'those who screwed up' (Interview, 9.4.18), while Larry speculated that it was a private space for students to impress the professors and establish close relationships by '送送小礼' (sending small gifts) and '说说好话' (complementing/saying nice words) (Interview, 8.30.18).

Due to their lack of knowledge on the purpose of office hour consultation, the majority of my participants had very limited experiences seeking support from their professors at the beginning of their freshmen journey at Hillside University. During their first month in college, some described that they '真想去又不敢去' (really wanted to take the opportunity, but were not brave enough to do so), while others never took the initiative in seeking support during office hours because they 'did not screw up' '没什么大问题问' (had no big questions to ask), '和教授没什么好说的' (had nothing special to talk with the professor) or simply felt worried that their low oral English proficiency would leave a bad impression in front of their professors (Interviews, 8.30.18, 9.4.18, 9.6.18). Due to their lack of knowledge on the office hour consultation, a perceived culturally incongruent practice, Chinese international students were unable to take full advantage of this very important academic resource. Since '[f]requent student-faculty contact in and out of classes is the most important factor in student motivation and involvement' (Chickering & Gamson, 1986: 3), their resistance to seeking support from their professors in turn put their overall academic well-being at a disadvantage during their initial college experiences.

Cultural Challenges of Chinese International Students' Communication in Social Contexts

In social contexts, Chinese international students' lack of cultural knowledge could exclude them from conversations with their native peers, resulting in misconceptions about their domestic peers, and further reducing their opportunities to socialize with American peers and engage in intercultural communication.

For instance, from the very start of the semester, Eva had complained that she was frequently isolated from conversations by her American roommates: 'They kept on laughing and chatting about "keeping up with the credentials" or something... What credentials? Why they have to keep up? I totally have no idea what they were talking about...' (Interview, 9.4.18). In this example, because of her lack of exposure to American media, the newly arrived international student was not able to understand the culture-specific topic *Keeping Up with the **Kardashians*** (which she misheard as 'credentials'), which is the name of a popular American reality television series. Due to this cultural barrier, despite her near perfect TOEFL score (115), Eva was excluded from conversations with her roommates.

Similarly, Pat was unaware of a culture-specific practice that Westerners often adopt to communicate with people they are not very familiar with – to use some non-controversial topic such as the weather as a conversation starter for small talk. He formed the misconception that Americans enjoyed chatting about topics which were '没营养的' (literal translation: nutrition-free, meaning superficial and meaningless). This resulted in his lack of interest in making friends with his American peers (Interview, 8.30.18). Pat shared his observations during history class. According to Pat, each time his American classmates saw each other before class, they would always spend about 10 minutes chatting about some 'meaningless topics' such as the weather (Interview, 8.30.18). Pat considered their behavior 'a total waste of time', and believed that his American classmates were keen on those 'meaningless' conversations because 'they must be afraid to let others know that they were lonely' (Interview, 8.30.18). He speculated:

她们每次都说这些没营养的东西，其实肯定是因为她们内心孤独，找不到别人说话，又怕被别人笑话。所以只能没话找话说，还常常笑出声，假装自己很开心。她们可以花上十分钟聊一下完全没意义的话题。我每次上课都听一个女生抱怨：啊，昨天好热！然后其他两个女生也随声附和。然后我就听她们接着说：我的宿舍好热啊，你的宿舍热吗？然后又能聊很久。。。在我们中国人看来，这简直难以理解——你和不熟的人有事就说，没事就闭嘴，谁会聊什么天气呢？*So what?* 聊了可以让天气变凉快吗？

Each time they always talked about those 'nutrition-free' stuff. This must be because they were very lonely at heart, and could not find friends to chat with. Since they were afraid to be laughed at being loners, they had to find stuff to chat about even though in reality they had nothing to say. They even pretended to be very happy by laughing out loud. They could spend 10 minutes talking about completely meaningless topics. Every time in class, I would hear one girl saying 'ah, it was so hot yesterday!' The other two girls would always agree with her. Then I heard that they would go on complaining about something like 'It was really hot in my dorm. How about yours?' Following this trend, they could continue their conversations for very long… From we Chinese's point of view, this was completely unbelievable—you talk to people you are not familiar with only when you have important things to say; otherwise, you remain in silence. Who will talk about weather? So what? By talking about it, the weather will get cooler? (Interview, 8.30.18)

By the same token, despite Matthew's confidence in his oral communication in social settings at the beginning of the semester, he later gave up his dream of dating an American girl due to what he described as unmanageable 'cultural differences' (Interview, 11.21.18). Matthew shared an unsuccessful experience communicating with a female domestic student. Despite Matthew's ability to understand her question, his lack of cultural knowledge of American popular sports made it extremely challenging for him to engage in the conversation:

我们聊天不到5分钟，她就突然问我 '*Who do you think will be the winner in tonight's game?*' 我当时就懵逼了。我连今晚有什么比赛都不知道，更不要说告诉她谁会赢了。太尴尬了。感觉他们美国女生都对体育特别感兴趣，什么*baseball, football*呀。我们中国人都不怎么关系这些体育项目的。文化差异太大，更不聊不到一起。

Less than 5 minutes into our conversation, she [the American girl] suddenly asked me, 'Who do you think will be the winner in tonight's game?' I was completely confused. I had no idea that there was a game that night, not to mention predicting the winner. It was too embarrassing. I feel American girls all have strong interest in sports, especially baseball and football. However, we Chinese do not care much about those kinds of sports. The cultural differences are too dramatic for us to communicate with each other. (Interview, 11.21.18)

Positive Influences due to Cultural Congruence

So far, culture has been discussed as a source of challenge for Chinese international students. All the cases above, be it subject learning in philosophy, music and mathematics, support-seeking from professors at their office hours or socializing with American peers, have indicated that when cultural incongruences occurred, Chinese international students were likely to face increasing languaging difficulties. Yet, it is worth noting that when cultural congruency is present, culture could also act as a positive force to balance out challenges from other aspects, such as English language difficulties and a heavy workload, to facilitate Chinese international students' languaging experiences in academic contexts.

For example, around half of the participants (Pat, Larry, Hugo, Shawn and Kristin) chose to take a course in the history department to fulfill one of the undergraduate core requirements of Hillside. Different from the courses provided by the philosophy department, in which students had no choice but to learn Western-centered knowledge, the history department offered students a much larger choice of classes. Thus, students were able to avoid culturally incongruent topics and select courses relevant to their own culture and interests, which resulted in their positive academic experiences.

All five Chinese international students who took history during their first semester ended up in Asia-related courses, which echoed their preferred cultural connections during content-subject learning. Kristin was enrolled in *Women in Modern Asian Society*, a 10-person discussion seminar, while the other four students chose to take *Asia in the World*, a lecture-style class composed of around 200 students. According to my participants, their rationales for choosing culturally congruent courses were three-fold. Firstly, knowing that history is a discipline with high linguistic demands in reading and writing, selecting a course with familiar topics would make it easier for them to tackle the reading and writing assignments. Secondly, my participants were very interested in the history of Asia back in China and they were curious to experience how Asian history was taught and viewed in Western education (Interviews, 8.30.18, 9.4.18). Lastly, the five participants mentioned that one of their biggest motivations in selecting courses on Asian history was because the professors for those courses were Chinese. While they were fully aware that having Chinese professors would not change the English-speaking nature of the courses, they claimed that this could at least provide them with some emotional support. As Larry put it,

'选课时一看到中国老师的名字就感觉亲切!' (During the course selection, I felt happy and relaxed the moment I saw Chinese professors' names!) (Interview, 8.30.18).

On taking these courses, my participants were faced with a heavy reading load and dense discipline-specific discourse that was 'constructed mainly through texts and [could] not easily be experienced hands-on' (Schleppegrell *et al.*, 2008: 176). Yet, owing to the cultural congruency of Asian history courses, neither the high linguistic demands nor the heavy workload in history exerted negative influences on Chinese international students' academic well-being. My participants explained that unlike their experiences in culturally incongruent courses such as philosophy, they felt 'superior', 'smarter' and 'more like an expert' in their history classes (Interviews, 8.30.18, 9.4.18). Their sufficient cultural knowledge on Asian history put them in a much more advantageous position compared to their American classmates. Despite the heavy workload and high linguistic demands in reading, the participants' perceived that cultural congruency not only lessened their academic difficulties but also motivated their content-subject learning. For example, describing his experience in history as 'exciting', Pat was thrilled that '终于有门课可以让我们秒杀所有美国人了' (finally there is a course in which we can beat all the American classmates easily) (Interview, 8.30.18). On *WeChat*, Pat posted a Chinese poem (see Figure 12.1) to express his passion for history. As shown in his poem, owing to his interest in learning Asian history, even tackling 50 pages of history reading in one night was not a problem (*WeChat* Observation, 10.10.18).

Concluding Remarks

This chapter closely examined the myth blaming Chinese international students' lack of English proficiency for all the challenges they face during their initial overseas college experiences. While English language proficiency is indeed one of the major challenges, it is inaccurate to assume that all difficulties facing Chinese international students are related to their limited ability to function linguistically in a new academic

	[Translation]
确认过眼神	Pat's post:
爱学这一门	I have firmly believed that
一晚五十页	Since I love this subject,
问题并不大	Finishing 50 pages of readings in
	one night
20 hours ago	Is going to be a piece of cake
	[liked by other Chinese peers]

Figure 12.1   An example of Pat's comment on history readings, 10/10/18

environment. It is important to think beyond language problems and situate Chinese international students' challenges in a broader context, especially in paying attention to the role culture plays in the process.

On the one hand, the term *Chinese international students* should not be associated with a static, homogeneous group, but rather a broad umbrella term for all international students of Chinese origin who have had various academic and language backgrounds. Given the heterogeneity of the group, it is therefore unfair to associate language difficulties with all Chinese international students. Considering their previous educational experiences, *regular high* students are more prone to be affected by the challenges of college academic linguistic demands compared with their *American high* counterparts. On the other hand, blaming English for the academic and social difficulties that Chinese international students encounter may mask the many challenges from culture, which could consequently lead to missed opportunities for the university support system to provide essential help as needed. Based on the findings of my study, when Chinese international students encountered cultural incongruences, they were likely to face many difficulties in their overall academic well-being. Courses with westernized content and expectations as well as academic practices that were perceived culturally incongruent were all examples of sources of challenges due to cultural aspects. Additionally, their lack of cultural knowledge may also hinder their ability to function linguistically in social settings and establish friendships with American students. Regardless of their high English proficiency, the cultural gap may lead to misconceptions about their American peers which could, in turn, discourage them from having meaningful conversations with domestic students to learn more about Western culture. In contrast, when cultural congruency was achieved, Chinese international students were likely to have positive experiences during their academic studies. In fact, owing to cultural congruency, the challenges from students' lack of English proficiency and heavy workload in certain courses were likely to be alleviated.

Because languaging is a social practice that never happens in a vacuum but occurs when multilinguals are actively navigating and negotiating their environments for communication purposes (Canagarajah, 2011; García, 2009; Jørgensen, 2008), it is important to situate participants' languaging experiences within the greater developmental contexts to look beyond language difficulties and consider the role of culture in their macrosystems (Bronfenbrenner & Morris, 2006). Raising awareness of influences from cultural factors could pave the way for the university support system to facilitate students' languaging success and overall academic well-being. To many, the phrase 'culture-related challenges' may sound depressingly meaningless, since it is impossible to eradicate the gap between Western and Eastern cultures. Yet, what I want to emphasize in this chapter is that in the context of supporting multilingual international students, many of the culture-related challenges, if fully understood, could be addressed by joint efforts from various parties in the university support system. To provide culturally and linguistically responsive instruction (e.g. Lucas & Villegas, 2010; Villegas & Lucas, 2002; Zhang-Wu, 2017), it is important to identify cultural gaps and take concrete action. For example, while it is impossible to completely overhaul the content of Western philosophy to focus on Eastern wisdom, creating an open and welcoming space that allows Chinese international students to bring their background knowledge to facilitate their understanding of the course content is helpful to strengthen cultural congruency. Ultimately, this will translate into more positive academic outcomes among students from culturally and linguistically diverse backgrounds. In Chapter 14, I provide more recommendations regarding how cultural congruency may be achieved to support Chinese international students from different levels of the university support system.

13 Myth 5: Chinese International Students are Well Supported in American Higher Education Linguistically and Academically

Introduction

As Anne Corbett (2016) once pointed out, 'no system of higher education and research can be purely national; neither higher education systems, nor the individuals within them, can prosper behind national walls'. The concept of the internationalization of higher education has received increasing attention in global society over recent years. On the one hand, the internationalization of higher education could bring about diverse perspectives and promote global collaboration. This outlook has been embraced by leaders of many internationally renowned higher education institutions. For instance, L. Rafael Reif, president of Massachusetts Institute of Technology, has publicly declared: 'As a community and as a practical force for good, MIT is... [d]elighted and energized by our diversity, with a meritocratic openness to talent, culture and ideas from anywhere' (November 9, 2016). Additionally, globalizing higher education by recruiting more and more international students could lead to substantial financial benefits. In the United States, the world's largest international host country, the continuously growing number of international students has exerted 'a significant positive economic impact' (Institute of International Education, 2020). In 2018 alone, international college students brought over $45 billion into the US economy (Institute of International Education, 2020).

A significant factor contributing to the growing internationalization of higher education is the influx of Chinese international students. According to a recent report from the Institute of International Education (2018), over the past decade China has been the leading country of origin for international students in the United States (33.2%), followed by India (17.9%) and South Korea (5.0%). Between 2006 and 2019, the number of Chinese international students pursuing overseas studies in the United States skyrocketed over five times, increasing from under 67,700 to 372,500 (Fischer, 2021). In fact, so many Chinese international students are studying in the United States that educational researchers Mengwei Su and Laura Harrison (2016: 913) noted in their article titled 'Being Wholesaled' that 'In an extreme case, 90% of the cohort at Ohio University's Master of Finance and Economics program (MFE) are Chinese'.

Given the welcoming attitude toward the internationalization of higher education in the United States and the soaring numbers of Chinese international students, a common assumption is that Chinese international students must be well supported in American higher education, both linguistically academically. Yet, is this really the case?

Drawing on data collected from semi-structured interviews, ongoing research memos, informal communications, bilingual language logs and *WeChat* observations, this chapter challenges the assumption by presenting how the university support system at Hillside has failed to support Chinese international students. In response to the inadequate institutional help, the participants ended up forming a strong within-group support system among themselves to facilitate their first-semester languaging experiences in college. The findings pave the way for discussing areas where American higher education could better support their multilingual international students, which is discussed further in Chapter 14.

'I don't think they care!': How the University Support System has Left Chinese International Students Under-Supported

In this section, my discussion focuses on two main sectors within the university support system that work closely with international student populations, namely the Office of International Students and Scholars (OISS) and faculty members. While both sectors have demonstrated their good intentions to care for international students, the support they provided was not always perceived sufficient in helping Chinese international students adjust to their initial languaging experiences in college.

'Just a format'? International students' perceptions on support from the OISS

According to its mission statement, the OISS at Hillside University aims to 'increase awareness of international student and scholar needs, promote intercultural competency across campus, and advocate for greater support for the international community'. Every year the OISS is responsible for planning and organizing international student orientation for first-year undergraduate and graduate students at Hillside. To better facilitate international freshmen's initial college experiences, the

OISS has also created a peer-to-peer support network which assigns upperclassmen as international assistants (IAs) to support newly arrived international students' initial academic and social adjustment at Hillside University.

Despite the good intentions of the OISS to support international students' overseas studies experiences, 11 of the 12 participants reported that they felt disappointed by the services provided by the OISS. Not only did they describe the OISS as 'just a format', but these Chinese international students also argued that the inadequate support from the OISS revealed Hillside's 'true motivations' in recruiting international students, which they believed were 'to make money', 'to increase diversity' and 'to boost up its ranking' (Interviews, 8.30.18, 9.4.18, 9.6.18).

The Chinese international students showed their strong dissatisfaction toward the international student orientation, complaining that it was 'poorly organized', 'too intense', 'too abrupt', 'boring' and 'very intimidating' because of its cultural incongruency and high linguistic demands (Interviews, 8.30.18, 9.4.18, 9.6.18). On the one hand, most participants found popular Western conventions such as icebreaker activities very uncomfortable and culturally incongruent, which hindered their languaging experiences. As *American high* graduate Rebecca complained, 'In China, people do not usually talk about personal stuff or hug each other unless they are close friends. Here, thanks to icebreakers, we were forced to act cheesy with strangers! Ugh... Excuse me, am I your friend?!' (Interview, 9.6.18). To most *regular high* students, the concept of icebreaker activities was even more challenging, as it was not only culturally incongruent but also entirely new. Struggling to figure out the purpose, expectations and rules of the icebreaker games while working through the discomfort of disclosing personal information and making physical contact with unfamiliar peers, the *regular high* students vented their disappointment blaming the organizers of the international student orientation for their lack of cultural sensitivity.

On the other hand, the orientation marked *regular high* students' very first experience communicating in an entirely English-speaking environment. When they were unable to join in the small talk with native speakers of English or they encountered communication breakdowns, these newly arrived Chinese international students tended to feel linguistically unprepared, embarrassed and helpless. These negative feelings further triggered their dissatisfaction toward the OISS, blaming it for not providing enough linguistic support prior to their arrival. As illustrated in Sarah's case (see Chapter 5), despite her high test of English as a foreign language (TOEFL) result and her strong desire to socialize with domestic students at the orientation, she found it almost impossible to have any meaningful conversation due to her inability to function linguistically upon immersion in an English-speaking environment: '虽然大家都很想聊天，但是大家说的话都听不太懂，就接不下

去，只能很尴尬地看着大家' (We all wanted to chat with each other, but since I could not understand what they said, I could not respond to their questions. The only thing I did was to stare at them, feeling very embarrassed) (Interview, 9.6.18). Sarah blamed the OISS for her negative experiences at the orientation, arguing that prior to the orientation, staff from the OISS should have offered international students opportunities to observe summer classes online and connect with domestic students via videoconferencing so as to get a sense of the authentic college-level linguistic demands and prepare themselves better prior to college entry.

In addition to their negative experiences at the international student orientation, 11 of the 12 participants were unhappy about their experiences with IAs. Although the IA program was established at the OISS with the good intention of providing newcomer international students with systemic, long-term, peer-to-peer support, my participants claimed that they did not feel any support from their IAs. Instead, they described the existence of the IA program as '走过场' or '形式化' (both meaning nothing but a format) (Interviews, 8.30.18, 9.4.18, 9.6.18). The most common complaint among my participants was that their IAs did not seem to care about them at all, and they seldom performed their many expected responsibilities such as frequent check-ins and long-term peer-to-peer support which they should have fulfilled based on the mission of the program. Half of my participants claimed that their contacts with their IAs were limited to the international student orientation, where they met each other for the first time. Despite their interest in getting to know more about their IAs and socializing with domestic students at the social gatherings organized by the OISS, the Chinese international students in my study soon realized that such events were poorly organized with an extremely low attendance rate. Bill shared his experience:

> 我就去过一次，本想找个机会和外国人说说话的。结果去了发现，加上我一共才这么几个人，太尴尬了。根本没人鸟这种活动，连我们自己的IA 都没去！我去了也谁都不认得，太无聊了。我反正以后再也不去了。。。

I only attended one social event organized by the OISS. Originally, I had planned to go there in the hope to meet and talk with some Americans. However, after I went there, I realized that including me, there were only a few students there. It was so embarrassing. Nobody cared about those events; even my IA ignored this event! I went there only to find that there was nobody that I knew there. It was so boring. Anyways, I will never go there again in the future… (Interview, 11.19.18)

Among the six participants who did somehow maintain connections with their IAs beyond the orientation, five shared negative experiences due to their IA's lack of cultural sensitivities. On the one hand, the participants complained that the small-group events organized by their IAs were somewhat culturally irrelevant, which made them feel unmotivated and intimidated to participate. For instance, Matthew received an invitation from his IA, to go kayaking. Yet, he had no idea what kayaking was, since it was not a common recreational activity in China. Consequently, Matthew decided to ignore the invitation and spent the weekend with his Chinese peers (Interview, 11.21.18). On the other hand, my participants felt marginalized and even discriminated against, complaining that some IAs showed a strong tendency to favor international students from other language and cultural backgrounds. For example, according to Shawn, all the Chinese students in his group were neglected after their first IA meeting. This was because his IA, an American upperclassman, was so passionate in learning and practicing Spanish with several Mexican international students in the group that he completely ignored everybody else (Interview, 8.30.18). Shawn still sounded furious when he reflected on this incident, 'It's Okay if you like Spanish and want to have more practice. But it's not Okay if you humiliate us by simply ignoring us!' (Interview, 8.30.18).

Despite their dissatisfaction with their IAs, however, my participants did not seem to be overly surprised by their lack of support. They told me that the lack of support from their IAs was 'highly predictable' and 'not surprising at all', since their IAs were busy college students who 'wanted to earn a decent stipend and brush up their resumes [by volunteering as IAs], but had no time to actually care about others' (Interviews, 8.30.18, 9.4.18, 9.6.18). Furthermore, since the low-quality services from their IAs were consistent across the international student community, my participants developed negative attitudes toward the OISS altogether. As Kristin explained:

> 本来我还觉的怎么IA都不管我，OISS 也没给我们什么特别的帮助，还有点不爽。后来一问周围同学，原来大家都一样，我也就完全不在乎了。直接忽略他们就好。

> Originally, I felt a little bit annoyed because I felt that I was left unattended by my IA and the OISS. But later, after asking around, it turned out that my friends were all in the same boat. Then I did not care anymore, I decided to directly ignore them [the OISS and IAs]. (Interview, 11.19.18)

Most participants' overall sentiment toward the OISS remained negative throughout their first semester in college. It is worth noting, however, that one student, Lily, who was the only student in my study to be assigned a Chinese upperclassman as her IA, shared very positive experiences with the services provided by the OISS. In addition to their shared cultural and language backgrounds, Lily's IA also happened to be from the same department studying the same major– applied psychology. Their identical backgrounds clearly benefited Lily, academically, culturally and emotionally. Throughout the semester, Lily's IA provided her with academic support, especially suggestions on course selections. Additionally, empathizing that newly arrived Chinese international students might feel homesick, Lily's IA frequently invited all the Chinese students in her group to Chinatown for dim sum and groceries, and showed them around local museums to familiarize them with American culture and history. Compared with her peers who were assigned domestic students as their IAs, Lily believed her shared culture and language background with her IA made it easier to seek support whenever necessary:

都是中国人，感觉就比较亲切，说什么都可以用中文，而且大家有什么问题直接都可以微信。不像是和美国*IA*，说什么都要发英文邮件很麻烦，而且又不熟，有什么事又觉得不好意思打扰他们。。。

Since my IA and I are both Chinese, we feel more connected, and can feel free to use Chinese whenever needed. If I have any questions, I can directly contact her via *WeChat*. However, if you have an American IA, then all communication has to be done via email in English, which is a lot of hassle. Moreover, you just don't feel close enough to them and thus feel shy to bother them with questions... (Interview, 9.6.18)

Lily's appreciation of the support she received from her IA could be observed in her *WeChat* public posts. For instance, as shown in Figure 13.1, Lily reported having had a great time at a social event organized by her IA, which she referred to as a 'mentor–mentee meeting' (*WeChat* Observation, 10.7.18). Toward the end of her *WeChat* post, Lily said that she felt sorry for a few friends who were not present at the event and offered them emoji kisses. Judging from her tone, it was very likely that this was not the first social outing organized by her IA, and students in Lily's group were very close to each other.

'It depends': International students' perceptions on support from faculty

Although, in general, my participants showed appreciation of the guidance and support they received from their professors throughout the semester, several students argued that the quality of faculty support needed to be considered on an individual basis. Among those Chinese international students who had mixed feelings toward their professors, the most common complaint was that while most of their professors showed sympathy toward their language struggles, few provided concrete support to facilitate their linguistic functioning in class. Almost all

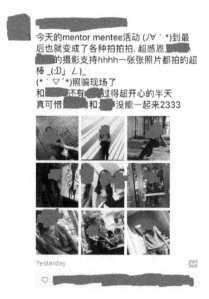

今天的mentor mentee活动 (/∀ ˋ ˙)到最
后也就变成了各种拍拍拍. 超感恩▮▮
▮▮▮的摄影支持hhhh一张张照片都拍的超
棒 _(:D」∠)_
(* ˋ ▽ ʻ*)照骗现场了
和▮▮还有▮▮过得超开心的半天
真可惜▮▮和▮没能一起来2333

Yesterday

[Translation]
Lily's post content: Today's mentor-mentee event [happy face emoji] turned into a photo shooting event. Big thanks to XXX who is a guru in taking pictures for us [laughing face emoji]

[shy face emoji] Let me show off some pictures from today

Had a great time with XXX and XXX. Unfortunately, XXX and XXX were unable to join us today [emoji showing kisses]

[Pictures from the event]

Figure 13.1   An example of Lily's experience with her IA, public *WeChat* post, 10/7/18

regular high students had, at some point, mentioned to at least one of their professors their concerns in relation to language barriers (Research Memo, 10.28.18). However, approximately half of the students reported that after hearing about their difficulties in English, their professors did not take any concrete action to help them. While almost all the professors showed sympathy on hearing their linguistic concerns, very few actually provided the students with additional linguistic or academic support, which included (1) initiating regular check-in meetings with the students; (2) requiring mandatory weekly office hour visits by the students; (3) recommending additional language resources; (4) connecting the students with some of their Chinese 'academic brothers and sisters' who had taken the same class in the past; and (5) promising to curve the students' score by focusing more on their content performance (Research Memo, 10.28.18).

In most cases, however, the professors were likely to either 'pretend as if nothing has happened' when they met again after the meeting, or do nothing except incorporate some 'random', 'unhelpful', 'funky' and 'totally irrelevant' Chinese expressions in their future communication to demonstrate their interest in and respect for the Chinese language and culture (Interviews, 11.19.18, 11.20.18). For instance, after Sarah had revealed her *regular high* educational backgrounds and concerns about her ability to function linguistically in English, one of her professors always tried to incorporate expressions like '你好' (hello), '谢谢' (thanks) and '不客气' (you're welcome) into their oral and email communication

(Interview, 11.20.18). Yet, Sarah was unhappy about that professor's frequent code-switching to Chinese. She complained that it not only embarrassed her in front of her American peers, but it was also unhelpful in improving her ability in linguistic functioning:

我觉得很无语啊。每次老师一说这些弱智的中文，美国同学就会一下都看着我，让我感觉好尴尬。其实他用不用中文我都不在乎啦，我的问题关键的是他得给我语言上的支持。弄到最后，我和他练习了几句中文，该*struggle*的地方我继续*struggle,* 一点用也没有。。。

I really felt speechless. Every time that professor used those stupid Chinese expressions to me, my American classmates would stare at me. This made me extremely embarrassed. In reality, I didn't really care about whether or not he could use Chinese; my only hope was to get support on language. Toward the end, I practiced a few Chinese expressions with him, but my struggles in English remained the same. This was totally unhelpful... (Interview, 11.20.18)

In even worse scenarios, two of my participants (Kristin and William) reported that they had professors who showed no empathy after learning of their difficulties in linguistic functioning, not to mention providing any comfort or concrete support. For example, Kristin decided to seek support from her history professor, who frequently described her essays as being 'in lack of depth' (Interview, 11.20.18). During their meeting, Kristin revealed her frustration at not being able to express her ideas clearly in English. She explained that despite her deep understanding, it was the language barrier that prevented her from providing a strong argument (Interview, 11.20.18). By confessing her weaknesses in English, Kristin had originally hoped that her professor would provide her with some concrete advice on how to meet the written linguistic demands of that course. Nevertheless, to her disappointment, Kristin's professor seemed to believe that it was her lack of effort rather than a language barrier that led to her unsatisfactory academic performances. 'You need to try harder', the professor told Kristin: 'History writing is hard for everybody!' (Interview, 11.20.18).

Similarly, William commented that the effectiveness of professors' support could be summarized in two words: 'it depends' (Interview, 11.20.18). Shortly after midterm, William contacted me through *WeChat* to share his painful experience of failing one of his exams. Despite his ability to comprehend and explain all the course concepts in Chinese, William was unable to accurately spell out the corresponding technical terms in English in the short-answers questions, which led to his unsatisfactory grade (Informal Communication, 10.30.18). William told me that he felt very guilty for letting his professor down and decided to post a sorry note on Twitter to apologize to the professor in public (Informal Communication, 10.30.18).

However, a few weeks later, William contacted me again, informing me that the professor had not only completely misunderstood his Twitter post, but also reported him to the Dean's office due to 'his public threat' (Informal Communication, 11.14.18). It turned out that right after sharing his frustration of failing the midterm exam due to his inability to spell discipline-specific jargon correctly, William mistakenly put down 'I am so sorry for my professor!!!!!!!!!' instead of 'I am so sorry for letting my professor down' which he had intended to say (Informal Communication, 11.14.18). Since the expression 'be sorry for somebody' was not an apology but rather a way to show sympathy, the professor mistook the post as a sarcastic way of showing William's anger, dissatisfaction or even hatred (Informal Communication, 11.14.18). This consequently led to William's miserable experiences in the Dean's office, as he desperately wanted to express himself yet without the linguistic ability to do so:

> 发了推特没多久，我就收到了一封邮件，说是来自Dean's Office，关于这个老师的课，想找我面谈。我当时很开心，还以为是这个老师觉得我由于语言障碍所以没考好，于是联系Dean's Office给我一个补考的机会。结果等我去了才知道，弄了半天，他认为我仇恨他，有心理问题，report了我去Dean's Office。。。太无语了，一上来，那个工作人员就说他愿意给我提供心理疏导。我当时就傻了，完全不知道怎么回事，我解释了半天他都没明白，我都不知如何是好。。。

Shortly after I posted the message on Twitter, I got an email from the Dean's Office. The email mentioned that somebody from the office would like to talk with me with regard to this professor's class. I was very happy then, believing that I was contacted, because the professor had understood my language barrier and spoken up for me to earn a second chance by having a make-up exam through the Dean's Office. Yet, it was not until I arrived at the appointment that I found out the professor must have misinterpreted my message, believing that I hated him and I needed psychological support. That's why he reported me to the Dean's Office... I was so speechless. Upon showing up at the meeting, the staff from the office told me that he would like to give me some psychological assistance. I was so confused. I was completely lost. Later, I tried to explain for a long time, but however hard I tried, he could not understand. I didn't know what to do... (Informal Communication, 11.14.18)

Although William was very frustrated over this incident, he felt lucky to be 'rescued' by another professor who was not only aware of the language difficulties that international students faced, but also offered him concrete support:

> 好在刚好我的另一个教授从这里经过，帮我解了围，还和*Dean's Office* 保证，说我是个好学生，每周都在去*office hour*，很努力，很积极，肯定不会仇恨老师。就是偶尔会有英语问题，所以导致了误会。然后我的教授还替我说话，说那个*report*我的教授一定是不了解国际生的困难，所以第一时间想到的不是和学生沟通，而是去打小报告。我当时真的好感动！

> Luckily, another professor of mine happened to pass by, who rescued me from the meeting. He assured the Dean's Office by saying that I was a good student, because I visited him during the office hours every week. Also, he added that I was a positive and hard-working person, who would surely not threaten or hate that professor. It must have been some language problems that had caused the misunderstanding. Later, he also spoke up for me, and said that the other professor must be someone who did not have a good understanding of the language difficulties of international students; therefore, his first instinct was to report me rather than to communicate with me. I was so grateful to him! (Informal Conversation, 11.14.18)

'We have to depend on each other!': Strong Within-Group Support among Chinese International Students

Faced with inadequate support from key units of the university support system, the Chinese international students formed a strong within-group support network to help each other survive their overseas studies at Hillside University and to cope with the many linguistic, academic, social and psychological challenges. As Sarah put it: '我们在中国小伙伴的互相支持下，在美国顽强地生活着' (Thanks to the mutual support among us [Chinese international students], we are still surviving fine in the United States) (Interview, 11.20.18).

'Our best mentors': Support from 'academic brothers and sisters'

All participants had experiences seeking support from Chinese upperclassmen, who they often referred to as 'academic brothers and sisters'. They generally found such academic support from Chinese upperclassmen beneficial, especially in guiding them through course selection and providing tips and advice on how to meet the oral linguistic demands in class.

With regard to course selection, most participants described the suggestions from their 'academic brothers and sisters' as the 'golden rule' (Interviews, 8.30.18, 9.4.18, 9.6.18). In fact, suggestions from Chinese upperclassmen were regarded as more precious than advice from their faculty advisors, because my participants believed that their 'academic brothers and sisters' were once in their shoes, which made it possible for them to evaluate and recommend courses from the viewpoint of Chinese international students (Interviews, 8.30.18, 9.4.18, 9.6.18). For instance, based on suggestions from his faculty advisor, Bill was originally enrolled in a course taught by a Chinese professor, hoping that their common Chinese backgrounds would help him succeed in the course. Nevertheless, Bill decided to drop that class immediately after hearing rumors from some of his 'academic brothers and sisters' that the Chinese professor had a tendency to be extra strict with Chinese students to show the university that he or she was not biased by their common ethnicity (Interview, 8.30.18).

Similarly, all the Chinese international students in my study held favorable attitudes toward the tips and advice provided by their 'academic brothers and sisters' on how to meet the oral linguistic demands (Research Memo, 9.14.18). The two most frequently adopted oral participation suggestions from Chinese upperclassmen were (1) to be patient and (2) to make connections to China.

The first piece of advice on being patient was addressing a common challenge encountered by many Chinese international students during group discussions. Since their American peers often talked very fast and frequently jumped back and forth into each other's speech, Chinese international students found it challenging to get the floor and contribute in oral discussions (Interviews, 8.30.18, 9.4.18, 9.6.18). In response to these difficulties in oral linguistic functioning, the 'academic brothers and sisters' shared their lived experiences and provided helpful tips. Based on the 'to be patient' strategy, the Chinese students were advised to stay silent, keep smiling and maintain direct eye contact with their American peers as they expressed their opinions. In this way, even though the Chinese students may not have the proper turn-taking strategy to have the floor during the discussion, eventually some American peers would be interested in knowing their opinions (Research Memo, 9.14.18). My participants found this strategy helpful, especially those who perceived themselves as introverts. Pat shared his experiences applying this strategy:

有时你越是想说，他们就越不让你说。你感觉插不上话，自然很郁闷，就更说不出了。但是，你要是有耐心，一直微笑地看着他们静静等，总有美国人会找你。要不然他们可能觉得冷落你半天不好意思，要不然就是他们好奇你对他们的观点有什么想法。就有一个美国人和我说 'You were smiling when I was talking. What do you think?'

Sometimes the more you want to talk, the more they [American peers] won't let you. If you cannot jump into the conversation, you surely will feel depressed and stressed, and will find it harder to express your opinions. But if you are patient enough, keeping on staring at them while smiling, eventually some Americans will find you. Maybe this is because they feel bad for ignoring you for quite a while, or maybe because they are curious about your thoughts on their opinions. Once there was an American student who gave me the floor by saying 'You were smiling when I was talking. What do you think?' (Interview, 8.30.18)

The second popular piece of advice from the 'academic brothers and sisters' was to make connections to China and Oriental funds of knowledge. This strategy was reported to be particularly useful by those who were enrolled in philosophy. Since the course content was heavily Western centered, Chinese international students were at a disadvantage in digesting course materials and contributing to oral participation. Additionally, the heavy reading load and frequent usage of technical terminologies in philosophy further added to Chinese international students' linguistic challenges. Using the strategy recommended by their 'academic brothers and sisters', my participants were able to draw on their background knowledge to show their expertise and engage in meaningful discussions. For example, when the whole class was comparing Plato and Aristotle's opinions, my participants adopted the strategy to intentionally make connections between Western schools of thought and the wisdom of famous Chinese philosophers such as Confucius. Since neither their philosophy professor nor their American peers were knowledgeable about Oriental philosophy, the Chinese international students were able to take advantage of their content expertise to gain the floor in oral discussions.

As a matter of fact, due to their shared language and cultural backgrounds, my participants regarded Chinese upperclassmen as their 'best mentors' toward the end of the semester, the academic support from whom was perceived as 'more convenient' than that provided by their professors (Interviews, 11.19.18, 11.20.18). For example, Sarah mentioned that because of the upcoming finals, she had many questions with regard to her computer science class (Interview, 11.20.18). According to Sarah, since she was not familiar with much of the technical jargon in computer science, whenever she needed to seek support from her professor, it usually took a long time for her to elaborate her questions and digest her professor's explanations (Interview, 11.20.18). However, when she sought help from her 'academic brothers and sisters' by communicating directly in Chinese via *WeChat* audio messages, she was able to express the questions and understand the explanations more quickly and easily (Interview, 11.20.18). She believed that since in Science, Technology, Engineering and Mathematic (STEM) courses it was more important to correctly solve the problems than learn to express discipline-specific technical jargon in English, it would be more efficient and effective to directly seek support from Chinese upperclassmen:

像这种*STEM*的课还是学长学姐来的快。大家直接中文交流，没有生词障碍，那些英文表达会不会都不重要，反正能把题目作对就好。

For these STEM related questions, support from the 'academic brothers and sisters' was more efficient. We could directly communicate in Chinese and do not need to worry about the barrier from unfamiliar vocabulary. It does not matter whether or not I know how to say those English expressions. For STEM problems, the key is to get the answers rights. (Interview, 11.20.18)

'We're all in the same boat': Support from Chinese freshmen peers

In addition to the helpful guidance from their 'academic brothers and sisters', the Chinese international freshmen were able to support each other emotionally, socially and academically (Research Memo, 9.21.18).

From the very beginning of the semester, the emotional support among Chinese international freshmen at Hillside was highly valued by my participants, who frequently described it as '一笔财富' (a treasure) and '温暖' (warm) (Interviews, 8.30.18, 9.4.18). Two participants explicitly pointed out that they had chosen to join Hillside over other elite universities because of its reputation of having a supportive Chinese international student community (Interviews, 8.30.18, 9.4.18). Matthew explained that since the total number of Chinese international freshmen was relatively small compared with many other universities, the students were more likely to know each other well and stick together

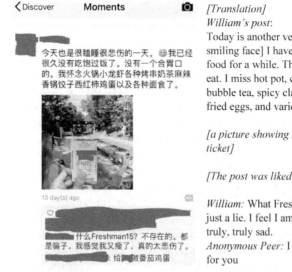

[Translation]
William's post:
Today is another very sleepy, sad day. [emoji smiling face] I have not had any appetite for food for a while. There's nothing that I want to eat. I miss hot pot, crawfish, Chinese barbecue, bubble tea, spicy clay pot, dumplings, tomato fried eggs, and various other Chinese food.

[a picture showing his hand holding a subway ticket]

[The post was liked by many other students]

William: What Freshman 15? It's not real. It's just a lie. I feel I am losing more weight. I feel truly, truly sad.
Anonymous Peer: I can cook tomato fried egg for you

Figure 13.2 Example of emotional support, William's public *WeChat* post, 9/15/18

when difficulties arose (Interview, 8.30.18). His view was supported by several other participants, who mentioned that owing to the support from their Chinese peers, they were able to conquer negative emotions due to language barriers, homesickness, loneliness and marginalization from the mainstream student group at Hillside (Interviews, 8.30.18, 9.4.18).

For instance, due to the stress of not being able to function linguistically in academic and social settings at the beginning of the semester, William felt depressed, homesick and had no appetite for any of the food served at Hillside Cafe (Informal Communication, 9.20.18). To vent his negative feelings, William posted on *WeChat* (see Figure 13.2), describing how miserable he felt and how much he craved Chinese food (*WeChat* Observation, 9.15.18). His post was liked by many Chinese peers, among whom some contacted him via personal message to offer him comfort (Informal Communication, 9.20.18). One of his peers even directly replied under his post, offering to make William tomato fried egg, a traditional Chinese dish that he had craved (see Figure 13.2). A week later, William told me that he felt so empowered and amazed by the emotional support from his peers that he felt 'very, very blessed' to be a member of the Chinese international student community at Hillside (Informal Communication, 9.20.18).

Such valuable mutual emotional support among Chinese international freshmen was present throughout the semester. An interesting pattern that was observed in the meantime was that the focus of Chinese international freshmen's support had shifted gradually with the passage of time. Earlier in the semester, Chinese international freshmen comforted each other and tried to form a strong support circle to reduce their initial college adjustment and homesickness, as illustrated by William's case above. As the semester progressed, Chinese international freshmen's mutual emotional support started to focus more on cheering each other up and relieving academic stress. For example, Larry was faced with a heavy workload at the end of the semester, and he vented his stress on

[Translation]
Larry's post content: I hope I can successfully survive this week [hoping face emoji]

[the post was liked by his peers]

Another student: I hope so too. I have a 4-page paper plus another exam from XXX professor, plus an expressionist painting (I have no idea about it at all)

Figure 13.3   Example of peers' emotional support, Larry's public post, 12/4/18

[Translation]
Pat's post content: Group study to review for the History final! Anybody who is still awake and would like to join me?

Pat: Can we use Hillside's group study room?
Another student: Count me in, count me in. I see hope to survive!

Figure 13.4 Example of peers' emotional support, Pat's public post, 12/10/18

WeChat wishing to survive his busy week (see Figure 13.3). The post was liked by a few peers, among whom one student showed empathy by commenting 'I hope so too' and shared her own burden and stress in order to comfort Larry (*WeChat* Observation, 12.4.18). In another example, Pat posted on *WeChat* around midnight, asking whether any peers who were still awake would like to form a study group to prepare for the history exam together (see Figure 13.4). In response to his post, a peer showed excitement about this idea, and not only immediately agreed to join him, but also expressed that he saw 'hope to survive' thanks to the late-night study group (*WeChat* Observation, 12.10.18).

Beyond emotional support, their mutual social support helped to provide Chinese international students with resources to tackle everyday problems. On my participants' *WeChat* posts, mutual social support frequently occurred throughout the semester, covering all dimensions of their daily life experiences, ranging from where to buy soy sauce, which Chinese restaurants had discounts, which bubble tea shop provided the most authentic Chinese drinks, to how to mail gifts to their friends and families in China among many others. In one *WeChat* post, for example, William asked about the distance between his current location and another city where his good friend lived (see Figure 13.5). A few minutes after posting, his problem was solved by his freshmen peers (*WeChat* Observation, 9.22.18).

[Translation]
William's post: My *WeChat* friends!!! How long does it take to travel from Anonymous City A to City B!!!

William: See you all soon!! I am so exacted!
Anonymous Peer: it takes 6 hours by car

Figure 13.5 Example of support seeking among peers, William's public *WeChat* post, 9/22/18

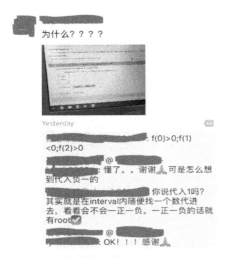

为什么？？？？

Yesterday

: f(0)>0;f(1)<0;f(2)>0

@
: 懂了。。谢谢🙏可是怎么想到代入负一的

你说代入1吗？
其实就是在interval内随便找一个数代进去，看看会不会一正一负。一正一负的话就有root✅

@
: OK！！！感谢🙏

[Translation]
Eva's post: Why????
[A picture showing that her answer to a math problem was wrong]

Anonymous Peer: f(0)>0; f(1)<0; f(2) >0
Eva @ Anonymous Peer: I got it... Thanks [grateful emoji] But how did you think of using -1 as an example
Anonymous Peer: Are you talking about using 1 as an example? In fact, I randomly picked numbers within the interval to see whether both positive and negative results would show up. Once we see one positive and the other negative, then it will have root [emoji showing correct answer]
Eva @ Anonymous Peer: OK!!! Thank you [grateful emoji]

Figure 13.6   Example of support seeking among peers, Eva's public *WeChat* post, 9/18/18

Last but not least, their mutual academic support was beneficial in providing quick solutions to difficult homework questions. Being able to ask, answer and discuss academic problems drawing on their shared linguistic resource, Mandarin, made my participants feel at ease when clarifying their statements, raising follow-up questions and double checking their understanding (Interviews, 11.12.18). For instance, in her *WeChat* post, Eva asked for help with her math homework (see Figure 13.6). Immediately after she posted a picture of the question and put down the word 'why' followed by four question marks, another Chinese freshman peer not only posted detailed explanations, but also answered Eva's follow-up questions (*WeChat* Observation, 9.18.18). Tapping into their rich communicative repertoires, the two students engaged in multilingual and multimodal communication to solve the math problem (see Figure 13.6).

Concluding Remarks

This chapter has challenged the myth assuming that Chinese international students are well supported linguistically and academically by the university support system. Despite the rising popularity of the internationalization of higher education and Chinese international students' interest in pursuing overseas studies in the United States, the university support system at Hillside did not provide sufficient resources to facilitate participants' initial languaging journeys in college. Yet, since developing individuals are not passive recipients of their external factors but active change agents who have the power to alter their trajectories (Bronfenbrenner & Morris, 2006), the Chinese international students ended up forming a strong within-group support system to collaboratively cope with their linguistic and academic difficulties, which consequently facilitated their emotional, social and academic well-being during their initial languaging journeys in college. In this process, the Chinese international students tapped into multilingual and multimodal resources in their communicative repertoires (e.g. Mandarin, English, numbers, emojis and images) to fulfill communication purposes. This reflects the nature of languaging as a social practice, in which languagers adopt their agency to pick, choose and creatively combine relevant codes in their linguistic repertoires to facilitate meaning-making and navigate various contextual situations (e.g. Canagarajah, 2011; Jørgensen, 2008; Pennycook, 2010; Swain, 2006).

It is worth noting, however, that while in the short term (i.e. during their initial college experiences) the within-group support system that the Chinese international students established in response to the failing university support system was found to be beneficial emotionally, socially and academically, excessive reliance on the within-group support system among Chinese international students may lead to enclaved experiences in the long run. Socializing and seeking support exclusively within the Chinese international student community throughout their college studies may potentially deprive students of many valuable opportunities for intercultural communication and thus lead to segregated experiences. For instance, as reflected in her weekday and weekend bilingual language logs, Sarah's enclaved experiences somewhat defeated the purpose of her overseas studies (see Chapter 5). Sarah was so dependent on her Chinese friend circles that she felt isolated in her American higher education experiences. Therefore, although it is important to acknowledge the many benefits of such a strong within-group support system, merely depending on efforts from the Chinese international student community is not enough to facilitate students' long-term success in their overseas studies. To put it another way, joint efforts from the university support system are indispensable. In Chapter 14, the concluding chapter of the book, I discuss concrete suggestions on how to improve the quality of institutional support.

14 Revisiting Myths and Realities

Introduction

I opened the book with an overview of the need to study Chinese international students' initial languaging journeys in American higher education institutions. Based on my review of the literature on the gap between Chinese international students' English as a foreign language (EFL) education in China and the linguistic demands of American higher education, I presented my theoretical framework as well as my study design (Part 1). Drawing attention to the within-group dynamics among Chinese international students, I then proposed a continuum to capture their academic and language experiences prior to college entry and presented the case studies of five focal participants representing each of the categories on the continuum (Part 2). In Part 3, I shifted my focus back to all 12 participants and strived to debunk five commonly held myths about Chinese international freshmen's linguistic functioning and cross-cultural experiences. In this chapter, I first revisit and revise the theoretical framework of the study based on my research findings. Informed by the updated theoretical framework, I discuss the implications for Chinese international students, for American higher education support systems as well as for research methodological innovation. Finally, I close the book pointing out the limitations of the study and directions for future research.

Revisiting the Integrated Model of the Theoretical Framework

As detailed in Chapter 2, the theoretical framework that guided my study is an integrated model of the Bioecological Model of Human Development (Bronfenbrenner & Morris, 2006) and the concept of languaging (e.g. Canagarajah, 2011; García, 2009; Jørgensen, 2008). Such a theoretical framework allowed a close investigation of my participants' first-semester language and academic experiences across time and contexts; from this framework, participants' languaging journeys were examined as a developing process rather than a static concept. To be specific, in Chapters 5 and 6, I presented the data on five focal participants following the developmental stages of the semester as indicated in the chronosystem. In Chapters 9 through 13, I organized the general findings of the study into five myths and realities, capturing the participants' multimodal and multilingual languaging experiences across their micro, meso, exo and macrosystems.

Reflecting on the findings of my research, I customized the original model to better capture Chinese international students' first-semester experiences in American higher education. An updated theoretical framework of Chinese international students' initial overseas college experiences is shown in Figure 14.1. Compared with the original model presented in Chapter 2, the following changes have been made to reflect the specific characteristics of Chinese international students' transitional languaging experiences during their first semester in college.

Firstly, at the exosystem, I added a few more elements that were found to be influential based on my participants' experiences, including the large number of Chinese international students, their socioeconomic status (SES), tutors, teaching assistants (TAs) and the Office of International Students and Scholars (OISS). Secondly, I specified major factors in the chronosystem of Chinese international freshmen, namely the different stages during the semester as well as their previous language and education experiences. This decision was made based on the findings of

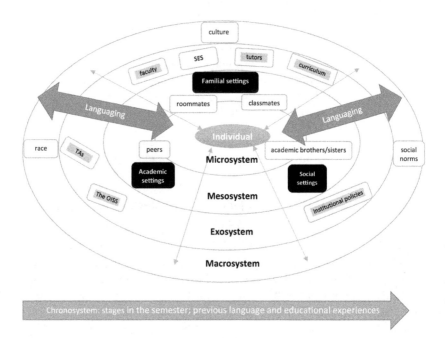

Figure 14.1 Integrated model revisited: Chinese international students' initial experiences

my research, in which I recognized that participants' first-semester college experiences may vary across different stages of the semester (e.g. in the first week of the semester vs around final exams) and are heavily dependent on their previous language and academic experiences prior to college entry (e.g. experiences with English-medium instruction, familiarity with American high school curricula).

Thirdly, I generated some bidirectional arrows, pointing from individuals back to their surrounding micro, meso and exosystems. By doing so, this revised model emphasizes the power of developing individuals as change agents. While the various contextualized factors in micro, meso and exosystems are constantly shaping Chinese international students' initial overseas college experiences, my participants also exerted counterforces against influences from these three layers of environments. In other words, rather than being passive recipients of external influences, individuals may also have the power to change their most immediate environment (e.g. at the microsystem, Chinese international students form a strong within-group support system), to make active decisions in the interactions between factors in the microsystem and beyond (e.g. at the mesosystem, Hugo chose to socialize mainly with newly arrived Chinese students in academic and social settings to preserve his heritage language and culture) and to cope with challenges encountered in the indirect environment (e.g. at the exosystem, William aggressively sought support from his professors through office hour consultations).

Last but not least, while the majority of the external forces in the exosystem may be difficult to change, I have identified six external factors (colored in grey, Figure 14.1) that could possibly be addressed by American higher education to better facilitate Chinese international students' initial languaging experiences. These factors include faculty, TAs, tutors, curricula, the OISS and institutional policies. In the following sections, I draw on the revised theoretical framework to inform my discussion of the research implications for Chinese international students and the university support system.

Implications for Chinese International Students' Successful College Adjustment

Chinese international students, situated at the center of the framework, are constantly influenced by their direct and indirect environments (micro, meso, exo and macrosystems) and the passage of time (chronosystem). Yet, as illustrated in Figure 14.1, instead of being passive recipients, they have the power to take an active role in determining how they respond to various external forces. To embrace their agency and take the initiative to cope with the challenges posed by their environments at the initial stage of their overseas college experiences, Chinese international students are advised to (1) understand their within-group variability through a developmental perspective and (2) take advantage of both within- and beyond-group support systems.

Understanding within-group variability from a developmental perspective

One of the themes that persisted throughout the semester was the divide between the *American high* and *regular high* Chinese international students. Whether it was their linguistic functioning in academic and social settings or their coping strategies, there were substantial differences between the two groups. Generally speaking, the *regular high* participants were comparatively more likely to resort to their heritage language, socialize with peers with similar backgrounds and experience various degrees of difficulties in their linguistic functioning across contexts. In contrast, the *American high* participants demonstrated relatively smoother transcultural and translingual processes during their first semester at Hillside, were less likely to encounter language difficulties and showed more familiarity with American culture, curricula and content-subject learning via English.

Beyond the dichotomy of *regular high* and *American high* students, I further proposed a continuum to capture Chinese international students' within-group variability and categorized them into five groups based on their previous language and education experiences (see Chapter 4). As reflected in the continuum (see Table 4.1), my participants' different degrees of cultural, linguistic and academic acculturation prior to college entry already positioned them at different starting points on arriving at Hillside University. To be specific, the students who had least exposure to the English language or to native speakers of English, as well as the American education system were those who attended the so-called traditional *regular high* schools in China. These students were the least prepared for college studies overseas on arriving at Hillside. Next on the continuum were students from the so-called foreign language *regular high* schools in China. While also unfamiliar with American high school curricula, these students were in a slightly more advantageous position at the beginning of their overseas college journeys given their experiences of having native speakers as their English teachers. In the middle of the continuum were students from the so-called international department within *regular high* schools in China. These students engaged in test preparation for overseas college studies and were familiar with American high school curricula, putting them in a more acculturated position compared with their traditional and foreign language *regular high* peers. Depending on the school, however, the international department *regular high* students may or may not have been exposed to native English speakers as their teachers, making them prone to challenges in linguistic functioning. Toward the right end of the continuum were students who had spent three to four years in American high schools. Their previous years of immersion in American high schools had prepared them to meet the oral and written linguistic demands of college, leading to their smoother college adjustment compared to peers with different language and academic backgrounds. Therefore, compared with their *regular high* peers, *American high* students demonstrated significantly fewer struggles linguistically, academically and culturally.

Interestingly, however, despite the importance of such a continuum in understanding Chinese international students' within-group variability and their degree of readiness for overseas college studies, none of the participants in my study seemed to have noticed their unique challenges and advantages given their previous language and education experiences. Instead, the participants insisted on categorizing themselves based on the dichotomy of *American high* or *regular high* students. This led to persistent tensions between the two groups. On the one hand, the *regular high* students showed unfavorable attitudes toward their *American high* peers, especially with regard to their frequent English usage and friendship with domestic students. They interpreted these as deliberate acts by *American high* students to show off their high English proficiency. For instance, Bill complained to me that one *American high* student living on the same floor always 'show[ed] off' by talking to him in English (Interview, 11.19.18). Bill commented with contempt, '都是中国人，你装什么逼假装ABC？也不看看你其实也有口音！' (We are all Chinese. How dare he shows off by pretending to be a Chinese American? Before he talks, he should understand that he has an accent too!) (Interview, 11.19.18). On the other hand, the *American high* students compared their *regular high* counterparts to 'sticky rice' who stuck together talking in Chinese, and criticized their reluctance to step out of their comfort zones (see Rebecca's case in Chapter 6). Such tensions remained throughout the Chinese international students' first-semester college experiences studying at Hillside University.

The constant divide between the two groups of Chinese international students, however, did not infer that the seemingly linguistically struggle-free *American high* students were superior compared with their *regular high* counterparts. Instead, it simply illustrated the distinct stages the participants were at in terms of their linguistic acculturation into an English-speaking environment. Compared with their *regular high* peers, the three *American high* students had been immersed in English-medium instruction and American high school curricula for at least three years prior to college entry, during which they had gone through various linguistic and cultural adjustments. By the time they arrived at Hillside, they were naturally placed at a more advanced stage in their linguistic transition. In other words, rather than being superior or completely linguistically problem-free, *American high* students might be better defined as 'ex-strugglers' who had already experienced the many challenges and difficulties of linguistic acculturation during their high school years in America. In contrast, *regular high* international freshmen were still at the beginning stage of their linguistic transition. Therefore, they were naturally more prone to various linguistic, academic and cultural challenges.

From a developmental perspective, the tensions between the two groups of students identified in my study were largely due to their lack of awareness of the contrasting linguistic transitional stages in which they were situated. To be specific, instead of interpreting *American high* students' frequent English usage and friendship with American peers as deliberate actions to mimic Chinese Americans or to show off their high English proficiency, it is more likely that such behaviors naturally reflected the characteristics of those international students' advanced stages during their linguistic acculturation. In fact, when *regular high* students eventually reached similar stages later in their overseas studies, they also demonstrated such a tendency of frequent English usage and socialization with domestic students. By the same token, *regular high* students were likely to socialize with their own kind and frequently resort to their heritage language because they were still at the earlier phases in their linguistic transition. They needed the additional linguistic, emotional and academic support from peers with similar language and education backgrounds to facilitate their transition into English-speaking academic and social contexts. It is again highly possible that *regular high* students' 'sticky rice' behavior toward which their *American high* peers showed unfavorable attitudes might be something they themselves had already experienced years ago when they first arrived in American high schools.

Understanding their initial college experiences from a developmental perspective could benefit *American high* and *regular high* students alike. To be specific, not only would it reduce their biases and hostility toward each other, but it could also encourage these developing individuals to actively seek support to cope with the challenges from their layers of surrounding external systems. It is true that *American high* Chinese international students are already at relatively advanced stages of academic and linguistic acculturation. Yet, socializing and supporting their *regular high* peers provides valuable opportunities for *American high* students to reflect on their initial transcultural, translingual and transnational transitions when they first entered American high schools years ago. Such reflections help American high students understand the developmental nature of their languaging journeys, which could facilitate their further acculturation and benefit their future studies at an American higher education institution in the long run.

On the contrary, *regular high* students are still at the early stages in their academic and linguistic acculturation, and thus face various challenges studying in an unfamiliar cultural and linguistic environment. If they can view the two groups' differences in linguistic functioning through a developmental perspective, the *regular high* students are more likely to seek support from their *American high* peers. Given their identical age and shared heritage language, cultural background and experiences with Chinese elementary and middle school education, *American high* students have excellent potential to function as peer mentors to support *regular high* students. In particular, they have great potential to function as an alternative resource when the university support system fails to provide assistance as needed. For example, due to the high demand for writing support around midterm, it proved extremely competitive to make appointments with tutors to seek writing support from Hillside Writing Center. Lily was fortunate that under such circumstances she could send her essays to an *American high* classmate who was experienced in academic English writing and also had substantial knowledge of the norms and thought processes of Chinese writers (Interview, 11.19.18). Similarly, Larry found the support of his *American high* peers effective and beneficial because of their familiarity with some discipline-specific expectations in American education. He shared his experiences in chemistry class:

> 在中国化学课我们一般做实验，把结果简单记录一下就好。在美国这里，老师叫我们详细观察，要把实验报告写的越详细越好。我都不知道格式怎么写，也不知道如何详细描述。每次班里美国同学都在做实验时拼命打字记录，我都不知到怎么写。好在有个美高女生和我一个班，她每次实验报告都几乎满分，因为她在美高都练过。我就跟她学，在她的帮助下，我的报告也都有平均分以上了。

In China, when we did experiment in chemistry class, usually we only needed to briefly document the results. However, in the US, the professor required us to observe carefully and provide as much details as possible for the lab reports. I did not know what the format of writing should be; nor did I have any idea about how to describe in detail. Every time, the American students were typing like crazy to take notes on the details of the experiment, but I did not have any idea how to write a report. Luckily, there was an "American high" girl in my class. She received near-perfect scores for all her lab reports, because she had experiences with writing reports in high school. So I asked for help from her. Under her guidance, I was able to achieve above-average scores on my reports. (Interview, 11.20.18)

Taking advantage of both within- and beyond-group support systems

As mentioned in Chapter 13, the Chinese international students formed a strong within-group support system that demonstrated great potential to benefit its members, academically, socially and emotionally.

For one thing, their shared mother tongue allowed newly arrived Chinese international students to communicate freely, be it to seek academic support, to ask for help in social dimensions or to establish close friendships. For another, when the university support system to some extent failed to facilitate a smooth translingual, transcultural and transnational transition, the strong network from the within-group support system could orient newcomer Chinese international students during their initial overseas college experiences and reduce the cultural shock.

Yet, I argue that in order for Chinese international students to fully exercise their power to fight against challenges from their environments, it is important to strike a balance in their navigation of within- and beyond-group support systems. In other words, in addition to seeking support from their Chinese peers, it would also be beneficial if Chinese international students explored and took advantage of the university support system.

Despite its many advantages, relying exclusively on a within-group support system may lead to enclaved experiences, which could ultimately have a negative impact on Chinese international students, academically, socially and psychologically. For instance, as illustrated in the stories of Matthew (see Chapter 5), depending excessively on his Chinese peers to solve academic challenges not only made him accidentally acquire misinformation from course readings, but also discouraged him from trying to meet the oral linguistic demands in mathematics. Similarly, in the case of Sarah (see Chapter 5), her overreliance on the companionship of her Chinese peers, especially her roommate, both added to her psychological burden of feeling suffocated and segregated, and prevented her from socializing with domestic peers.

In contrast, when participants managed to resort to both within- and beyond-group support systems, they were likely to have a smoother initial college experience. This is probably because since both support systems have their limitations, strategic reliance on both could provide Chinese international freshmen with the greatest support as needed. For example, due to his traditional *regular high* school background, William had initially been positioned in the least advantageous position on the developmental continuum. Yet, owing to his support seeking from not only his close Chinese peers but also his American professors and peers, William made substantial progress in his linguistic functioning and initial academic adjustment (see Chapter 5). Additionally, different from Matthew and Sarah, he was able to maintain his close circle of Chinese peers while also establishing friendships with domestic students, which further facilitated his psychological well-being and accelerated his initial college transition. As a result, toward the end of the semester, William ended up at a relatively more advanced developmental stage compared with many of his peers who had had more exposure to American culture and language.

Implications for How American Higher Education Support Systems could Better Support Newcomer Chinese International Students

Based on the findings of my research, I have identified six factors, including the OISS, institutional policies, curriculum, faculty, TA and tutors, which could be enhanced to provide Chinese internationals students with better support during their initial languaging experiences studying in American higher education institutions (highlighted in green/grey in Figure 14.1). These factors touch on university administration as well as higher education curriculum and instruction. Informed by the revised theoretical framework, I present implications for both areas.

University administration

The university leadership plays an important role in supporting international students' translingual, transcultural and transnational adjustment as well as their academic well-being at large (Williams, 2013). Drawing on the findings of my study, instead of adopting an English-only policy at the local context to help multilingual international students 'learn English', university officials from various support divisions need to cultivate a welcoming attitude toward cultural and linguistic diversity across the institution. Multilingual international students should be treated as individuals with the ambition to cultivate global citizenship rather than English language learners who are desperate to assimilate at the cost of leaving their diverse funds of knowledge outside of the classroom door. It is recommended that alongside American higher education institutions' aggressive plan to attract international applicants, emphasis should also be put on their commitment to support students from culturally and linguistically diverse backgrounds. Higher education leadership needs to understand the dynamics and developmental nature of multilingual students' transcultural and transnational languaging practices and take concrete action to create an embracing environment and to provide training, workshops, events and colloquiums to raise cross-cultural awareness among all members of the university community.

Working closely and directly with international student populations, the OISS plays an important role in facilitating those learners' academic, linguistic and psychological well-being during their overseas studies. Informed by the findings of my study, it is recommended that the OISS take concrete steps to support Chinese international students' initial college adjustment before, on and after arrival in the United States. A few months prior to the start of the fall semester, the OISS could provide opportunities for multilingual international students, especially those with no previous schooling backgrounds in the United States, to experience authentic English-speaking environments through virtual seminars, online workshops and remote meetings with their IAs prior to the start of the semester. If possible, the incoming international students could also be invited to 'sit in' on a few sessions of summer courses through remote education platforms in order to get a sense of the discipline-specific linguistic demands and course expectations. These activities could alleviate international college freshmen's initial linguistic shock and contribute to their long-term college success. For instance, 30 minutes of virtual participation in a college-level math lecture would raise the incoming international students' awareness of the different expectations and linguistic demands of Western mathematics courses. This would make it possible for international students to preview discipline-specific vocabulary and expressions over the summer in preparation for their upcoming college studies overseas.

During international student orientation, which takes place on international students' arrival, the OISS should explicitly explain the dynamics and within-group variabilities among international students from the same cultural and ethnic backgrounds. Students need to be trained to adopt a developmental perspective to understanding the prolonged process of linguistic acculturation. This will not only help prevent ongoing tensions between *regular high* and *American high* students, but also facilitate important mutual support among the international student community. Based on the findings of the study, *American high* students may serve as a crucial source of support for their *regular high* peers due to their shared cultural background, higher English proficiency and better understanding of the American education system. In addition, foundational academic knowledge and social skills should also be explicitly taught during international student orientation to facilitate Chinese international students' smooth transition from secondary to higher education, from China to the United States and from Chinese to an English-speaking environment. Mini lessons on topics such as the purposes of office hour visits, how to make appointments with professors through email correspondence and common ways to initiate a casual conversation with American peers could function as beneficial resources that would facilitate Chinese international students' navigation of American higher education.

Throughout the semester, the OISS needs to promote cultural and linguistic congruences in every stage of its activity planning and implementation. It is important for the OISS to design activities that strike a balance between introducing Western culture and connecting to the international students' cultural and ethnic backgrounds. For instance, not only should international students be invited to experience Western traditions such as Halloween and Thanksgiving, but they also need to be provided with ample opportunities to cherish their own cultural traditions. One possible solution is to encourage international students to volunteer and help organize institution-wide events that represent their cultural backgrounds (e.g. Lunar New Year, Mid-Autumn Festival). Through these experiences, international students could be empowered by their role as cultural ambassadors. This could, in turn, motivate them to learn about other cultural traditions and participate in the various other events hosted by the OISS.

Furthermore, the OISS needs to be more mindful about their IA training and placement. Extensive professional development support should be provided to IAs to raise their cross-cultural awareness and welcoming attitudes toward diversity and inclusion. It is hoped that in this way, they would treat their mentees with proper respect and plan social events that are relevant to their cultural and linguistic backgrounds. Additionally, based on Lily's positive experiences, it is suggested that if possible, upperclassmen who have extensive knowledge of international students' linguistic and cultural backgrounds could be recruited as IAs and paired with newcomer international students. In this way, newly arrived international students are less likely to feel isolated and would be more comfortable in approaching their IAs for communication and support.

Tertiary-level curriculum and instruction

Tertiary-level curriculum and instruction exert a direct influence on international students' initial college experiences (Fry *et al.*, 2008). Based on the findings of the study, it is necessary for higher education teaching forces (e.g. faculty members, TAs and tutors) to have access to professional development training, in which they learn about the importance of delivering culturally and linguistically responsive instruction to serve the needs of their bilingual students. It is hoped that through these opportunities, they could acquire foundational knowledge about important topics such as second language acquisition and emergent bilinguals' writing styles influenced by their cultural backgrounds, as well as strategies to engage bilingual international students in course discussions. In particular, since newly arrived international students' linguistic transition is a prolonged process and it is natural for multilingual languagers to constantly draw on the resources in their rich linguistic repertoires to fulfill communicative purposes, college educators need to be equipped with the knowledge to create a safe space for translanguaging practices in their classroom (Canagarajah, 2011; García, 2009; García & Wei, 2014; Jørgensen, 2008). In this way, students are encouraged to strategically draw on their home language to facilitate their comprehension and learning. As suggested in Chapter 10, mandating a classroom-level English-only policy is both unnecessary and harmful for first-semester college freshmen. For one thing, going against the nature and agency of multilingual students' languaging practices (Jørgensen, 2008), an English-only policy would create an extra hurdle for Chinese international students' acculturation into a new language environment, as they are discouraged from using their home language as a bridging tool during their initial college adjustments. For another, from a developmental perspective, with their natural advancement to more linguistically and academically accultur-ated stages, Chinese international students will naturally prefer English over home language usage in academic contexts.

As Richards *et al.* (2007: 68) wisely pointed out, 'Although the cur-riculum may be dictated by the school system, teachers teach it. Where the curriculum falls short in addressing the needs of all students, teach-ers much provide a bridge...'. Since language is a hidden curriculum across the disciplines (Brisk & Zhang-Wu, 2017), while it is important to familiarize multilingual international students with campus resources and direct them to various support services (e.g. the university writing center), content-subject professors need to recognize their responsibility in guiding students to meet the linguistic demands across the disciplines (Zhang-Wu, 2021b). All instructors, especially content-subject profes-sors, need to create a safe space for their newly arrived international students by delivering culturally and linguistically responsive instruction and inviting them to draw on their multilingual and multicultural funds of knowledge (e.g. de Jong *et al.*, 2013; Gallagher & Haan, 2018; Lucas & Villegas, 2011, 2013; Zhang-Wu, 2017). For instance, while it may be unrealistic for professors of Western-centered courses such as philoso-phy to teach philosophical ideologies representing every international students' culture, it is highly feasible to incorporate global perspectives into these classes. One way to achieve this is to encourage international students to make explicit connections between the course content and the beliefs and practices in their own culture. Such a practice can benefit international and domestic students alike. Not only will international students be empowered by resuming the role of cultural ambassadors and content experts in the learning process, but they may also find it easier to contribute to oral discussions in class. Meanwhile, domestic students are exposed to diverse perspectives in this process, which could raise their cross-cultural awareness.

Furthermore, college educators should also be made aware of the within-group variabilities among international students from the same ethnic group and the corresponding pedagogical implications. It is hoped that by understanding the various developmental stages these inter-national students are at and the different degrees of support students need, faculty members could better tailor their instructional practices. For example, in response to some newly arrived Chinese international students' lack of oral class participation at the beginning of the semes-ter, instead of directly deducting grades, faculty members could initiate private check-in meetings to see if the students need additional language assistance to facilitate their listening comprehension and oral production in English. Furthermore, when possible, faculty members may connect international college freshmen with their 'academic brothers and sisters' who share the same cultural and ethnic background and have taken the course in the past. These upperclassmen play important roles in their within-group support system and serve as excellent resources to provide newly arrived international students with additional language, academic and psychological support.

Implications for Research Methodology

Integrating digital ethnography (Pink *et al.*, 2016) with traditional data collection methods, this exploratory qualitative study has shed light on research methodological innovation. Without any material incentives, I have yielded a participant retention rate of 100% over the course of one academic semester. Because of their substantial commitment to research participation, none of my participants dropped out of the study over the course of four months, during which they (1) participated in two semi-structured interviews and two talks-around-texts interviews; (2) allowed daily observations on their *WeChat* social media usage; (3) responded to informal communication initiated by me about their linguistic and academic experiences whenever necessary; (4) provided at least two writing samples; and (5) documented and reported their weekday and weekend language usage by completing a 48-hour language log.

As a matter of fact, in addition to the perfect retention rate, many of my participants showed extraordinary passion in research participation; they took the initiative in providing me with much more data than expected. For example, while I had originally asked for two writing samples per student (expected total: 24 samples for 12 participants), the students shared with me a total of 37 writing samples which was more than 1.5 times my original plan, among which 29 fell into the predetermined data collection window (Weeks 5–7). Similarly, I had originally planned to initiate informal conversations with participants through *WeChat* only to make clarifications about their public posts so as not to add extra burden to their already stressful academic and linguistic transition. Unexpectedly, however, more than half of my participants initiated *WeChat* conversations with me in order to share their languaging experiences and major life events during their first semester in college. As a result of these participant-initiated conversations, I was able to yield much richer data than expected. To be specific, without the voice messages from Larry late at night, I would never have known the severity of the tensions between *regular high* and *American high* Chinese international students in their private *WeChat* group chats (I was only granted access to observe their public posts). By the same token, without Sarah's *WeChat* call on a Sunday afternoon, I would never have known about her constant dilemma between her desire to socialize with domestic students and her fear to be seen as a traitor by her Chinese peers throughout her first semester in college.

Two reasons stand out as contributing factors to the perfect retention rate of this study. Firstly, the culturally congruent social media platform, *WeChat*, played an important role in collecting non-intrusive, multimodal data. Through daily observations of the participants' public posts, this social media application provided me with the unique opportunity to conduct intensive digital ethnography over time without adding additional stress or burden to the participants. Since all the information had been made public based on the participants' preferences, there was little concern about intruding on the participants' privacy or requiring extra effort from them to report to me about their first-semester experiences. This could largely explain why I was able to consistently collect digital observation data on the focal participants' experiences even during periods when they were extremely busy due to midterm and final exams. Furthermore, owing to online observations informed by digital ethnography (Pink *et al.*, 2016), I was also able to yield rich multimodal data in the form of videos, audios, bilingual text, pictures, emojis, animations, and memes. All these provided a vivid picture of their multilingual and multimodal languaging experiences (Canagarajah, 2011; García, 2009; Jørgensen, 2008) during their initial linguistic, academic and social adjustment in an American higher education institution.

Secondly, my identity as a multilingual individual and once a *regular high* Chinese international student established a unique bond and sense of trust between the participants and me. On the one hand, owing to my language background, I allowed participants to choose the media of communication throughout all stages of the data collection; regardless of their decision to communicate in Chinese, English or translanguage between the two, I responded accordingly in the language forms preferred by the participants to make them comfortable. For instance, when communicating with *American high* student Rebecca, I noticed her preference for expressing herself in English. Therefore, I made sure to ask interview questions in English and responded to her *WeChat* messages in English. Occasionally, when she decided to shift back to Chinese in order to discuss any cultural-specific topics, I would also join the conversations using Chinese. In contrast, when chatting with many of the *regular high* students who still lacked confidence in their oral English and felt more comfortable communicating in Chinese, I tried to avoid English usage during all written and oral communication to reduce their anxiety.

On the other hand, my insider identity and lived experiences as an international student from China played an extremely positive role in establishing a sense of trust and a bond with my participants. This consequently led to their gracious support in research participation and open-hearted sharing of the details of their journeys. In fact, the overwhelming support from my participants was evident during my participant recruitment at the international student orientation. As I was handing out the recruitment flyers, a few students immediately friended me through *WeChat* and expressed their interest in supporting my research by volunteering as research participants. One student (Shawn) even approached me to express his admiration of my commitment to advocate for multi-lingual international students. On finishing the first round of interviews, almost all the students encouraged me to reach out to them if I needed any additional information. Around two weeks after the anchor interviews, I received a few *WeChat* messages from my participants, asking me about the progress of my project and inviting me to contact them whenever I needed more information. Interestingly, after knowing of my ambition to turn this research into a book, my participants became even more committed to the project. For example, Shawn assured me via *WeChat* that no matter what the commitments for participation were, he would 'always be there' to support me. Similarly, William often joked that he could not wait to 'become a celebrity' owing to his role as one of the main characters in my book project, and contacted me regularly to provide updates on memorable events during his initial bilingual linguistic functioning.

The bonding and trust established throughout the semester far transcended the traditional researcher–participant relationship. My research participants perceived me as a legitimate member of the Chinese international student community. Instead of using my first name Qianqian, they chose to call me '学姐' (academic older sister) throughout the data collection process. This sense of trust allowed my participants to share with me many insider views and provided me with rich multimodal data that might never have been possible to yield had I not been accepted as part of their community. This unique insider researcher position indeed benefited my data collection in many ways. Yet, I also strived to simultaneously adopt an outsider stance, trying to place my participants 'at a distance' (Kessen, 1991: 189) to minimize the possibility of imposing my own assumptions on the participants, inhibit their idea expressions and skew data analysis.

Reflecting on this one semester journey working closely with a group of Chinese international freshmen, I would like to align myself with Dwyer and Buckle (2009) and advocate for an integration of insider and outsider stances in qualitative research. Rather than treating the two identities as separate entities, I believe that adopting an insider–outsider positionality and approaching my participants from a stance in between is beneficial in navigating through a third space of 'paradox, ambiguity, and ambivalence, as well as conjunction and disjunction' to bring out the richness and complexity of the phenomenon under study (Dwyer & Buckle, 2009: 60).

Concluding Remarks: Limitations, Future Directions and Reflections

Despite my study's potential and many promising strengths, I would like to draw readers' attention to its potential limitations. Although integrating multiple resources and triangulating multimodal data to examine myths and realities about Chinese college freshmen's initial languaging experiences in the United States, this project is highly contextualized in nature: the findings and corresponding implications are based on the first-semester languaging journeys of 12 Chinese freshmen studying in one specific higher education institution in the United States. Given the small sample size and contextualized nature of the study, my research findings fall short in providing strong implications for Chinese international students' long-term linguistic functioning in American higher education. Yet, it is worth noting that since the aim of this exploratory qualitative study was to understand the complex phenomenon in relation to international freshmen's linguistic transition rather than to generalize, this underlying limitation is unlikely to jeopardize the overall rigor of the study (Marshall, 1996). While I never intended to generalize the results of the project across all higher educational contexts among all Chinese international students studying in Anglophone countries, it is hoped that the findings and implications of the current exploratory study shed light on identifying (1) research-informed pedagogical practices to enhance Chinese international students' initial college adjustment and linguistic functioning; (2) dimensions and areas where international student host institutions may need to improve to facilitate those students' transitional experiences and academic well-being; and (3) directions for future research.

This study has pointed to various directions for future research. Firstly, given the prolonged process of bilinguals' linguistic acculturation, it would be interesting to replicate the present study using a long-term design to closely follow a group of international students throughout their four years in college. By doing this, the nuances and patterns of their growing ability to function linguistically in American higher education could be identified in order to better understand their long-term languaging journeys and how they adapt their agencies to navigate their layers of external developmental systems during their overseas college studies. Furthermore, while this study explored Chinese international students' experiences solely from the angle of the college freshmen themselves, it would be interesting for future research to examine the same phenomenon by bringing in the voices of other parties indicated in the theoretical framework, such as professors, university administrators and domestic students. Are there gaps between faculty's and students' perceptions on how to support multilingual international students' initial languaging experiences? How do domestic students perceive the quality of institutional support for multilingual international students? These are some interesting questions which need to be explored in future research.

Additionally, although this in-depth qualitative study has drawn attention to many nuances and dynamics among Chinese international students' initial college experiences, it would be beneficial to triangulate those qualitative findings with quantitative analysis on the rich data collected using digital ethnography via *WeChat*. In this way, it is possible that some additional patterns with regard to the participants' linguistic functioning, especially their language usage in social settings, could be identified. Moreover, throughout my contact with the participants, translanguaging was observed throughout the *WeChat* postings, personal communication, interviews and talks around texts. It would be interesting to revisit the data and explore when, how and why did the Chinese international students adopt translanguaging, and whether such patterns changed over time. Also, since there is a lack of empirical research examining the cross-linguistic associations among adults with advanced multilingual proficiencies (Proctor & Zhang-Wu, 2019), in-depth analysis could be conducted on students' writing samples to explore the translingual practices between Mandarin Chinese and English and how students draw on their cultural funds of knowledge in conducting written communication in English.

Last but not least, while this project focused extensively on Chinese international students' languaging experiences in their micro, meso and exo systems, future research could pay more attention to how they navigate the macrosystem. Specifically, in their experiences negotiating this complex, racialized world, how do power and race play a role in their languaging processes? How does the zero-point epistemology of English (Mignolo, 2009; Pennycook, 2019; Zhang-Wu, 2021a) affect Chinese international students' languaging decisions across contexts?

This study is one of the pioneers in the field to use a combination of online observations informed by digital ethnography (Pink *et al.*, 2016) and traditional data collection methods to explore Chinese international students' languaging journeys across academic and social contexts during their first semester studying in an American higher education institution. Different from most previous studies on similar topics (e.g. Jiang, 2014; Wang, 2016; Xue, 2013; Yeh & Inose, 2003), which examined non-native English-speaking international students' experiences through a somewhat deficit view, focusing almost entirely on their English language barriers in the new academic environment, this study has positioned multilinguals as active decision makers who strategically deploy all resources from their linguistic repertoire to fulfill communicative purposes (e.g. Canagarajah, 2011; Creese & Blackledge, 2015; García & Kleifgen, 2020; Jørgensen, 2008). Rather than merely focusing on the stories of the strugglers who were newcomers to the English-speaking environment, balanced attention has been given to the linguistically problem-free journeys of those Chinese international students who were at more advanced phases during their linguistic acculturation. This has not only highlighted important within-group variabilities among the broad category of 'Chinese international students', but it has also extended the understanding of multilingual international students' languaging journeys by viewing them from a developmental perspective.

The significance of the study is two-fold. On the one hand, the findings have shed an important light on US higher education administration and instruction in order to better serve the needs of its growing international student population from culturally and linguistically diverse backgrounds. On the other hand, the methodological implications from the study have also opened up many future research possibilities to take an insider–outsider stance to conduct intensive digital ethnography through culturally responsive social media applications to explore minoritized populations' experiences in a non-intrusive manner.

This book has investigated the first-semester languaging journeys of Chinese international students and provided research-based tips and advice for these students and institutional support systems. Despite its many endeavors to facilitate Chinese international students' initial college adjustment and academic well-being, there are still countless questions to be explored, especially during the current global crisis. The Covid-19 global pandemic has triggered widespread negative sentiments toward Chinese nationals, which adds another layer to Chinese international students' challenges in pursuing overseas education in Western countries. Under such circumstances, it is more important than ever to continue researching how to improve their translingual, transcultural and transnational journeys from an insider–outsider perspective. Challenges await, and I must not put down my pen.

Appendix A

Interview Protocols

Anchor Interview at the Beginning of the Semester

- The language of the interview is determined based on interviewees' preferences.
- These questions only provide a basic guideline. Due to the nature of the semi-structured interview, each participant will be given slightly different questions/prompts based on their responses.

(1) **Can you tell me a little bit about your English learning experiences back in China?**
   (If participant remains silent, the following aspects will be covered in prompts to get more information)
   - (a) Length of study
   - (b) English classroom size, learning style, instructional style
   - (c) TOEFL preparation and TOEFL score
   - (d) Self-evaluation of English proficiency

(2) **Why did you choose to pursue overseas studies at Hillside University in the United States?**

(3) **What courses are you taking? Tell me about them.**
   (If participant remains silent, the following aspects will be covered in prompts to get more information)
   How do you perceive your language experiences at Hillside University?
   - (a) Any language difficulties? If so, in what aspects? Why?
   - (b) How do you evaluate your performance during classroom discussions/participation/teamwork?
   - (c) How do you feel about your current experiences compared with your previous English learning experiences in China?

(4) **How does it feel to be an international student at Hillside?**
(If participant remains silent, the following aspects will be covered in prompts to get more information)
    (a) Identity as a non-native-speaking international student
    (b) Perceptions of the English language in relation to Chinese

(5) **In what ways do you think the university supports (or fails to support) Chinese international students?**
(If participant remains silent, then prompt him/her to discuss with regards to their language experiences in particular)

Second Interview at the End of the Semester

- The language of the interview is determined based on interviewees' preferences.
- These questions only provide a basic guideline. Due to the nature of the semi-structured interview, each participant will be given slightly different questions/prompts based on their responses.

(1) **How are you recently? How do you describe your first-semester experiences at Hillside University?**
(If participant remains silent, the following aspects will be covered in prompts to get more information)
    (a) What is your favorite class? Why?
    (b) What is the course that you find the most challenging? Why?
    (c) Do you feel stressed? If yes, how so?

(2) **Tell me about your friendships/social life.**
(If participant remains silent, the following aspects will be covered in prompts to get more information)
    (a) Who do you usually hang out with? Why?

(3) **What are some of your major areas of growth regarding your English proficiency as well as academic studies?**

(4) **Is there anything you would wish to have done differently regarding your language and academic experiences?**
(If participant remains silent, the following aspects will be covered in prompts to get more information)
    (a) Anything you feel regretful about regarding your language experiences?
    (b) Anything you feel regretful about regarding your academic experiences?

(5) **How does it feel to be an international student at Hillside?**
(If participant remains silent, the following aspects will be covered in prompts to get more information)
  (a) Identity as a non-native-speaking international student
  (b) Perceptions of the English language in relation to Chinese

(6) **In what ways do you think the university supports (or fails to support) Chinese international students?**
(If participant remains silent, then prompt him/her to discuss with regards to their language experiences in particular)

Appendix B

Genre-Based Rubrics

Argument: Purpose and Stages	1	2	3	4
Purpose				
Verb tense				
Title				
Thesis statement				
Evidence				
Reinforcement of position				
Cohesiveness				

Argument: Language	1	2	3	4
Audience awareness				
Use of technical vocabulary for evidence				
Types of sentences				
Use of person				
Modality				
Evaluative vocabulary				
Grading				
Text connectives				
Cohesive paragraphs				
Additional Notes				

Criteria:

(1) The student writer needs extensive help developing that aspect of the genre.

(2) There are gaps in the writer's understanding of the specific aspect. The writer will benefit from a teacher-student conference.
(3) The student needs to revise one or two instances in their paper regarding the feature.
(4) The student writer has mastered the feature.

Adapted from Brisk (2015).

Explanation: Purpose and Stages	1	2	3	4
Purpose				
Verb tense				
Title				
Identifying statement				
Explanation sequence				
Conclusion				
Coherent text				

Explanation: Language	1	2	3	4
Verb groups				
Adjectivals				
Adverbials				
Use of clause complexes				
Audience				
Voice				
Text connectives				
Lexical ties (collocation)				
Additional Notes				

Criteria:

(1) The student writer needs extensive help developing that aspect of the genre.
(2) There are gaps in the writer's understanding of the specific aspect. The writer will benefit from a teacher-student conference.
(3) The student needs to revise one or two instances in their paper regarding the feature.
(4) The student writer has mastered the feature.

Adapted from Brisk (2015).

Recount: Purpose and Stages	1	2	3	4
Purpose				
Verb tense				
Title				
Orientation				
Sequence of events				
Record of events				
Conclusion				
Coherent text				
Paragraph formation				

Recount: Language	1	2	3	4
Verb groups				
Noun groups: Describes nouns with adjectivals				
Packs noun groups in place of multiple clauses				
Adverbials				
Use.of clause complexes				
Use of dialogue (quoting)				
Audience				
Voice				
Text connectives				
Track participants through reference ties				
Additional Notes				

Criteria:

(1) The student writer needs extensive help developing that aspect of the genre.
(2) There are gaps in the writer's understanding of the specific aspect. The writer will benefit from a teacher-student conference.
(3) The student needs to revise one or two instances in their paper regarding the feature.
(4) The student writer has mastered the feature.

Adapted from Brisk (2015).

Report: Purpose and Stages	1	2	3	4
Purpose				
Verb tense				
Title				
General statement				
Information				
Conclusion				
Cohesiveness				
Audience				
Voice				

Report: Language	1	2	3	4
Participants				
Noun groups lexical ties				
Adjectivals				
Clause complexes				
Cohesive paragraphs				
Additional Notes				

Criteria:

(1) The student writer needs extensive help developing that aspect of the genre.
(2) There are gaps in the writer's understanding of the specific aspect. The writer will benefit from a teacher-student conference.
(3) The student needs to revise one or two instances in their paper regarding the feature.
(4) The student writer has mastered the feature.

Adapted from Brisk (2015).

References

Allard, E.C. (2017) Re-examining teacher translanguaging: An ecological perspective. *Bilingual Research Journal* 40 (2), 116–130.

Andrade, M.S. (2006) International students in English-speaking universities: Adjustment factors. *Journal of Research in International Education* 5 (2), 131–154.

Arnold, K.D. and Casellas Connors, I. (November 2017) The 'Anti-Instagram': Using Visual Methods to Study the College Experiences of Underrepresented Students. Paper presented at the Annual Meeting of the Association for the Study of Higher Education, Houston, TX.

Association of International Educators (2018) NAFSA International Student Economic Value Tool. See https://www.nafsa.org/Policy_and_Advocacy/Policy_Resources/Policy_Trends_and_Data/NAFSA_International_Student_Economic_Value_Tool/ (accessed 11 June 2019).

Azmat, F., Osborne, A., Le Rossignol, K., Jogulu, U., Rentschler, R., Robottom, I. and Malathy, V. (2013) Understanding aspirations and expectations of international students in Australian higher education. *Asia Pacific Journal of Education* 33 (1), 97–111.

Bailey, A. (2007) *The Language Demands of School: Putting Academic English to the Test.* New Haven, CT: Yale University Press.

Bailey, A.L. and Heritage, M. (eds) (2008) *Formative Assessment for Literacy, Grades K-6: Building Reading and Academic Language Skills across the Curriculum.* Thousand Oaks, CA: Corwin Press.

Ball, S.J. (1993) Education markets, choice and social class: The market as a class strategy in the UK and the USA. *British Journal of Sociology of Education* 14 (1), 3–19.

Ball, S.J. (2003) *Class Strategies and the Education Market: The Middle Classes and Social Advantage.* New York: Routledge.

Barton, D. and Lee, C. (2013) *Language Online: Investigating Digital Texts and Practices.* London: Routledge.

Bayley, S., Arnol, J., Fearnside, R., Misiano, J. and Rottura, R. (2002) International students in Victorian universities. *People and Place* 10 (2), 45–55.

Beckett, G. and Li, F. (2012) Content-based English education in China: Students' experiences and perspectives. *Journal of Contemporary Issues in Education* 7 (1), 47–63.

Benda, J., Dedek, M., Girdharry, K., Gallagher, C., Lerner, N. and Noonan, M. (2018) Confronting superdiversity in US writing programs. In S.K. Rose and I. Weiser (eds) *The Internationalization of US Writing Programs* (pp. 79–96). Boulder, CO: University Press of Colorado.

Bird, C.M. (2005) How I stopped dreading and learned to love transcription. *Qualitative Inquiry* 11 (2), 226–248.

Blair, A. (2016) Academic uses of language (re) defined: A case of emergent bilinguals engaging in languages and literacies in and outside of school. *Linguistics and Education* 35, 109–119.

Blommaert, J. and Rampton, B. (2011) Language and super-diversity. *Diversities* 13 (2), 1–22.

Brand, M. (2004) Collectivistic versus individualistic cultures: A comparison of American, Australian and Chinese music education students' self-esteem. *Music Education Research* 6 (1), 57–66.

Brisk, M.E. (2015) *Engaging Students in Academic Literacies: Genre-Based Pedagogy for K-5 Classrooms*. New York: Routledge.

Brisk, M.E. and Zhang-Wu, Q. (2017) Academic language in K-12 contexts. In E. Hinkel (ed.) *Handbook of Research in Second Language Teaching and Learning. Third Edition* (pp. 82–100). New York: Routledge.

Brisk, M.E., Burgos, A. and Hamerla, S. (2004) *Situational Context of Education: A Window into the World of Bilingual Learners*. Mahwah, NJ: Lawrence Erlbaum Associates.

Bronfenbrenner, U. (1979) Contexts of child rearing: Problems and prospects. *American Psychologist* 34 (10), 844–850.

Bronfenbrenner, U. (1989) Ecological systems theory. In R. Vasta (ed.) *Six Theories of Development* (pp. 187–249). Greenwich, CT: JAI Press.

Bronfenbrenner, U. (1993) The ecology of cognitive development: Research models and fugitive findings. In R.H. Wozniak and K.W. Fischer (eds) *Development in Context: Acting and Thinking in Specific Environments* (pp. 3–44). Hillsdale, NJ: Erlbaum.

Bronfenbrenner, U. and Morris, P.A. (2006) The bioecological model of human development. In R.M. Lerner and W.E. Damon (eds) *Handbook of Child Psychology* (pp. 793–828). Hoboken, NJ: John Wiley & Sons, Inc.

Brown, P. (1990) The 'third wave': Education and the ideology of parentocracy. *British Journal of Sociology of Education* 11 (1), 65–86.

Brown, P. (1995) Cultural capital and social exclusion: Some observations on recent trends in education, employment and the labour market. *Work, Employment & Society* 9 (1), 29–51.

Canagarajah, A.S. (2006) The place of world Englishes in composition: Pluralization continued. *College Composition and Communication* 57 (4), 586–619.

Canagarajah, S. (2011) Codemeshing in academic writing: Identifying teachable strategies of translanguaging. *The Modern Language Journal* 95 (3), 401–417.

Canagarajah, S. (2012) *Translingual Practice: Global Englishes and Cosmopolitan Relations*. London: Routledge.

Cargill, M., O'Connor, P. and Li, Y. (2012) Educating Chinese scientists to write for international journals: Addressing the divide between science and technology education and English language teaching. *English for Specific Purposes* 31 (1), 60–69.

Chang, M.J., Park, J., Lin, M.H., Poon, O. and Nakanishi, D.T. (2007) *Beyond Myths: The Growth and Diversity of Asian American College Freshmen, 1971–2005*. Los Angeles, CA: Higher Education Research Institute, UCLA.

Charmaz, K. (2014) *Constructing Grounded Theory*. Thousand Oaks, CA: Sage.

Cheng, R. and Erben, A. (2011) Language anxiety: Experiences of Chinese graduate students at US higher institutions. *Journal of Studies in International Education* 16 (5), 477–497.

Chickering, A. and Gamson, Z. (1986) Seven principles for good practice in undergraduate education. *AAHE Bulletin* 39, 3–7.

Cho, Y. and Bridgeman, B. (2012) Relationship of TOEFL iBT® scores to academic performance: Some evidence from American universities. *Language Testing* 29 (3), 421–442.

Christie, F. (1985). Language and schooling. In S. Tuchudi (Ed.), *Language, Schooling, and Society* (pp. 21–40). Upper Montclair, NJ: Boynton/Cook.

Christie, F. (2012) Language education throughout the school years: A functional perspective. *Language Learning* 62 (1), 1–247.

Clark, M.R. (2005) Negotiating the freshman year: Challenges and strategies among first-year college students. *Journal of College Student Development* 46 (3), 296–316.

Clark, N. (September 1, 2009) What Defines an International Student? A Look Behind the Numbers. See https://wenr.wes.org/2009/09/wenr-september-2009-feature (accessed 20 May 2020).

Coffin, C. and Donohue, J.P. (2012) Academic literacies and systemic functional linguistics: How do they relate? *Journal of English for Academic Purposes* 11 (1), 64–75.

Coffin, C., Curry, M.J., Goodman, S., Hewings, A., Lillis, T. and Swann, J. (2005) *Teaching Academic Writing: A Toolkit for Higher Education*. London: Routledge.

Corbett, A. (2016) Post-Brexit options for UK universities. *University World News*. See http://www.universityworldnews.com/article.php?story=20160927183505420 (accessed 20 May 2020).

Corbin, J. and Strauss, A. (2007) *Basics of Qualitative Research: Techniques and Procedures for Developing Grounded Theory* (3rd edn). Thousand Oaks, CA: Sage.

Creese, A. and Martin, P. (eds) (2003) *Multilingual Classroom Ecologies*. Clevedon: Multilingual Matters.

Creese, A. and Blackledge, A. (2010) Translanguaging in the bilingual classroom: A pedagogy for learning and teaching? *Modern Language Journal* 94 (1), 103–115.

Creese, A. and Blackledge, A. (2015) Translanguaging and identity in educational settings. *Annual Review of Applied Linguistics* 35, 20–35.

Creswell, J.W. and Miller, D.L. (2000) Determining validity in qualitative inquiry. *Theory into Practice* 39 (3), 124–130.

Cummins, J. (1980) The cross-lingual dimensions of language proficiency: Implications for bilingual education and the optimal age issue. *TESOL Quarterly* 14 (2), 175–187.

Cummins, J. (1981) Empirical and theoretical underpinnings of bilingual education. *Journal of Education* 163 (1), 16–29.

Cummins, J. (2008) BICS and CALP: Empirical and theoretical status of the distinction. In B. Street and N.H. Hornberger (eds) *Encyclopedia of Language and Education*: Vol. 2. Literacy (2nd edn, pp. 71–83). New York: Springer.

Dale, T.C. and Cuevas, G.J. (1987) Integrating mathematics and language learning. In J.A. Crandall (ed.) *ESL through Content-Area Instruction: Mathematics, Science, Social Studies* (pp. 9–54). Englewood Cliffs, NJ: Prentice Hall Regents.

Daly, J., Kellehear, A. and Gliksman, M. (1997) *The Public Health Researcher: A Methodological Approach*. Melbourne: Oxford University Press.

de Jong, E.J., Harper, C.A. and Coady, M.R. (2013) Enhanced knowledge and skills for elementary mainstream teachers of English language learners. *Theory into Practice* 52 (2), 89–97.

DiCerbo, P.A., Anstrom, K.A., Baker, L.L. and Rivera, C. (2014) A review of the literature on teaching academic English to English language learners. *Review of Educational Research* 84 (3), 446–482.

Dika, S. (2012) Relations with faculty as social capital for college students: Evidence from Puerto Rico. *Journal of College Student Development* 53 (4), 596–610.

Donahue, C. and Foster-Johnson, L. (2018) Liminality and transition: Text features in postsecondary student writing. *Research in the Teaching of English* 52 (4), 359–381.

Douglas, J., Douglas, A. and Barnes, B. (2006) Measuring student satisfaction at a UK university. *Quality Assurance in Education* 14 (3), 251–267.

Dwyer, S.C. and Buckle, J.L. (2009) The space between: On being an insider-outsider in qualitative research. *International Journal of Qualitative Methods* 8 (1), 54–63.

Echevarria, J.J., Vogt, M.J. and Short, D.J. (2013) *Making Content Comprehensible for Elementary English Learners: The SIOP Model*. Upper Saddle River, NJ: Pearson Education.

Eggins, S. (2004) *Introduction to Systemic Functional Linguistics*. New York: A&C Black.

ETS (2012) TOEFL Test Makes Impacts on China. See https://www.ets.org/s/toefl/newslet ter/2012/19378/ww/china_impact.html (accessed 14 February 2019).

ETS (2019a) Improve Your Skills. See https://www.ets.org/toefl/ibt/scores/improve (accessed 14 February 2019).

ETS (2019b) The TOEFL iBT® Test: Improving Your Listening Skills. See https:// www.ets.org/toefl/ibt/scores/improve/advice_listening_high (accessed 14 February 2019).

ETS (2019c) TOEFL iBT® Free Practice Test Transcript. Accessed February 14, 2019. See https://www.ets.org/s/toefl/pdf/free_practice_test.pdf (accessed 14 February 2019).

ETS (2020a) The *TOEFL iBT®* Test. See https://www.ets.org/toefl (accessed 17 May 2020).

ETS (2020b) About the *TOEFL iBT®* Test. See https://www.ets.org/toefl/test-takers/ibt/ about (accessed 17 May 2020).

Fang, Z. (2005) Scientific literacy: A systemic functional linguistics perspective. *Science Education* 89 (2), 335–347.

Fang, Z. (2008) Going beyond the fab five: Helping students cope with the unique linguistic challenges of expository reading in intermediate grades. *Journal of Adolescent & Adult Literacy* 51 (6), 476–487.

Fang, Z. and Schleppegrell, M.J. (2010) Disciplinary literacies across content areas: Supporting secondary reading through functional language analysis. *Journal of Adolescent & Adult Literacy* 53 (7), 587–597.

Fang, Z., Lamme, L.L. and Pringle, R.M. (2010) *Language and Literacy in Inquiry-Based Science Classrooms, Grades 3–8*. Thousand Oaks, CA: Corwin Press.

Feng, A.W. (2005) Bilingualism for the minor or the major? An evaluative analysis of parallel conceptions in China. *International Journal of Bilingual Education and Bilingualism* 8, 529–551.

Feng, J. (2007) Making the grade. *Beijing Review* 50 (36), 24–25.

Fereday, J. and Muir-Cochrane, E. (2006) Demonstrating rigor using thematic analysis: A hybrid approach of inductive and deductive coding and theme development. *International Journal of Qualitative Methods* 5 (1), 80–92.

Fischer, K. (March 11, 2021) Is This the End of the Romance between Chinese Students and American Colleges? *The Chronicle of Higher Education*. See https://www.chr onicle.com/article/is-this-the-end-of-the-romance-between-chinese-students-and-u-s -colleges (accessed 21 March 2021).

Fraiberg, S., Wang, X. and You, X. (2017) *Inventing the World Grant University: Chinese International Students' Mobilities, Literacies, and Identities*. Boulder, CO: University Press of Colorado.

Fry, H., Ketteridge, S. and Marshall, S. (eds) (2008) *A Handbook for Teaching and Learning in Higher Education: Enhancing Academic Practice*. Abingdon: Routledge.

Gallagher, C.E. and Haan, J.E. (2018) University faculty beliefs about emergent multilinguals and linguistically responsive instruction. *TESOL Quarterly* 52 (2), 304–330.

Gao, X. and Xu, H. (2014) The dilemma of being English language teachers: Interpreting teachers' motivation to teach, and professional commitment in China's hinterland regions. *Language Teaching Research* 18 (2), 152–168.

García, O. (2009) Education, multilingualism and translanguaging in the 21st century. In T. Skutnabb-Kangas, R. Phillipson, A. Mohanty and M. Panda (eds) *Social Justice through Multilingual Education* (pp. 140–158). Bristol: Multilingual Matters.

García, O. and Kleifgen, J.A. (2020) Translanguaging and literacies. *Reading Research Quarterly* 55 (4), 553–571.

García, O. and Wei, L. (2014) *Translanguaging: Language, Bilingualism and Education*. New York: Palgrave Macmillan.

Ginther, A. and Yan, X. (2018) Interpreting the relationships between TOEFL iBT scores and GPA: Language proficiency, policy, and profiles. *Language Testing* 35 (2), 271–295.

Glaser, B.G. and Strauss, A.L. (1967) *The Discovery of Grounded Theory: Strategies for Qualitative Research*. New York: Aldine.

Gottlieb, M. and Ernst-Slavit, G. (2014) *Academic Language in Diverse Classrooms: Definitions and Contexts*. Thousand Oaks, CA: Corwin Press.

Griffin, W., Cohen, S.D., Berndtson, R., Burson, K.M., Camper, K.M., Chen, Y. and Smith, M.A. (2014) Starting the conversation: An exploratory study of factors that influence student office hour use. *College Teaching* 62 (3), 94–99.

Guest, G., MacQueen, K.M. and Namey, E.E. (2012) *Applied Thematic Analysis*. Thousand Oaks, CA: Sage.

Gynne, A. and Bagga-Gupta, S. (2015) Languaging in the twenty-first century: Exploring varieties and modalities in literacies inside and outside learning spaces. *Language and Education* 29 (6), 509–526.

Halliday, M.A. (1973) *Explorations in the Functions of Language*. London: Edward Arnold.

Halliday, M.A. (1984) Language as code and language as behaviour: A systemic-functional interpretation of the nature and ontogenesis of dialogue. *The Semiotics of Culture and Language* 1, 3–35.

Halliday, M.A. (1985) *An Introduction to Functional Linguistics*. London: Edward Arnold.

Halliday, M.A. (1994) *Functional Grammar*. London: Edward Arnold.

He, D. and Li, D.C.S. (2009) Language attitudes and linguistic features in the 'China English' debate. *World Englishes* 28, 70–89.

He, D. and Zhang, Q. (2010) Native speaker norms and China English: From the perspective of learners and teachers in China. *TESOL Quarterly* 44 (4), 769–789.

Hellsten, M. (2002) Students in Transition: Needs and Experience of International Students in Australia. Paper presented at the 16th Australian International Education Conference, Hobart, Tasmania.

Hellsten, M. and Prescott, A. (2004) Learning at university: The international student experience. *International Education Journal* 5 (3), 344–351.

Hendrickson, B., Rosen, D. and Aune, R.K. (2011) An analysis of friendship networks, social connectedness, homesickness, and satisfaction levels of international students. *International Journal of Intercultural Relations* 35 (3), 281–295.

Heng, T.T. (2018) Different is not deficient: Contradicting stereotypes of Chinese international students in US higher education. *Studies in Higher Education* 43 (1), 22–36.

Hill, K., Storch, N. and Lynch, B. (1999) A comparison of IELTS and TOEFL as predictors of academic success. *English Language Testing System Research Reports* 2, 52–63.

Hornberger, N.H. (2004) The continua of biliteracy and the bilingual educator: Educational linguistics in practice. *International Journal of Bilingual Education and Bilingualism* 7 (2 & 3), 155–171.

Hornberger, N.H. and Hult, F. (2008) Ecological language policy. In B. Spolsky and F. Hult (eds) *The Handbook of Educational Linguistics* (pp. 280–296). Malden, MA: Blackwell.

Hornberger, N.H. and Link, H. (2012) Translanguaging and transnational literacies in multilingual classrooms: A biliteracy lens. *International Journal of Bilingual Education and Bilingualism* 15 (3), 261–278.

Huong, T. (2001) The predictive validity of the International English Language Testing System (IELTS) test. *Post-Script* 2 (1), 66–94.

Institute of International Education (2018) 'International Student Totals by Place of Origin, 2012/13-2017/18'. Open Doors Report on International Educational Exchange. See http://www.iie.org/opendoors (accessed 11 January 2020).

Institute of International Education (November 2019) Number of International Students in the United States Hits All-Time High. See https://www.iie.org/Why-IIE/Announc

ements/2019/11/Number-of-International-Students-in-the-United-States-Hits-All-Ti me-High (accessed 17 May 2020).

Institute of International Education (2020) International Students. Accessed May 17, 2020. See https://www.iie.org/Research-and-Insights/Open-Doors/Data/International-Stu dents

International TEFL Academy (May 19, 2020) What are Salaries for English Teachers in China? See https://www.internationalteflacademy.com/blog/what-are-salaries-for-en glish-teachers-in-china (accessed 1 June 2020).

Jenkins, J. (2006) Current perspectives on teaching world Englishes and English as a lingua franca. *TESOL Quarterly* 40 (1), 157–181.

Jiang, H.D. (2003) Lun jichu jiaoyu jieduan de shuangyu jiaoyu [On bilingual education at the basic education stage]. *Tianjin Shifan Daxue Xuebao* 4 (1), 52–56.

Jiang, X. (2014) Chinese biology teaching assistants' perception of their English profi ciency: An exploratory case study. *The Qualitative Report* 19 (21), 1–24.

Jin, L. and Cortazzi, M. (2006) Changing practices in Chinese cultures of learning. *Lan guage, Culture and Curriculum* 19 (1), 5–20.

Johnson, P. (1988) English language proficiency and academic performance of under graduate international students. *TESOL Quarterly* 22, 186–168. doi:10.2307/3587070

Jørgensen, J.N. (2008) Polylingual languaging around and among children and adoles cents. *International Journal of Multilingualism* 5 (3), 161–176.

Kachru, B.B. and Nelson, C.L. (1996) World Englishes. *Sociolinguistics and Language Teaching* 11, 71–102.

Kagawa, M., Hune, S. and Park, J. (2011) Asian American college students over the decades: Insights from studying Asian American first-year students from 1971 to 2005 using survey research data. *AAPI Nexus: Policy, Practice and Community* 9 (1–2), 119–126.

Karuppan, C.M. and Barari, M. (2010) Perceived discrimination and international stu dents' learning: An empirical investigation. *Journal of Higher Education Policy and Management* 33 (1), 67–83.

Kerstijens, M. and Nery, C. (2000) Predictive validity in the IELTS test: A study of the relationship between IELTS scores and students' subsequent academic performance. *IELTS Research Reports* 3, 85–108.

Kessen, W. (1991) Commentary: Dynamics of enculturation. In M.H. Bornstein (ed.) *Cul tural Approaches to Parenting* (pp. 185–193). Hillsdale, NJ: Erlbaum.

Krausz, J., Schiff, A., Schiff, J. and Hise, J.V. (2005) The impact of TOEFL scores on placement and performance of international students in the initial graduate account ing class. *Accounting Education: An International Journal* 4 (1), 103–111.

Krefting, L. (1991) Rigor in qualitative research: The assessment of trustworthiness. *American Journal of Occupational Therapy* 45 (3), 214–222.

Kuh, G., Kinzie, J., Schuh, J. and Whitt, E. (2010) *Student Success in College: Creating Conditions that Matter*. San Francisco, CA: Jossey Bass.

Law, W.W. and Ho, W.C. (2009) Globalization, values education, and school music edu cation in China. *Journal of Curriculum Studies* 41 (4), 501–520.

Lee, M.E. (2014) Shifting to the world Englishes paradigm by way of the translingual approach: Code-meshing as a necessary means of transforming composition peda gogy. *TESOL Journal* 5 (2), 312–329.

Lee, J.S. and Oxelson, E. (2006) 'It's not my job': K-12 teacher attitudes toward students' heritage language maintenance. *Bilingual Research Journal* 30 (2), 453–477.

Leininger, M.M. (1985) Ethnography and ethnonursing: Models and modes of qualitative data analysis. In M.M. Leininger (ed.) *Qualitative Research Methods in Nursing* (pp. 33–72). Orlando, FL: Grune & Stratton.

Lenkeit, J., Caro, D.H. and Strand, S. (2015) Tackling the remaining attainment gap between students with and without immigrant background: An investigation into the equivalence of SES constructs. *Educational Research and Evaluation: An International Journal on Theory and Practice* 21 (1), 60–83.

Li, M. and Baldauf, R. (2011) Beyond the curriculum: A Chinese example of issues constraining effective English language teaching. *TESOL Quarterly* 45 (4), 793–803.

Li, W. (2018). Translanguaging as a practical theory of language. *Applied linguistics*, 39(1), 9-30.

Li, Z. (April 27, 2020) English education in China: An evolutionary perspective. *People's Daily Online*. See http://en.people.cn/n3/2020/0427/c90000-9684652.html (accessed 13 January 2021).

Light, R.L., Xu, M. and Mossop, J. (1987) English proficiency and academic performance of international students. *TESOL Quarterly* 21 (2), 251–261.

Light, R.L., Teh-Yuan, W. and Weinstein-Shr, G. (1991) Soviet students at U.S. colleges: Social perception, language proficiency and academic success. *TESOL Quarterly* 25, 179–185.

Lillis, T. and Scott, M. (2008) Defining academic literacies research: Issues of epistemology, ideology and strategy. *Journal of Applied Linguistics* 4 (1), 5–32.

Lim, D.Y. (2015) Exploring and identifying predictors that affect Asian American college students' sense of belonging: How do I fit in? Unpublished doctoral dissertation, University of Maryland.

Lin, C. (2006) Culture shock and social support: An investigation of a Chinese student organization on a US campus. *Journal of Intercultural Communication Research* 35 (2), 117–137.

Lippi-Green, R. (2012) *English with an Accent: Language, Ideology and Discrimination in the United States.* New York: Routledge.

Liu, O.L., Schedl, M., Malloy, J. and Kong, N. (2009) *Does Content Knowledge Affect TOEFL iBT TM Reading Performance? A Confirmatory Approach to Differential Item Functioning.* Princeton, NJ: English Testing System.

Lucas, T. and Villegas, A.M. (2010) The missing piece in teacher education: The preparation of linguistically responsive teachers. *National Society for the Study of Education* 109 (2), 297–318.

Lucas, T. and Villegas, A.M. (2011) A framework for preparing linguistically responsive teachers. In T. Lucas (ed.) *Teacher Preparation for Linguistically Diverse Classrooms: A Resource for Teacher Educators* (pp. 55–72). New York: Routledge.

Lucas, T. and Villegas, A.M. (2013) Preparing linguistically responsive teachers: Laying the foundation in preservice teacher education. *Theory into Practice* 52 (2), 98–109.

Ma, Y. (2020) *Ambitious and Anxious: How Chinese College Students Succeed and Struggle in American Higher Education.* New York: Columbia University Press.

Macaro, E. and Han, S. (2020) English medium instruction in China's higher education: Teachers' perspectives of competencies, certification and professional development. *Journal of Multilingual and Multicultural Development* 41 (3), 219–231.

Macedo, D. (2000) The colonialism of the English only movement. *Educational Researcher* 29 (3), 15–24.

MacSwan, J. and Rolstad, K. (2003) Linguistic diversity, schooling and social class: Rethinking our conception of language proficiency in language minority education. In C.B. Paulston and R. Tucker (eds) *Sociolinguistics: The Essential Readings* (pp. 329–340). Oxford: Blackwell.

Marshall, M.N. (1996) Sampling for qualitative research. *Family Practice* 13 (6), 522–526.

Martin, P. (2009) 'They have lost their identity but not gained a British one': Non-traditional multilingual students in higher education in the United Kingdom. *Language and Education* 24 (1), 9–20.

Martirosyan, N.M., Hwang, E. and Wanjohi, R. (2015) Impact of English proficiency on academic performance of international students. *Journal of International Students* 5 (1), 60–71.

Mervosh, S. (January 27, 2019) Duke University Apologizes Over Professor's Email Asking Chinese Students to Speak English. See https://www.nytimes.com/2019/01/27/us/megan-neely-duke-chinese.html (accessed 17 May 2020)

Mignolo, W.D. (2009) Epistemic disobedience, independent thought and decolonial freedom. *Theory, Culture & Society* 26 (7–8), 159–181.

Miles, M.B., Huberman, A.M. and Saldaña, J. (2014) *Qualitative Data Analysis: A Methods Sourcebook.* Thousand Oaks, CA: Sage Publications.

Mori, S.C. (2000) Addressing the mental health concerns of international students. *Journal of Counseling & Development* 78 (2), 137–144.

Morton, J., Storch, N. and Thompson, C. (2015) What our students tell us: Perceptions of three multilingual students on their academic writing in first year. *Journal of Second Language Writing* 30, 1–13.

National Association for Music Education (2014) 2014 Music Standards. See https://nafme.org/my-classroom/standards/core-music-standards/ (accessed 7 January 2019).

National Bureau of Statistics of China (2020) China Average Yearly Wages. See https://tradingeconomics.com/china/wages (accessed 17 May 2020).

Neuby, B.L. (2012) Chinese student success in an applied academic environment. *Journal of Public Affairs Education* 18 (4), 683–693.

New Oriental Education and Technology Group (2020) Test Preparation. See http://www.neworiental.org/english/what/201507/8214171.html (accessed 17 May 2020).

Norris, S.P. and Phillips, L.M. (2003) How literacy in its fundamental sense is central to scientific literacy. *Science Education* 87 (2), 224–240.

Nunan, D. (2003) The impact of English as a global language on educational policies and practices in the Asia-Pacific region. *TESOL Quarterly* 37, 589–613.

O'Connor, M.T. (2017) Everybody knows everybody?: Investigating rural secondary students' language choices in response to audience across argument writing experiences. Doctoral dissertation, Boston College.

Pan, M. (2007) Explorations in the Minban system of higher education. *Chinese Education and Society* 40 (5), 83–91.

Park, H.Y. (2016) *Culture Clash: Korean International Students in an American High School: English Language Only!* Scotts Valley, CA: On-Demand Publishing.

Park, J., Lin, M., Poon, O. and Chang, M. (2008) Asian American college student and civic engagement. In P. Ong (ed.) *The State of Asian America: Trajectory of Civic and Political Engagement* (pp. 75–98). Los Angeles, CA: LEAP Asian Pacific American Public Policy Institute.

Patton, M.Q. (2002) Two decades of developments in qualitative inquiry: A personal, experiential perspective. *Qualitative Social Work* 1 (3), 261–283.

Pennycook, A. (2010) *Language as a Local Practice.* New York: Routledge.

Pennycook, A. (2019) From translanguaging to translingual activism. In D. Macedo (ed.) *Decolonizing Foreign Language Education: The Mis-teaching of English and Other Colonial Languages* (pp. 169–186). London: Routledge.

Pew Research Center (2016) Mobile fact sheet: Who owns cellphones and smartphones. See http://www.pewinternet.org/fact-sheet/mobile/ (accessed 2 September 2018).

Pink, S., Horst, H.A., Postill, J., Hjorth, L., Lewis, T. and Tacchi, J. (2016) *Digital Ethnography: Principles and Practice.* Los Angeles, CA: Sage.

Poe, M. and Zhang-Wu, Q. (2020) Super-diversity as a framework to promote justice: Designing program assessment for multilingual writing outcomes. *Composition Forum* 44, 1–15.

Proctor, C.P. and Zhang-Wu, Q. (2019) Cross-linguistic relations among bilingual and biliterate learners: Interdisciplinary perspective and convergences. In V. Grover, P. Uccelli, M. Rowe and E. Lieven (eds) *Learning through Language* (pp. 218–234). Cambridge: Cambridge University Press.

Qian, Y.W. (2003) Fenceng duoyuan de shenhua shuangyu jiaoxue shiyan [Promote experimentation with bilingual education at multiple levels and in plural ways]. *Shanghai Jiaoyu Keyan* 7, 53–57.

Rao, Z. (2010) Chinese students' perceptions of native English-speaking teachers in EFL teaching. *Journal of Multilingual and Multicultural Development* 31 (1), 55–68.

Reif, R. (November 9, 2016) With our eyes on the future. See https://president.mit.edu/speeches-writing/our-eyes-future (accessed 17 May 2020).

Renn, K.A. and Arnold, K.D. (2003) Reconceptualizing research on college student peer culture. *The Journal of Higher Education* 74 (3), 261–291.

Rice, P.L. and Ezzy, D. (1999) *Qualitative Research Methods: A Health Focus* (Vol. 720). Melbourne: Oxford University Press.

Richards, H.V., Brown, A.F. and Forde, T.B. (2007) Addressing diversity in schools: Culturally responsive pedagogy. *Teaching Exceptional Children* 39 (3), 64–68.

Rinard, B.J. (2011) *The Persuasive and Evaluative Essays of Adolescent English Learners: How Context Shapes Genre*. Davis, CA: University of California, Davis.

Robertson, M., Line, M., Jones, S. and Thomas, S. (2000) International students, learning environments and perceptions: A case study using the Delphi technique. *Higher Education Research & Development* 19 (1), 89–102.

Rowntree, M.R., Zufferey, C. and King, S. (2016) 'I don't just want to do it for myself': Diverse perspectives on being successful at university by social work students who speak English as an additional language. *Social Work Education* 35 (4), 387–401.

Royer, D.J. and Gilles, R. (1998) Directed self-placement: An attitude of orientation. *College Composition and Communication* 50 (1), 54–70.

Royer, D.J. and Gilles, R. (2003) *Directed Self-Placement: Principles and Practices*. Cresskill, NJ: Hampton Press.

Ryan, G.W. and Bernard, H.R. (2003) Techniques to identify themes. *Field Methods* 15 (1), 85–109.

Saldana, J. (2009) *An Introduction to Codes and Coding. The Coding Manual for Qualitative Researchers*. Thousand Oaks, CA: Sage.

Sang, Y. and Hiver, P. (2021) Using a language socialization framework to explore Chinese students' L2 reticence in English language learning. *Linguistics and Education* 61, 100904.

Sawir, E. (2005) Language difficulties of international students in Australia: The effects of prior learning experience. *International Education Journal* 6 (5), 567–580.

Scarcella, R. (2003) *Academic English: A Conceptual Framework*. Santa Barbara, CA: The University of California Linguistic Minority Research Institute Technical Report 2003-1.

Schertzer, M.J., Robinson, R., Landschoot, T., Ghosh, A., Liberson, A. and Hensel, E. (2014, November) Effect of office hour participation on student performance. In *ASME 2014 International Mechanical Engineering Congress and Exposition* (pp. V005T05A027–V005T05A027). New York: American Society of Mechanical Engineers. See https://proceedings.asmedigitalcollection.asme.org/proceeding.aspx?articleid=2204905

Schleppegrell, M.J. (2004) *The Language of Schooling: A Functional Linguistics Perspective*. New York: Routledge.

Schleppegrell, M.J. (2007) The linguistic challenges of mathematics teaching and learning: A research review. *Reading & Writing Quarterly* 23 (2), 139–159.

Schleppegrell, M.J., Greer, S. and Taylor, S. (2008) Literacy in history: Language and meaning. *The Australian Journal of Language and Literacy* 31 (2), 174–187.

Shanghai Curriculum and Teaching Materials Reform Commission (1999) *Mianxiang ershiyi shiji Shanghaishi zhongxiaoxue waiyu xueke jiaoyu gaige xingdong gangling: 2000–2010* [*Programme for 21st Century-Oriented Reform on Foreign Language*

Curriculums for Primary and Secondary Schools in Shanghai: 2000–2010]. Shanghai: Shanghai Education Press.

Shen, P. and Feng, Y.P. (2005) Tuijin shuangyu jiaoxue de tansuo yu shijian [Exploring and implementing bilingual instruction]. *Zhongguo Daxue Jiaoxue* 2, 24–31.

Sherry, M., Thomas, P. and Chui, W.H. (2010) International students: A vulnerable student population. *Higher Education* 60 (1), 33–46.

Smith, R.A. and Khawaja, N.G. (2011) A review of the acculturation experiences of international students. *International Journal of Intercultural Relations* 35 (6), 699–713.

Snow, C.E. and Uccelli, P. (2009) The challenge of academic language. In D.R. Olson and N. Torrance (eds) *The Cambridge Handbook of Literacy* (pp. 112–133). Cambridge: Cambridge University Press.

Song, Y.Q. and Yan, H.C. (2004) Kaizhan shuangyu jiaoxue de kexingxing ji wenti tantao [A discussion of the feasibility of bilingual instruction and related issues]. *Jilin Gongcheng Jishu Shifan Xueyuan Xuebao* 20 (1), 20–22.

Statista (2019) Most popular global mobile messenger apps as of January 2019, based on number of monthly active users (in millions). See https://www.statista.com/statistics/258749/most-popular-global-mobile-messenger-apps/ (accessed 1 September 2019)

Stecklow, S. and Harney, A. (December 23, 2016) Exclusive: Chinese Education Giant Helps its Students Game the SAT. [News Report] See https://www.reuters.com/article/us-college-china-testing-exclusive/exclusive-chinese-education-giant-helps-its-students-game-the-sat-idUSKBN14C1G7 (accessed 17 January 2019).

Su, M. and Harrison, L.M. (2016) Being wholesaled: An investigation of Chinese international students' higher education experiences. *Journal of International Students* 6 (4), 905–919.

Swain, M. (2006) Languaging, agency and collaboration in advanced second language proficiency. In H. Byrnes (ed.) *Advanced Language Learning: The Contribution of Halliday and Vygotsky* (pp. 95–108). London: Continuum.

Thornbury, S. and Slade, D. (2006) Teaching conversation: Approach, design, procedure and process. In S. Thornbury and D. Slade (eds) *Conversation: From Description to Pedagogy* (pp. 274–325). Cambridge: Cambridge University Press.

Tran, T. and Baldauf, R. (2007) Demotivation: Understanding resistance to English language learning: The case of Vietnamese students. *The Journal of Asia TEFL* 4, 79–105.

Turkan, S., De Oliveira, L.C., Lee, O. and Phelps, G. (2014) Proposing a knowledge base for teaching academic content to English language learners: Disciplinary linguistic knowledge. *Teachers College Record* 116 (3), 1–30.

United Nations Educational, Scientific and Cultural Organization Institute of Statistics (2020) International (or Internationally Mobile) Students. See http://uis.unesco.org/en/glossary-term/international-or-internationally-mobile-students (accessed 17 May 2020).

Villegas, A.M. and Lucas, T. (2002) Preparing culturally responsive teachers: Rethinking the curriculum. *Journal of Teacher Education* 53 (1), 20–32.

Wait, I.W. and Gressel, J.W. (2009) Relationship between TOEFL score and academic success for international engineering students. *Journal of Engineering Education* 98 (4), 389–398.

Wang, K.T., Heppner, P.P., Fu, C.C., Zhao, R., Li, F. and Chuang, C.C. (2012) Profiles of acculturative adjustment patterns among Chinese international students. *Journal of counseling psychology*, 59(3), 424–436.

Wang, L., Wang, K.T., Heppner, P.P. and Chuang, C.C. (2017) Cross-national cultural competency among Taiwanese international students. *Journal of Diversity in Higher Education* 10 (3), 271–287.

Wang, M. (2016) The impact of cultural values on Chinese students in American higher education. *The Qualitative Report* 21 (4), 611–628.

Wang, X. and Li, Y. (2014) 'English fever' in China has reached a watershed. *International Higher Education* 75, 13–14.

Warner, J. (2018) What Is First-Year Composition? See https://www.insidehighered.com/blogs/just-visiting/what-first-year-composition (accessed 17 May 2020).

White, L.E. (2012) English-Only Policy and Belief in the United States. See The University of New Hampshire Scholar's Repository: https://scholars.unh.edu/honors/21

Williams, D.A. (2013) *Strategic Diversity Leadership: Activating Change and Transformation in Higher Education*. Sterling, VA: Stylus Publishing, LLC.

Wong, J.K. (2004) Are the learning styles of Asian internationals culturally or contextually based? *International Education Journal* 4 (4), 154–166.

Woodrow, L. (2006) Academic success of international postgraduate education students and the role of English proficiency. *University of Sydney Papers in TESOL* 1, 51–70.

Wright, W.E. (2004) What English-only really means: A study of the implementation of California language policy with Cambodian-American students. *International Journal of Bilingual Education and Bilingualism* 7 (1), 1–23.

Wu, Y. (April 27, 2006) English 'fever.' *China Daily*. Op-ed article. See http://www.chinadaily.com.cn/opinion/2006-04/27/content_577941.htm (accessed 17 May 2020).

Wyer, K. (October 19, 2007) More Asian Americans meeting obstacles to academic success, survey shows. See http://newsroom.ucla.edu/releases/counter-to-popular-belief-majority-39558

Xie, X. (2010) Why are students quiet? Looking at the Chinese context and beyond. *ELT Journal* 64 (1), 10–20.

Xue, M. (2013) Effects of group work on English communicative competence of Chinese international graduates in United States institutions of higher education. *The Qualitative Report* 18 (7), 1–19.

Yan, K. and Berliner, D.C. (2011) Chinese international students in the United States: Demographic trends, motivations, acculturation features and adjustment challenges. *Asia Pacific Education Review* 12 (2), 173–184.

Yeh, C.J. and Inose, M. (2003) International students' reported English fluency, social support satisfaction, and social connectedness as predictors of acculturative stress. *Counselling Psychology Quarterly* 16 (1), 15–28.

Yin, R. (2003) *Case Study Research: Design and Methods* (3rd edn). Thousand Oaks, CA: Sage.

Yoon, E. and Jepsen, D.A. (2008) Expectations of and attitudes toward counseling: A comparison of Asian international and US graduate students. *International Journal for the Advancement of Counselling* 30 (2), 116–127.

You, X. and You, X. (2013) American content teachers' literacy brokerage in multilingual university classrooms. *Journal of Second Language Writing* 22 (3), 260–276.

Yu, L.P. (2004) Guanyu zhongxiaoxue shuangyu jiaoxue de sikao yu jianyi [Reflections on and suggestions about bilingual education at the primary and secondary levels]. *Dangdai Jiaoyu Kexue* 9, 29–31.

Yu, L. and Suen, H.K. (2005) Historical and contemporary exam-driven education fever in China. *KEDI Journal of Educational Policy* 2 (1), 17–33.

Zawacki, T.M. and Cox, M. (eds) (2014) *WAC and second language writers: Research towards linguistically and culturally inclusive programs and practices*. Parlor Press LLC.

Zhang, F.J. (2003) Wo xiang zhongxiaoxue yuwen shuangyu jiaoxue polengshui [Against bilingual instruction in the Chinese language arts classroom]. *Jichu Jiaoyu Waiyu Jiaoxue Yanjiu* 5, 18–20.

Zhang, J. and Goodson, P. (2011) Predictors of international students' psychosocial adjustment to life in the United States: A systematic review. *International Journal of Intercultural Relations* 35 (2), 139–162.

Zhang, Y. and Mi, Y. (2010) Another look at the language difficulties of international students. *Journal of Studies in International Education* 14 (4), 371–388.

Zhang-Wu, Q. (2017) Culturally and linguistically responsive teaching in practice: A case study of a fourth-grade mainstream classroom teacher. *Journal of Education* 197 (1), 33–40.

Zhang-Wu, Q. (2018) Chinese international students' experiences in American higher education institutes: A critical review of the literature. *Journal of International Students* 8 (2), 1173–1197.

Zhang-Wu, Q. (2019) Exploring the bilingual linguistic functioning of first-semester Chinese international students. Unpublished doctoral dissertation, Boston College.

Zhang-Wu, Q. (2021a) (Re)Imagining translingualism as a *verb* to tear down the English-only wall: 'Monolingual' students as multilingual writers. *College English* 84 (1), 121–137.

Zhang-Wu, Q. (2021b) Preparing monolingual teachers of multilingual students: Strategies that work. In U. Lanvers, A. Thompson and M. East (eds) *Language Learning in Anglophone Countries: Challenges, Practices, Solutions*. London: Palgrave Macmillan.

Zhu, S.P. (2004) Zhongguo muqian yi jubei le kaizhan shuangyu jiaoyu de tiaojian [China is ready for bilingual education]. *Jiaoshi Bolan* 7, 23–24.

Zhu, Z. (May 8, 2017) Influx of Chinese students creates cultural challenges. See https://news.jrn.msu.edu/2017/05/influx-of-chinese-students-creates-cultural-challenges/ (accessed 17 May 2020).

Zi, M. (December 29, 2004) New Oriental Guilty of Copyright Violation. [News Report] See http://www.chinadaily.com.cn/english/doc/2004-12/29/content_404573.htm (accessed 10 October 2018).

Index

CPSIA information can be obtained
at www.ICGtesting.com
Printed in the USA
JSHW050741300422
25437JS00003B/37